D1499340

Duet for Two Voices

HUGH CAREY

DUET FOR TWO VOICES

*An informal Biography of Edward Dent
compiled from his Letters to Clive Carey*

CAMBRIDGE UNIVERSITY PRESS

CAMBRIDGE
LONDON   NEW YORK   MELBOURNE

Published by the Syndics of the Cambridge University Press
The Pitt Building, Trumpington Street, Cambridge CB2 1RP
Bentley House, 200 Euston Road, London NW1 2DB
32 East 57th Street, New York, NY 10022, USA
296 Beaconsfield Parade, Middle Park, Melbourne 3206, Australia

© Cambridge University Press 1979

First published 1979

Printed in Great Britain by Ebenezer Baylis & Son Ltd.
Leicester & London

Library of Congress cataloguing in publication data
Carey, Hugh.

Duet for two voices.

Includes index.

1. Dent, Edward Joseph, 1876-1957.
2. Musicians – England – Biography.
I. Dent, Edward Joseph, 1876-1957.
II. Carey, Clive. III. Title.
ML423.D37C4 780'.01'0924 [B] 78-62115
ISBN 0 521 22312 1

Contents

He was a tall, weakly built young man, whose clothes had to be judiciously padded on the shoulder in order to make him pass muster. His face was plain rather than not, and there was a curious mixture in it of good and bad. He had a fine forehead and a good large nose, and both observation and sympathy were in his eyes. But below the nose and eyes all was confusion, and those people who believe that destiny resides in the mouth and chin shook their heads when they looked at him.

Philip himself, as a boy, had been keenly conscious of these defects. Sometimes when he had been bullied or hustled about at school he would retire to his cubicle and examine his features in a looking-glass, and he would sigh and say, 'It is a weak face. I shall never carve a place for myself in the world.' But as years went on he became either less self-conscious or more self-satisfied. The world, he found, made a niche for him as it did for everyone. Decision of character might come later – or he might have it without knowing. At all events he had got a sense of beauty and a sense of humour, two most desirable gifts . . . All the energies and enthusiasms of a rather friendless life had passed into the championship of beauty.

E. M. Forster, *Where Angels Fear To Tread* (1905) p. 116

'You look on life as a spectacle; you don't enter it; you only find it funny or beautiful. So I can trust you to cure me. Mr. Herriton, isn't it funny?'

E. M. Forster, *Where Angels Fear To Tread* (1905) p. 313

I always imagine Dent as the Serpent telling Eve about the Apples. 'My dear Eve . . .' pointing at blemishes on them, with back-hits at God and Adam, and a rumour that the Holy Ghost was *enceinte*. But so kindly.

Rupert Brooke, Letter to Geoffrey Keynes, March 1911

Preface

I never thought that I should be the biographer of the Old
Serpent – a name Edward Dent acquired from the occasion
of *The Magic Flute* in 1911: when he appeared before the
curtain to announce that Mrs Fletcher could not sing
Pamina the shrill excited voice of a well-briefed child cut
through the momentary silence with 'Is that the Serpent,
Mummy?'. I used to meet him occasionally when my
uncle, Clive Carey, took me to the opera at Sadler's Wells,
and between the acts Dent, his chin characteristically
tucked below his shoulder, let fall a few aphorisms about
the performance. By then he was stooping and cadaverous,
and very deaf, but his comments were pithy enough and
wonderfully like the imitations in which his friends delighted. Evidently he was vastly learned, and I was too
ignorant to make much of him.

Of my uncle I knew both much and little. My father and
his brother and sisters took one another for granted.
Margery painted, Clive sang, Gordon wrote and taught,
Dorothea apparently could do many things but didn't;
none of them ever suggested that any of the others were
really *good* at what they did, and all tended to depreciate
their own work. Thus, while I loved to hear Clive sing folk-
songs downstairs at the piano or at school concerts, or on
gramophone records, and much as I enjoyed the infectious
charm of his company, I knew little of his real eminence.
When we went to Sadler's Wells together I was aware that
he was in some way in charge, but he gave no indication of
being an important person. Sometimes I used to join him
and his wife at the end of his (and my) day's teaching and
we would go to a Chinese restaurant together, but he never
mentioned that his pupils included Elsie Morison and
Joan Sutherland. In his last years I visited him almost
every weekend; it could still be fun, for his charm never
entirely left him; by now I knew what I wanted to ask him
about the past, but he was not often able to remember.

After his death I found myself, by the courtesy of other
members of the family who had recently by force of

circumstances been less close to him, the heir to a great collection of letters. From these it was clear that Clive had meant to attempt a memoir of Edward Dent, his old friend and mentor. There were answers from one or two friends to whom he had written for 'old serpentine letters', and he had tried to sort his own, but energy and powers of organisation had failed him; a request for a brief biography of Dent from the Dictionary of National Biography had been set aside and the task was not attempted.

When I mentioned that I was sorting and transcribing the large amount of material that had come into my hands, many friends encouraged me to continue. Jill Vlasto led me to a number of Clive's letters in the Rowe Music Library at King's College, Cambridge; Frank Howes and John Dykes Bower cast their more expert eye on the letters and reported well of them; Keith Falkner helped in the search for a publisher; Evelyn Broadwood with diligent loyalty played his part in arranging a commemoration of Edward Dent and Clive Carey at Sadler's Wells; Philip Radcliffe answered my questions with enthusiasm and kindness; friends helped with their typewriters and the book took shape.

I must emphasise that the outcome is not a full-dress biography either of Dent or my uncle. Where there are gaps, they have been left unfilled. For some readers it may be disappointing that there is nothing about Dent's work as Professor in organising the faculty of Music at Cambridge; for others that Clive's work in folk-song and dance, as a recitalist or with the English Singers, receives scant attention. The reason is that they did not write to one another about them, or perhaps in a few instances that Clive's letters on these topics have not survived. I have never felt myself competent to write Dent's life, but I believe that through the medium of his prolific correspondence he came near to writing it himself.

Once the text was complete, it became clear that much would be gained by contemporary illustrations. Again as an amateur in a professional world I discovered the remarkable helpfulness of their colleagues at Cambridge and at Sadler's Wells. Geoffrey Keynes generously lent the programme of the first Marlowe Society performance and, on behalf of Rupert Brooke's trustees, allowed quotations from his letters; George Rylands gave other useful information; Geoffrey Dent kindly sent photographs of Ribston Hall in his uncle's boyhood; and Mrs Frida

viii

Knight lent pages from her sketchbook. Dennis Arundell also opened his scrapbooks and his memories of Cambridge music, and the Fitzwilliam Museum provided Mrs Cockerell's lovely designs for the costumes for *The Fairy Queen*; Nick Furbank handed on some photographs he had collected as E. M. Forster's biographer. For the later years the Rowe Music Library, the Mander and Mitchenson collection, and the Victoria and Albert Museum were helpful, and Harry Lloyd lent his design for Clive's production of *Riders to the Sea*. The early years of opera at the Old Vic are hard to illustrate – probably Lilian Baylis thought photographs an unnecessary waste of scarce resources.

Had he not been busy with greater matters, my cousin Anthony Elliott could have written this book better than I have done. It is a great regret that he is not here to enjoy the book that I would so gladly have dedicated to him.

Crawley, Winchester

1. *Introduction*

The young don at King's: Dent,
c. 1902.

'We may be able to do our jobs a great deal better than the professional gang, but we always behave as if we were amateurs. We frequent the society of amateurs and feel uncomfortable with professionals. We refuse to concentrate on one thing and are no good at pushing ourselves continually; we are too much artists and too little business men.'

This extract from a letter written to Clive Carey in 1924 may explain why in 1976, when I write, Edward Dent's centenary year, there is need for an introduction. For more than fifty years of English music Dent was at the hub of the wheel; by accepting a professorship in Adelaide Clive Carey, it is true, was just then moving to the circumference. During the years before 1914, both had made Cambridge the centre of their life, influence, and friendships; in the post-war world they never perhaps fully regained the sense of hope and discovery that had culminated in their production of *The Magic Flute* in 1911. This should have been followed three years later by Purcell's *Fairy Queen*, last performed in England on stage in 1693. Production had to wait till 1920.

Although the authors of the *Concise Oxford Dictionary of Opera* state that 'his influence upon English operatic life and its relationship to the European scene is incalculable', Dent lingers obstinately in the footnotes; his translations begin to be 'dated', but otherwise he was so successful that his work is probably taken for granted. Now that the objects have been attained, it is hard to realise that so much needed to be achieved. We do now have a public for opera sung in English by English singers, and even composed by Englishmen; contemporary music is performed and widely understood in Europe.

Not all Dent's judgements have stood the test of time – he would deplore the continued popularity of Elgar and of much of Puccini – but to read his letters is to be reminded how rarely he backed a loser; and his backing was persistent, costly and painstaking. With meticulous antiquarian

I

scholarship that might have become merely conservative he combined a radical impatience, so that if one associates him very properly with rediscovery, notably of Scarlatti and the operas of Mozart, one must not overlook his championship of new music – his chairmanship of the International Society of Contemporary Music, his help to Roberto Gerhard to settle in Cambridge in 1938, and his advocacy of Bartók.

This account of his work is virtually an unintended autobiography. Dent was a prolific correspondent, and my uncle, Clive Carey, kept almost every letter which Dent addressed to him, beginning in 1902 and finishing only a few weeks before Dent's death in 1957. No doubt by reading all Dent's published work, aided by Lawrence Haward's bibliography, one could write another book, assuming that one had the qualifications to evaluate the soundness of each essay or review; but it would be a different and a drier one. Dent worked largely, as befits a don at King's College, Cambridge, through friends and friendships; he liked to get to know a man well enough to be able to criticise him frankly yet without offence; and few men have used correspondence more diligently to keep friendships in repair. To Clive, who, apart from Lawrence Haward and J. B. Trend, was perhaps his closest friend, he wrote more than four hundred extant letters, keeping also a substantial number of Clive's replies.

Mr Clive Carey, baritone, *c.* 1902.

The letters may be the manifestations of frustrated creativity as an original composer; they represent a necessary output of self-expression. He rarely changed a word or blotted a line, writing with a fluency far greater than his legibility. He is rarely trivial, in the sense of concerning himself with ephemeral things – meals and engagements, time-tables and tittle-tattle to amuse an hour or arrange a meeting. Inevitably each reader will subject him to different criteria. To some the in-fighting over the appointment of officers of a university musical society appears unimportant; to others the programme of an Italian town band, or the behaviour of a group of Englishmen on a continental express. The highlights may be obvious – *The Magic Flute* production, a description of the first performance of Holst's *Planets*, discussion of the future of opera in England, almost extinguished in the Second World War; the problem is what to exclude.

Fate has dealt kindly with the memory of some of Dent's friends while obscuring others. Shall the editor of his

Dent's family home, Ribston Hall, near Wetherby.

letters treasure each mention of Rupert Brooke while omitting Mrs Jenkinson's Mozart afternoons; retain Glyndebourne and jettison Glastonbury? If a document purports to be social history – and letters between friends can hardly fail to be that – it is tempting to include every word, annotating each obscurity so that there is an understanding of the passing reference to some little-known person or event. But a man must be a giant to receive such treatment, and modern publishing costs enable us to accord this only to the few, subsidised by the funds of some learned foundation.

What makes it hard to be selective with Dent is not only the wide variety of his interests, not all of which are likely to be shared by any individual reader, but still more the lucidity and wit of his prose. A long-forgotten concert may best remain in limbo, even if its choice of programme has some interest, but one discards it with reluctance: 'We at last tackled the Bach, but as Gray had copied some of the parts, and Levitt in his sweet innocence had begun by copying others from Gray instead of from the score the result was unspeakable. Letters never coincided, the first violins had two bars too many and the cellos six too few besides half bars, three-quarter bars and all sorts of

3

vagaries! Gallia goes as swimmingly as such a saturated solution of sugar could . . .'. Does it matter what the Cambridge University Musical Society played in 1904, still less how they played it? In the end much depends on your interest in, and affection for, the writer himself, and your enjoyment of his wit and style.

Travels in Italy and Germany before the First World War in his company had something of the quality and observation of Samuel Butler; even when he was searching with uncanny prescience for autograph MSS of Scarlatti he wore his learning lightly, pausing to strike up a friendship with some young student met at a railway station, hearing whatever music the local opera house provided. As a personality he takes his acknowledged place in literature as the original of Philip Herriton in Forster's *Where Angels Fear To Tread*; as a musician, now primarily as a writer on opera and as a translator. His letters show the animation behind these masks; the asperity which characterised much of his talk and writing comes from a generous heart.

Ribston Hall, the saloon in Dent's boyhood.

4

A family group at Ribston, *c.* 1890. Dent sits beside his mother with his three sisters behind, his father and brother stand together on the right.

At the time when his correspondence with Clive Carey began, Dent was twenty-six, newly elected into a fellowship at King's College, and Carey nineteen, organ scholar of Clare College. Dent came from the landed gentry – his home was Ribston Hall, a large estate between York and Harrogate; his father had been a Conservative Member of Parliament. However, he was a natural agnostic, sceptical of all 'establishments', academic or musical, with a Socratic tendency to question fundamental assumptions. Greek, too, was the value he placed on the friendship of men, as did his contemporaries at King's, Forster and Lowes Dickinson. For his fellowship he had submitted a setting for voices and orchestra of the first chorus of Shelley's *Hellas*. His means enabled him to be independent, but his temperament would in any case have made him so. He was not without fashionable prejudices; radicalism does not always redeem a man from being a snob. His anti-Semitism was marked but not undiscriminating – readers of Rupert Brooke's letters or of John Buchan can observe how

5

Choristers at King's: Clive Carey with his younger brother Gordon, c. 1896.

Francis and Elizabeth Carey, c. 1887.

widespread was this trait among university men before the First World War. He also found it hard to believe that any British composer could write well without the advantage of a university – or more particularly of a Cambridge – education, and his dislike of Elgar's (and Sullivan's) music and his antipathy to Beecham reflect this prejudice. In 1902, when his letters to Clive Carey begin, he was still uncertain whether his future lay in composition or in scholarship. Already he was fluent in German and Italian; the work on Alessandro Scarlatti, whose publication in 1905 was to establish his reputation, was nearing completion.

Clive Carey in 1902, and indeed throughout his equally long life, was less secure. His father, Francis Carey, naturally anxious and unassertive, had married Elizabeth Harrowell in 1877, when he was thirty-seven and his bride some twelve years younger. She was as forceful as he was mild. Francis Carey had retired prematurely from the City to Burgess Hill in Sussex, and the family of five children strained his limited resources. The three elder children, all girls, played, wrote and painted with more than usual skill – indeed Clive's first published songs were settings of his

6

Dent's contemporaries: a King's
College group, May Week 1900.

sister Winifred's poems. Clive (and his younger brother,
Gordon) both made their first acquaintance with Cambridge as choristers of King's. From there Clive went as a
scholar to Sherborne (where Louis Napoleon Parker
presided over the music), returning to Cambridge as an
organ scholar in 1900, at seventeen somewhat younger
than the average undergraduate of his day. Already he had
something of a reputation as a singer, composer, pianist
and conductor, and was combining rather sporadic study at
Clare with work in London at the Royal College of Music,
where he was Grove Scholar in Composition. Throughout
his life he combined exceptional charm and artistic sensi-
bility with a deep, though not always apparent, self-
distrust. At Cambridge he needed the friendship both of
contemporaries and older friends and received it in abund-
ance – George Lyttelton and Alwyn Scholfield; Percy
Lubbock and Edward Dent; and among the older men
Monty James, Provost of King's, and 'Daddy' Mann, the
organist.

Dent was probably jealous of these last, for his dislike
and distrust of 'reverence' and the college chapel ensured
that he would have little sympathy with men whose
affections were firmly rooted there. Moreover, Dent and
some of his contemporaries thought that Monty James's

7

distinction as a palaeographer and in apocryphal studies was something of a deliberate withdrawal from the abrasion of contemporary life and thought; the Provost's reported saying that the three most boring topics are politics, economics and sex (all of them subjects to which Kingsmen have made a distinctive contribution) did not endear him to Dent and some other contemporaries of Morgan Forster and of Maynard Keynes.

2. *Chiefly Scarlatti*

When his correspondence with Clive Carey began in June 1902, Dent was in Paris, pursuing his Scarlatti studies. In the first letter he asked Clive to let him know how far the second violin part went in a copy of some motets which he had been making in Brussels the previous year, but had not had time to complete, as he would shortly be returning there to finish it. The instructions began like this: 'If you will ascend into my upper chamber (but be careful, as I let my rooms for the King's ball and you may find a young lady there – however by the time this reaches you I think she will be gone) you will find on the top of the tall bookcase opposite the window some portfolios', and continued for several lines.

It was typical of him at this age that he was 'frightfully bored with Paris and perpetually cold', though in the same letter he describes a Sunday night at the Opéra-Comique – he was disappointed by *Le Domino Noir* and nearly suffocated by the want of ventilation; it was preceded by 'a stupid little one-act thing of E. Reyer's called *Maître Wolfram* in which the hero is organist of the cathedral at Bonn and there is a chorus of University students who sing the most approved Biergarten stuff, and Wolfram directs on a chamber organ till he falls dead. It was pretty in a way but most boring'; the following Thursday he went to a concert in aid of those who had suffered in the eruption of Mont Pelée in Martinique (scenes from Rameau and Jannequin's *Les Oiseaux* the principal attractions). Not being in a Bayreuth mood he failed to attend *Crépuscule des Dieux* with Richter conducting.

Meanwhile he had discovered two Scarlatti autographs in the library, neither noted in the catalogue, but 'old Weckerlin the librarian was so sniffy and incredulous when I showed him the first that I shan't say anything about the second'.

Nearly a year passed before the next letter (May 1903), written from Florence during a thunderstorm; Dent was spending a few days there, paying a round of calls 'which I

Nº4. "Stop! Stop!! Stop!!! Zat is 'orrible." D.A.Cº Copyright
AN ORCHESTRAL REHEARSAL.

We practise the Aristophanes again on Saturday at 4.30, tea at 4. I hope you will come as it will be a great help. It went decently: but the terms are funny! Ever, S.D.

A postcard from Dent, 1904.

oddly enough rather enjoy, as they are all very cordial and delightful'. He had been working at old operas, and seeing a few: *Traviata* at Palermo, *Barbiere* at Naples, and *Lucia di Lammermoor* at Florence. 'I am crazy for Donizetti Bellini and early Verdi and don't wish ever to hear a note of Wagner again.' Boito's *Mefistofele*, heard at Rome, was glorious – 'I wish you would make Gray do it again at the C.U.M.S.,[1] the prologue I mean, which is quite good for a concert, as all the action takes place behind the scenes!'

Dent's particular irritation was that Dr Hugo Goldschmidt, who wrote a 'fairly good book' on Italian opera in the seventeenth century, was now using the bibliography of Scarlatti which Dent had published the previous November, and preceding him 'like a pilot engine to a royal train' about a fortnight ahead. 'I expect he will publish something stupid about it all (at Montecassino the Prior who is a friend of mine said he thought Goldschmidt knew no Italian) and get all the credit of my work: he being German and well known: I being an unmusical Englishman and young into the bargain . . . However, I can't imagine that he was received with more cordiality and kindness than I am by all these dear people.' Already his journey had taken him to Palermo, Naples, Montecassino, Florence, Bologna ('an Italian Cambridge, and if it wasn't the worst climate in Italy I would go and live there'), and Modena. Meanwhile, the Cambridge University Musical Society was performing Sullivan's *Golden Legend*; Dent was glad he was not in Cambridge to hear it.

By the time the correspondence was resumed, in March 1904, to run unbroken at monthly intervals or less till 1919, Clive had become better known in Cambridge and outside it and Dent (who kept the unimportant letters which Clive was writing to him at this period) was watching jealously over his progress as a singer and songwriter and over his popularity and friendships. The particular occasion of his success had been the performance of the Greek play in December 1903, *The Birds* of Aristophanes, set to Parry's music. Parry had written a new Parabasis for Clive, as

[1] The C.U.M.S. (Cambridge University Musical Society) gave its first concert in 1844. From 1873, when Stanford (an undergraduate member since 1870) became the conductor, it began to undertake concerts of major choral works, commonly drawing upon the services of professional orchestral players from London. By 1900, when Alan Gray was its conductor, most of the orchestra was resident in Cambridge; Clive Carey used to help by taking orchestral rehearsals. The C.U.M.C. (Musical Club) was a smaller body founded in 1889, holding weekly meetings for chamber music, and supplying professional classes in ensemble work.

The Birds of
Aristophanes, 1903:
the antics of the owl.

PUBLISHED BY C.F. KNOWLES. CAMBRIDGE.

The chorus in silhouette.

leader of the chorus, to sing, and this had won considerable acclaim. Contemporary newspapers, and Cambridge also, paid what to a modern reader appears disproportionate attention to the occasion, with two- and three-column reviews, illustrations, silhouettes and postcards.

Dent was now in Münster, combining Scarlatti studies with thoughts of Clive; 'Scarlatti reminds me of you perpetually. I think he would have liked your stuff – not that it is very much like his.' Work in the library was bitterly cold, in spite of a greatcoat and quite a respectable doormat borrowed from down below to keep his feet warm. Two-hour shifts, enormous meals with resultant torpor, followed by walks to regain warmth and settle the lunch – 'it is a truly dreadful thing when you walk until you are fit to drop and *still* feel that the digestive process is only on the way to completion' – composed the daily routine, which Dent found blunting to the finer sensibilities. 'Scarlatti is not for beefy persons: that's why old Hubert [Parry] doesn't care for him.' He described a concert which included 'I know that my Redeemer liveth for the benefit of the soprano solo (a middle-aged person in a most becoming grey and black dress)' and Brahms' Requiem – 'the chorus were well drilled – but they evidently thought it very

LÄMMER- RED- KING-
GEYER. SHANK. VULTURE. FISHER. COCK.

Mᴿ J. P. GABBATT. Mᴿ J. CLAGUE. Mᴿˢ W. R. C. ADCOCK.

...IOTT. Mᴿ T. W. HAWARD. Mᴿˢ H. M. J. F. DE P. ANTO LEITE.

difficult music and they never dared let themselves go at all. It was hopelessly dull, and the righteous souls were as dreary as righteous souls probably are. After the soprano solo which the lady sang in tune, but with reachings and screechings like a pussy-cat on a channel steamer, I thought I preferred supper to singing.' Easter at Münster would have been unendurable; the holiness of the town was too overwhelming: people did nothing but go to church – with occasional drunks – and the bells, ringing a diminishing triad ♭♩ ♩ ♩ were maddening, except when Dent conceived the happy notion of thinking of an A at the bottom which immediately made it part of the Parabasis – 'I've forgotten the words, but I can never forget the sound of your voice in them.'

Thence, after an extra day cataloguing Pergolesi for a friend, to Stendal by train, and on to Schwerin. At Stendal at the Schwarzer Adler Dent walked into the restaurant, found it only moderately lighted, 'and the proprietor billing and cooing with a female who I am quite willing to believe was his wife. I did not inquire.' On the next day, while he was at the Tangermünde two more Englishmen turned up – 'they sent me their kind regards or whatever it might have been, so I concluded that I had been fortunate to escape them'.

At this period Dent was a considerable walker, with a critical curiosity about architecture and landscape. At Tangermünde they had spoiled the old ruined castle by making a public garden with staircases and terraces leading up to this absurdity; at Stendal there was a fair, with several merry-go-rounds and steam organs all playing loudly and simultaneously, which disturbed his reading of G. E. Moore's *Ethics* – 'but I don't mind it much in the open air and it amuses me to watch the people'. The railway journey from Stendal to Schwerin shows Dent twice in typical vein; there was a wait while the local train was attached to the Berlin–Hamburg express: 'the opportunity was seized by a party of English 'Arries to get out and have a drink and make the usual wild beasts of themselves that they do. I suppose this was a "Polytechnic" tour to Beautiful Berlin and Happy Hamburg.' But in the slowest of slow trains he had a charming companion, a first-year student at Heidelberg. 'He had an hour to wait in Schwerin, so we lunched together and by the time he went away he had quite decided to come and take the Agricultural Tripos at Cambridge and play violoncello at the Club

– in three years' time.' Charming young foreigners met at railway stations are a recurrent element in Dent's travels, whereas he resents other Englishmen abroad.

To reproduce all the vignettes of Dent as traveller, opera-goer or wandering scholar which emerge from his vast output of letters is impossible. This from Schwerin must stand for many (5 April 1904):

'I went to the opera last night: *Der Polnische Jude* by Karl Weir and *Hänsel und Gretel*. I got there just as it began but it was rather awkward: the attendant took my ticket away and pushed me hastily in at a door, shut it immediately and I found myself in Egyptian darkness, at the top of a rather steep sloping gangway, the overture just beginning. I had not the remotest idea where my seat was except that it was 127 and there was no-one to show me to it; so there I waited trying vainly to get used to the Bayreuthian twilight. The overture was interminable and I stayed there till the end of the first act; and in the interval I found my seat – miles off and four people to pass by.

'The theatre is good for sound; at least I suppose it is, as everybody seemed to be singing and playing fortissimo all through, except in the places where it would exhaust my paper, pen and ink to write down an adequate number of "f's". The decorations were the climax of vulgarity: I never saw such horrible German taste. I never heard of Karl Weir and his Polish Jew before. It is in two acts and appears to be post-Wagnerian. It was quite pleasant to listen to, but not interesting. The best thing was the ballet, a polka, and a very, very slow German waltz. You know the story, of course: Erckmann-Chatrian's *Juif Polonais* that I read at a private school for French lessons & Irving's Bells that I have never seen. It always attracts composers and I don't wonder, but it is most impracticable as an opera because it doesn't make a good stage development. *Hänsel und Gretel* was done fairly, the four horns out of tune at the start: the angels very fearful: and the children all in training for Barnums. Gretel carried it off somehow, though she was very "bien nourri" as Prout says an orchestral score ought to be, especially in the middle parts . . .'

While Dent pursued Scarlatti on to Hamburg in search of more fragments among the books of the musicologist Chrysander which had been deposited there, Clive was producing and performing in his own operetta *Edwin and Angelina* in parish halls in Burgess Hill and Bedford. He

'An entirely new and moderately original comic Opera'. Here Angelina (Nellie Sargent) adopts a typically melodramatic pose.

The conductor (Clive) and the company: *Trial by Jury* at Cambridge.

had also attended a performance of *The Dream of Gerontius* given in a packed Queen's Hall. Dent, who used to refer to it disparagingly as 'Gerry's Nightmare', may not have welcomed Clive's enthusiastic description – 'I stick more firmly than ever to my opinion of it. It seems to me to have real inspiration about it and to be really sincere'; nor did he relish Clive's using his talents on the kind of facile music that he stigmatised in a later letter as 'an entirely new and moderately original comic opera'. An entry in Clive's diary for 15 October 1903 illustrates the dislike that some contemporaries had for Elgar's oratorios: 'When I got to the College [Royal College of Music] I came into the presence of Stanford, who was suffering from a bad cold and also from Elgar's "Apostles", of which he had heard the first performance the morning before, and which he said he never wanted to hear again. He was so delighted with my "Love on my Heart" that he brought in Charles Wood to hear it. He said, among other things, that he liked it better than the whole of "The Apostles"!' Posterity has forgotten Clive's settings of Bridges' poems, while Elgar's oratorios enjoy a revival.

After a very brief interlude in Cambridge, where one suspects that his affection for Clive was becoming a little uncomfortable ('Why did you sport your door? Otherwise I might have had a look at you when I brought the peonies on Sunday morning: though I would not have waked you'), and lunch with his mother in London ('dear good soul – it would never enter her head to cut the sermon in order to see her prodigal son! She returned from church in the most fetching of bonnets and gave me a contemptible lunch'), Dent was back working at the archives in Florence. In Milan *en route* he had preferred the company of a 'charming young man from the far end of Italy – a wine grower from Gallipoli – doing his military service, more or less of the seed of Abraham, I think, but very charming' to seeing the Duse in Maeterlinck's *Monna Vanna*. His sister joined him at Florence and was a very agreeable companion, sharing his enjoyment of hot weather and meals redolent of oil and garlic, with the most delicious wine in the world. There was a little bitterness in the thought that Clive would be in London hearing opera 'in more congenial company. I wish I could take you to a provincial Italian opera performance with a bawling tenor and a screaming soprano and an orchestra of "fifty professors" that plays at an unsteady fortissimo all the way through and drowns everything except the conversation and the singing of the audience.'

Percy Lubbock on holiday.

At this time Clive's friendship with Percy Lubbock, then a young civil servant, later Fellow of Magdalene and a well-known man of letters, was flourishing to a degree that Dent consciously or subconsciously resented, though Lubbock was a close friend and contemporary of his own. Dent wanted Clive to come to Italy to learn Italian, but he was hesitating. 'I suppose if Percy says "Dresden" to Dresden you go. Very well, go to Dresden and learn Saxon with an American accent, and eat horrible stodgy meals and hear horrible stodgy operas and make yourself agreeable to silly English schoolgirls and go into raptures over Raphael's Madonna and the beautiful Frau Salbach and all the other wonderful things in the so-called "Elbflorenz". It is vastly superior to the Arno Dresden you know.' Meanwhile, with his sister helping in copying some of Scarlatti's letters, and also proving a useful critic of the MS of his book, Dent was able to leave a suffocating Florence and battle with the last chapter amid the fragrant Spanish-chestnut woods of Cutigliano, writing in the garden with notebooks and portfolios heaped up round him on the ground. The company at the pension belonged very much to what one thinks of as Forster's Italy: two elderly German spinsters, one of them an authoress; an elderly Englishman, ex I.C.S., struggling with Italian ('less interesting'); an elderly Venetian ('not quite refined enough for my sister's taste, so I sit next to him at meals'); and a German honeymooning couple ('who are of no importance').

By July (1904) the chapter was written and the MS of the book was on its way with Dent's sister to London. From Modena, where he did a lot of good work, but suffered much from fleas and mosquitoes, after parting with his sister in Milan, he went to Piacenza, where they were not so aggressive. He had enjoyed having her with him, but was relieved to be alone again, noting the drawbacks to travelling even with the most agreeable of women: 'it becomes worse when she has indifferent health and a constitutional difficulty in making up her mind'. The labours at Modena had been increased by Dent's discovery that an opera ascribed in Paris to Scarlatti was really by Stradella; this entailed some rewriting, but his sister was at hand to make him tea with an 'Etna' in the middle of the long afternoon's work.

Now that Scarlatti was off his hands, he could take out his sketch-book, though in 1904 foreigners with sketch-books were viewed with some suspicion after a spy scare in Messina; but holiday plans went adrift – somehow he could not get other people to make plans in a businesslike manner. He lamented his fatal habit of trying to turn acquaintances into friendships by post: disagreeable as he might be in English, he discovered himself to be the most charming of correspondents in Italian, yet after most affectionate correspondence for twelve or eighteen months when eventually a meeting took place there was nothing to say. Evidently the letters had been read on both sides as pure literature and there was no attraction of personality. At Florence he talked with a pleasant Hungarian who admired the *Times Literary Supplement*, so Dent gave him some copies of the *Independent Review* ('better for his politics'); at Pistoia he made the acquaintance of two of the elegant young men, extremely friendly, but had no illusions about the basis of their friendship – 'I think as a matter of fact they liked my cigarettes which I bring from Cambridge.'

While Dent was writing affectionately, almost compulsively, Clive had been writing more songs, scoring two vocal quartets, and 'doing Italian opera like anything', with Caruso and Scotti in all of them. The possibility of the Italian holiday was slender, as he was penniless and his father could give him nothing. Dent went to Arezzo for

Petrarch celebrations, enduring the constant society of four or five American professors; in August he was in Rome, working a little in very hot weather, commanded by his publisher to add fifteen pages to his book, sitting in the Pincio gardens in the afternoon and strolling in the park of the Villa Borghese in the evening. There were no Englishmen, much less an Englishwoman; the English tea-rooms were all shuttered and padlocked ('so is the English Church, I expect'[1]), and there was the wine of Frascati and peaches which combined all the excellences of peaches, apricots and apples. The only drawback was the distance between places; if you went in trams you were sure to acquire numerous fleas.

Trouble persisted over the Scarlatti book, with Breitkopf and Härtel refusing to allow the catalogue of operas to be reprinted. Dent now moved to Fano, chosen because of its cheapness and sea-bathing, but there was no music as the military band was on manoeuvres and the town band on strike ('from what I know of small town bands in Italy it is very fortunate'). He was generously providing a holiday for an invalid Sicilian who had had nervous troubles 'though to his credit be it said that it does not imply in his case, as it generally does in Italy, the result of too great a partiality for female society'.

It was by now agreed that Clive should travel out in mid-September with Percy Lubbock to Verona, where Dent would join them; meanwhile he went back to Modena to write an introduction to the book, whose manuscript had temporarily been lost in transit. Apart from a 'café chantant' there was no entertainment; the previous month the theatre was on, but the plays were mostly not suitable to take his sister to. Already the year before he had sampled the 'café chantant' – 'dreadful females who could neither sing nor dance and were not even pretty. All they could do was to kick up their skirts and make eyes at the elegant young gentlemen in the front row who posed as connoisseurs of female beauty.'

It was remarkable how much one could see in September if one chose to wander through the provincial towns which Dent had just been through on his way from Fano: *Tosca* at Carpi; *Traviata*, *Trovatore* and *Rigoletto* in a cheap open-air theatre at Bologna; *La Serva Padrona* and *Il Maestro di Cappella* at Gubbio; at Citta di Castello, Donizetti's *Maria*

---

[1] A deliberate reference to a lifelong agnosticism, which Clive did not share.

di Rohan; at Orvieto, Gluck's *Orfeo* and the *Maestro di Cappella*. Dent also sent Clive the idea for an Offenbach opera 'which you may write, as I don't suppose I shall ever realise my great ambition to be simultaneously professor of music at Cambridge, and the idol of Paris and the Continent generally for operas à la Offenbach which can't *possibly* be done in England!' The theme was that the Vatican had suddenly heard that the King of Italy had abdicated, restoring Rome to the Popes; and that a gay and giddy Pope would start – in spite of strikes and the modern problems of city management – to restore a golden age, turning the Sistine Chapel into a 'café chantant' with a 'revised version' of Michelangelo's 'Last Judgement' painted by Paris poster artists. Dent appended a suitable can-can.

The projected Italian holiday took place in September. As might have been foreseen, the *ménage à trois* was not always a happy one, with Dent very proprietory about Italy and Clive's introduction to it. After a leisurely journey to Venice via Milan, Bergamo, (where they heard *Lohengrin* conducted by Tullio Serafin), Verona and Padua, Clive and Percy Lubbock were joined by Dent on the platform at Vicenza. Clive's diary reads: 'We had much looked forward to his arrival, but when he came he disappointed us – I think our British appearance and behaviour were too much for him. At any rate, he was not good tempered, that is to say, at times he wasn't – one could never be certain what he would be like the next minute. He addressed only about three remarks to me during the first day or so, and snapped very much at the new songs I showed him. It was really rather pathetic after the pleasure Percy and I had been feeling at the idea of seeing "our Dent"! I suspect he was hurt at my not having come out to stay with him before, feeling that I would not have come except for Percy; also perhaps because we had been running about Italy so close behind him (he left Padua the day we arrived) without letting him know . . After Tuesday, he was more of his old self, and his aggressive, anti-English remarks were not so numerous!'

Perhaps an incident in Verona which Clive describes in his diary was the germ of E. M. Forster's *A Room With a View*, for Dent was writing regularly to Forster at this period . . . 'When we first arrived we had a superb big balcony out of Percy's room, but we were asked to move because there were some English ladies who had the other

The Italian holiday: Dent leaves the party at Iseo.

19

room opening on to it, and they wanted ours for the rest of their party. We discovered afterwards that the room was merely wanted for the ladies' maid, or perhaps that they could have the whole balcony to themselves – a party of three!'

Dent returned to Cambridge at the beginning of October, just in time to join Clive at the Leeds Festival. He had been reading *Armide* and *Alceste* towards his lectures, and commented on how dreary Gluck's melody was; the best *music* was in the ballets; yet how essentially dramatic was his point of view. A production was in consideration in which Clive would play Apollo. At Leeds *Everyman*, an oratorio by Walford Davies, was to receive its first performance, and Dent hoped it was not as 'depressingly solemn' as its composer. Their reaction is not recorded, but the oratorio was well received. Unfortunately, at the end of the week, Clive became quite seriously ill; he had to cut down on his activities, giving up an organist's post in Uxbridge and temporarily much of his work with the orchestra of the Musical Society at Cambridge.

3. Edwardian Summers

From October 1904 Dent was back in Cambridge. Much of the content of his letters is small talk about the C.U.M.S., Alan Gray (organist of Trinity) its conductor, and C. B. Rootham, who took over from him. Rootham plays a constant, almost obsessional, part in Dent's life at Cambridge; they were exact contemporaries, and their ambitions and attitudes were in frequent conflict. Rootham was a prolific and not always sufficiently self-critical composer, an extrovert, often bewildered by the 'political' arts in which Dent revelled and excelled. The first mention of Rootham in Clive's diary is typical: 'We stayed quite late discussing Wagner, Strauss, Brahms, English music and Elgar, on whom Rootham is exceedingly keen. I wish he didn't lay the law down so much, though!' (3 May 1903). Dent's is equally characteristic: 'Rootham very kindly took me for a walk yesterday and then gave me tea. He has bought a Bechstein grand and is rather uneasy as to where to find room for it. But it was of course necessary to the dignity of his position. While the kettle was boiling he sat down to the pianoforte and said, "Now I want you to tell me what you think of this theme – I won't tell you who it's by!" I was tempted (but resisted) to assure him that there was no need whatever to tell me.'

The first batch of proofs of the Scarlatti were in hand by early October, no small achievement by those who had to decipher Dent's handwriting, and it is not surprising that he liked the look of it better in print, though he found himself bothered with small details of printing: 'I also discover how vague I am about such trifles as punctuation and spelling.'

Although it may not be without interest to trace the evolution of taste as reflected in the programmes of C.U.M.S., or the frustrating vagaries of its rehearsals ('We trudged through Dazu ist erschienen at the sort of pace one goes across a ploughed field in autumn at the end of a long and wet walk'), much in the letters of 1904–5 is of very esoteric significance. If Dent did not write with so much

More postcard humour: a few lines from Percy Lubbock to Clive Carey.

zest (and malice), especially if some manoeuvre was *very* confidential, or if great oaks did not grow from little acorns, omission would be easier. In November he first saw *Dr Faustus* performed at the Guildhall in Cambridge by the Elizabethan Stage Society, and was glad to be introduced to so fine a piece of literature, but both the performance and Arnold Dolmetsch's music were 'the most priggish and self-conscious absurdity I ever saw'. A few years later he was to play an important part in the Marlowe Society's first production, arranging the music, and still later on to translate Busoni's opera. His criticism of Clive's vocal quartets, performed at the R.C.M. was typically frank – he used to take pains to get to know a composer well enough to make such comments – 'I maintain that the quartets are beautiful and beautifully written for the voices when you can get mediocre singers who will sacrifice their individualities and try to get a good blend.' Plunket Greene ('the pea green man') was giving a recital at the Aeolian Hall of three of Clive's Bridges songs and Stanford's new 'Songs of the Sea' in November – he sang them again in February with Arthur Somervell's 'A Shropshire Lad' cycle – and was proving difficult, wanting something more 'rushy'; Dent produced a specimen 'hitherto unpublished, by Ernest Liddle and Maude Valerie Walker, revised and fingered or rather thumbed by Samuel (and Tom) Walker'.

The expression mark is 'with ever decreasing accuracy of intonation to the end', and the words, 'The birds that sing in autumn ever among the golden tinted leaves, (Plunkie, are you snarling there below . . .)'

Scarlatti was at last on the verge of publication, and Dent sent Clive a cutting – 'I attribute it to my uncle's curate or some such person' – which appeared in the Society and Personal column of the *Yorkshire Herald*, sandwiched between news of the King of Portugal at Chatsworth and an announcement that the Prince and Princess of Wales had left York House for Sandringham.

'Mr Arnold, the publisher, has lately made an announcement which cannot fail to interest scholars, littérateurs and musicians – especially if they happen to be natives of Yorkshire. It is to the effect that he will shortly publish an important monograph on Alessandro Scarlatti by Mr Edward J. Dent, Fellow of King's College, Cambridge. A Sicilian by birth, the great composer produced his first opera in 1680 at the court of Queen Christiana of Sweden, subsequently migrated to Rome, and finally to Naples, where he died in 1725. Mr Dent has made researches in all the principal libraries in Europe for manuscripts relating to Scarlatti, and has been so far successful that his work may be expected with eagerness. Mr Dent is a younger brother of Major Dent, of Ribston Hall, the popular owner of a large estate between York and Harrogate.' Dent added no further comment.

In December he was in Italy again, first Bordighera, then Rome. At Genoa he just missed *Manuel Menendez*, also played in 1904–5 at Milan, Zürich, Cairo, Breslau, Lisbon, Buenos Aires and Prague. He commented that he hoped success wouldn't turn the young composer's head; nowadays only an expert would know the name of its composer (Filiasi). In Rome he heard a fine *Aida*, and *Barbiere*, where the row was deafening, there was much horseplay and gagging – very traditional and exceedingly funny. He didn't wonder at its holding the stage as it does. This was, as usual in Italy, at a small theatre; the big opera houses went for the last Puccini, some stock Verdi, some Wagner and a little French stuff. As usual he went to *Mefistofele*, and was hoping to hear *I Lombardi*. In Genoa he had looked into an act of *La Forza del Destino* but did not make much of it without knowing the story, and left early as the air was so full of tobacco smoke that he could barely see the stage. On the way back he postponed his journey at Basle owing to the crowd of English with chaplain who were going by that train. 'Family prayers in the restaurant-car were not to my taste, and I stayed behind and saw a German farce all about beer.'

Again he was in Italy in April, breaking his journey to Palermo in Milan, Florence (where friends with a gramophone played records of Caruso in which his voice appeared to reach E♭ in the treble register) and Rome, where he discussed with Joachim his forthcoming Cambridge concert, quartets by Beethoven and Mozart. Dent was particularly delighted to see a poster, half stuck on two sheets, which announced LA BO LKIRIA, which was in fact a performance of *Die Walküre* in Italian. The audience was very small indeed.

When the summer term was over he came down to London for a few days: Duse as La Locandiera (Goldoni) and a grand performance of *The Huguenots*, which rather bored him, partly because in the 2s 6d amphitheatre seats the music, though clear enough, had lost all its guts by the time it reached him – 'and you do want guts to carry old Meyerbeer through'. He loved the overture because it was so cheap and must be horrible to the good Bach-and-Wagner-worshipper, and the tunes that he was told were vulgar. A children's play, *The Christening of Rosalys*, for which Dent had composed incidental music, was due for performance at the Botanic Gardens at Cambridge but it fell through. *Orphée* (with scenery largely from *The Ring*) in early July delighted him, though Eliza Parkina's French did not entitle her to Mademoiselle on the programme and stamped her as Elizabeth Parkinson; he came up for the first performance at Covent Garden of *Madame Butterfly*, but he never liked it.

By the end of July (1905) Dent was in Germany with a sketch-book, at Münster, Brunswick and Würzburg, where he coincided with a student festivity – processions through the town in strange costumes, with flags, in two-horse cabs, and orgies at restaurants with songs and beer *ad nauseam*. A Trinity undergraduate, a German over for the festival and something of a local hero, would have invited him to all the orgies but very creditably saw that Dent preferred loafing with a sketch-book. One suspects that it required no great perception to grasp that.

Clive meanwhile was reluctantly living in Munich, trying to learn the language and to increase his knowledge of German opera. His plans had miscarried and various friends had had to cry off or leave early. His diffidence condemned him to uncomfortable loneliness, so that a letter from Dent with a list of friends and a couple of introductions did not add much to his cheerfulness. A nervous young man may be excused for not presenting a letter to a man whom Dent described as 'a great invalid; he *was* rather too fond of his bottle. His conversation is at times obscene, but he is wonderfully well read and really musical . . . he is a bit grumbly, and will speak ill of most people, probably me included'; but Clive replied that he would certainly call on him – 'let us hope he won't be in the clutches of the bottle (or the bottle in his clutches) when I go'. He wondered whether the *Flying Dutchman* was worth 20 marks. Dent meanwhile meandered on via Wertheim to Bamberg, and the letter telling of Clive's disappointments in his arrangements took a week to catch up with him. Characteristically, though he thought that it was good for Clive and his German to be left quite alone, he offered to come next day if a telegram was sent. As to the *Flying Dutchman*, done in one act at Munich and Bayreuth it must be fine, but as done at Dresden and most places, in three acts, with long pauses and bad lighting, it was very tedious. The verdict was that it was splendid if very well done.

There was no need for the telegram, and Dent remained at Bamberg for another day or two, finding it pleasing though not sketchable, the best part an old slum by the river with such endless detail that he would never manage the drawing of it and in ten minutes would be surrounded by all the little ragamuffins of the place. They spent a week together in Nürnberg, then Clive returned home after six weeks' attempt at German and Dent went down to Trieste. He was composing the incidental music for another children's play by Netta Syrett, *Princess Fragoletta*, which he described as 'a parody of Parsifal by Phil May, Aubrey Beardsley and Ludwig Richter' – they each appeared to have written one act. Dent sketched the music, and the chambermaid threw it away when he was paying a day's visit to Pola, much more interesting to him for its magnificent Roman remains than as the increasingly hideous headquarters of the Austrian Navy.

The routine continued: Cambridge during the term – and few letters, as Clive was also doing some teaching there – and journeys to Italy in the vacations. In December 1905 Dent was in Rome again; in Milan he had thought 10 francs too much to pay for a seat in the pit for Catalani's *Loreley*, an opera much admired by Toscanini. In Rome there was *Faust*, and a performance of Shakespeare's *Julius Caesar* in Italian prose. The proximity of the Forum and the Capitol gave the play a living force that Dent had not hitherto realised. A patriotic play about Lombardy in 1854 excited the audience to fervent anti-Austrian slogans. He hurried back to be in London for Stanford's 'Watts' Symphony, as usual taking in an act of an opera at Genoa on the way; this time it was Audran's *Miss Helyett*, which amused him. He stayed with an uncle and aunt in Nice and would have arrived there a day earlier had he known that *Samson and Delilah* was on; his aunt had shied away from modern French opera, having been considerably shocked by Charpentier's *Louise*.

In letters from Vienna in April (1906) there is mention for the first time of Mozart opera, which was to provide both Dent and Clive with a linked enthusiasm throughout their lives. Dent had heard an atrocious performance of *Die Zauberflöte* in Dresden; in Vienna he read a good deal in the libraries and made the 'shocking discovery' that *Figaro* was full of reminiscences of Sarti's opera *Fra i due litigante il terzo gode* (alluded to in the supper scene of *Don Giovanni*). He went twice to *Figaro* in Vienna, in a new translation with new scenery and dresses. Surprisingly he wrote that he couldn't judge of the translation, but 'it struck me as being good in making it very clear to everybody that Marcellina had once had a child by Bartolo, and that she was very anxious to get married to somebody. She was the most awful fright imaginable, and a delightful surprise after the usual Miss Bauermeister type. She was

Cambridge in May Week 1906: the Pitt Club lawn.

Another May Week occasion: Mrs Wright's barge.

very red in the face, and fat, with ferocious black eyebrows, and a fine moustache! and was ludicrously overdressed. She had also a rather harsh commanding voice, and a manner that was meant to be engaging. Basilio (Breuer the famous Mime) was delightful and I was especially amused by the way in which (being a music master) he conducted the peasants in their chorus in the 1st act. The trial scene was much exaggerated, which was a pity but it is a return to Beaumarchais' original, I believe. They cut "La Vendetta" (partly, I suppose, because it is too quick to sing in German) and as usual the songs for Marcellina and Basilio in the last act; also the opera was given in two acts (5 scenes: I 1 Figaro's room 2 Countess' boudoir. II 1 Throne Room 2 Colonnade with the garden (Letter duet, reception of peasants, fandango) 3 Sotto i pini del boschetto).'

There was much other musical gossip: two symphony concerts, practices with Signora Maddalena of Max Reger's variations on a theme of Beethoven op. 86; Mahler conducting at the opera with a knitting needle, and playing the recitatives in *Figaro* on a harpsichord, the bars for the introduction to 'Si vuol ballare' being played by one cello and one double bass.

After the summer term of 1906 Dent had determined to study abroad for a year, and Clive returned to Cambridge as a graduate student. Abortive negotiations took place for him to occupy Dent's rooms in King's – he would thus have had the run of the books and music – but as Clive himself had been in residence at Clare the precedent (which would cause no anxiety nowadays) was regarded as dangerous, and he went into digs near Magdalene (at £4 a month). The chief excitement of the summer was to be a Cambridge performance at the Scala Theatre in London of Messager's *Mirette*; the composer himself was to conduct, and Geoffrey Toye (then aged seventeen) was deputy; Clive was, of course, singing in this, and at the same time his four-part settings with orchestra of poems from W. E. Henley's 'Hawthorn and Lavender' were to be performed at a Palmer concert. Neither occasion reached expectations, and Dent was not afraid to criticise his enthusiastic but sub-professional friends. He was bored to death by *Mirette* – 'it seems to be a great deal longer than *Meistersinger*!' – in fact it had taken 3¾ hours; Goeffrey Toye's conducting was masterly – he had stepped into the breach when Messager was called urgently to Paris – but Clive's voice was disappointing; Francis Toye's voice sounded of

27

really beautiful quality at times, but his operaticisms were grotesque.

There is no purpose in quoting individual criticisms of Clive's songs now forgotten though still extant; in the Queen's Hall they sounded 'choppy', one was described as 'confused and messy' another as 'chaos', but the summary may bear repetition: 'Your stuff, when it came off, was natural and beautiful and – oh well, I think I had better not say the rest. You must write more instrumental music, or else solo songs, not quartets; write tunes if you can, and try to be clear. Try to conceive a *whole* movement in your head if you can before you write it down. Now I understand why the best songs I wrote were written in Venice, and in places where I hated sitting in a room to write, and forced myself to work out the whole thing in my head, *as a whole*.'

The advice may have been sound, but Clive knew that he had no ideas worth anything when he hadn't words, and that it was the *atmosphere* of words that suggested music to him, and so it remained.

London, even with successive nights at *Eugene Onegin*, *Armide*, and *Traviata*, could not hold Dent for long. In August he was at Fano again, deprived of his bathing because a storm had washed the bathing cabins out to sea, and making various not particularly interesting acquaintances. He volunteered to play at an impromptu dance, and thought he had done better than the local 'maestro' who was turned on – 'I think he must have been a waiter.' Gorki's *Nachtasyl* at the local playhouse – it seems an odd choice for a seaside resort in summer – bored him with its monotonous bestiality. There was a doss-house with some half-a-dozen beds in it on which people either died of consumption or were dead drunk, or tried to rape somebody; and to give a realistic air the two beds nearest the footlights were conspicuously provided with chamber pots.

The whole summer of 1906 was to be spent in Italy, and in October he was to start work in Berlin; he was wandering about in little places, chiefly on foot, living very cheaply and beating down everything as low as possible. One anxiety was the importunity of Miss Syrett about the music for the fairy play; she had some hope that Tree would produce it. If he did, he would certainly pull it about so much that it was not worth writing anything yet; Dent hoped that Clive would take it off his hands.

He had attended Mass in the Cathedral at Orvieto:

Zander & Labisch, Phot., Berlin 1906

Restaurant Italia ∴ Weingrosshandlung ∴ Inh. Elia Bartolini
Königin Augustastr. 19. Fernspr. Amt VI, 8589

Berlin W.,
den

Café life in Berlin.

'there was a squeaky little organ in the nave, with a sort of balcony, in which stood four singers, a youth who sang falsetto alto up to high G, apparently with considerable pain; a tenor who bleated like a goat; a dummy who sang nothing, and a bass who sang with energy and conviction. The music I should say was Italian about 1860 by some mediocre composer who had read some Haydn or eighteenth-century Italian masses, and done some elementary counterpoint. It made a huge row in the bare empty building and was ludicrously inconsequent, though surpassed by the organist's extemporisation during the elevation, which was indescribably absurd, every now and then breaking off into cadenzas and melodic fragments dimly reminiscent of the Traviata.'

The work in which Dent was involved was a series of articles for the eleventh edition of *Encyclopedia Britannica* on Italian composers of the seventeenth and eighteenth centuries. In Florence, too, he was helping Robert Cust with translation; he lunched with Vernon Lee (Violet Paget), then well known as an essayist and interpreter of Italian culture – 'she is said to be marvellously hideous, but I thought her rather nice-looking. But then I judge by Cambridge standards still!'

29

O'Neil Phillips.

His Berlin interlude lasted for some eight months. It produced many long, often uncomfortable, letters, for Dent's social life became very much dependent on the moods of a young and brilliant English pianist, O'Neil Phillips, a pupil of Busoni, with whom Dent himself had studied. The circle was indeed a strange one, appearing even stranger in Dent's succinct sketches: they included a barefoot dancer, a would-be pianist with a wooden leg, and a she-composer with hair like a Japanese chrysanthemum – 'one of those Du Maurier women who are always in the act of shaking hands'. The common factor was their adoration for Busoni and his wife. The Englishmen in Berlin, typically, were too dreadful for description: 'mostly floppy, with a great desire to be artistic'.

Surprisingly, the music was mostly French: Debussy and C. V. Alkan, Fauré, and D'Indy, who was there in person to conduct his *Symphonie sur un chant montagnard*. Dent was hearing much music for the first time; he had been led to believe that these composers were ugly, confused and quite incomprehensible but found them full of melody, clear and very logical, as a rule. He thought D'Indy greatly superior to Strauss (and D'Indy's music more intelligible than D'Indy's German!). He had come to Berlin for quiet, but found himself in a whirl of engagements, drinking and smoking too much, spending the evenings at an Italian restaurant in a Babel of divers tongues. In the set with whom he was, rather than the professors of the Hochschule, he might spend the whole winter without hearing a word of Brahms ('Oxford's favourite composer').

Clive, mostly in Cambridge rehearsing *The Eumenides* of Aeschylus (Stanford), in which he played the part of Athena, received news of wild parties in Berlin after the concerts, the bass notes of the piano sticking because a glass of wine had previously been broken on the keyboard, Busoni looking in very late and going for a walk after it was all over. O'Neil Phillips was proving a problem, for he could not afford to stay (although his rent was only £2 10s 0d a month), and was too proud to accept help from friends. Dent asked Clive whether he could raise some money for him, perhaps through Mrs Knatchbull,[1] whose protégé Phillips was, as payment for imaginary work done. If Dent's name was mentioned it would spoil what was at

[1] Dora Bright, 1863–1951, pianist and composer. Clive was a frequent visitor to her country house at Babington.

The Eumenides of Aeschylus
1906.
Athena and Orestes (Carey and
Scholfield).

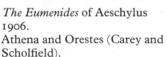

Rupert Brooke as the Herald.

the time a very good friendship; and he couldn't ask him
for piano lessons because he would hate them so. Busoni
wanted Phillips to stay, but the latter was even refusing
fees for playing. As for Dent's own work, all the *Encyclopedia* articles had to be completely rewritten; he was
supposed to be undertaking an edition of Purcell's *Indian
Queen*, and had promised to translate an article of Busoni's.
He was pushing on with a series of essays on musical
appreciation. Composition wouldn't come; he wondered
whether his abstention from Brahms might enable him one
day to write something that was not Brahms-and-water. In
December (1906) he had to lecture to the Berlin branch of
the International Musical Society, and, sidestepping a
request to speak on Scarlatti, he preferred to lecture on

Other views of *The Eumenides*: a
cartoon from *The Granta* (right)
and illustration from a review in
The Graphic (below).

Apollo
Mr E.H. Latter

Shade of
Clyt'mnestra
Mr E.J. Selwyn

Hermes
Mr G.G. Alderson

Leader of the Chorus
Mr F.A. Young

Athena
Mr F.C.S. Carey

Orestes
Mr A.F. Scholfield

Orestes, pursued by the Furies, seeks refuge
at the Temple of Athena

Leonardo Leo. This might also provide an excuse to bring Clive out to sing the musical illustrations; meanwhile Clive was to collect and send out a parcel of material. Dent was to lecture in German.

Relations with O'Neil Phillips became increasingly difficult. Dent believed wholeheartedly in his talents but not in his temperament; Phillips resented his rough tongue, and though Dent might write to Clive: 'I should not take the trouble to be rude to him if I did not think him worth it', he was not one of Dent's 'old gang' who could accustom himself to blunt criticism. 'The only music that has charms to soothe that savage breast is his own', Dent wrote, 'and after he has strummed his own works, with an occasional Chopin or Debussy intermezzo, for an hour or so at my pianoforte, he becomes quite pleasant.' Furthermore, Phillips was hurt if Dent wrote a letter or read during these sessions; he was jealous too of Dent's ability to get on faster with new acquaintances 'when they happen to be German, interesting and of the male sex', natural enough though it was with Dent's command of languages. Meanwhile Phillips made terrific progress with all females, young, old, American, German or English.

There are passing references to a stodgy recital from Donald Tovey, and a rehearsal of Mahler's Third Symphony ('very chaotic and not good'), praise for a wonderful chapter on Handel in Streatfeild's book on modern music, and fury that he hit upon what Dent thought was an entirely original idea of his own about Mozart. Clive is criticised for his generally dilettante attitude to his work – and, for once, retaliates: 'You went to Germany to write . . . and what do you do? Go to concerts, have supper with those Busoni people, quarrel with O'Neil and edit the Indian Queen.' He writes too very forcefully about Dent's tolerance of O'Neil Phillips in Berlin who 'stays there (on other people's money) long after Busoni has gone, mooning about, doing nothing except writing cynical and suggestive things to me, and doing his utmost, by saying rude and unpleasant things, to break off his friendship with Mrs Knatchbull, who really was entirely the cause of his going out, and has done her best to help him' – and more in this strain. Mrs Knatchbull, who composed and wrote under the name of Dora Bright, was a wealthy woman whose well-intended patronage was not always well-rewarded; Clive's mother nicknamed her 'Mrs Snatch'em' and resented her possessiveness.

Dora Knatchbull and friends, July 1909. Left to right, Francis Jekyll, Francis Toye, A.M. (unidentified), Dora Knatchbull, O'Neil Phillips.

Clive's letter cleared the air and elicited a thoughtful response: 'It is in vain that I tell O'Neil that I must cultivate the art of talking because I have no other accomplishments; he can both dance and play, and is good-looking as well . . . If I remonstrate he tells me not to preach, and I have such a horror of doing that that I relapse into silence. If I try to be agreeable he merely shows me that he considers me to be a hypocrite. Am I a brute because I can't do with friends who are not clever and ready-witted? . . . Yet I can't say that I have squeezed O'N dry; his playing is still a genuine pleasure to me, and his personality is at its best when he plays. Unfortunately I once took up a book when he was playing ostentatiously for his amusement and not for mine; and that has never been forgiven!'

The long letter ends with what was unusual for Dent, a 'Now I must stop.' What drew him away was a piano recital by Busoni. The previous evening Dent had been to hear Strauss conduct a revival of *Falstaff*; although it was not a good performance he was going again on Saturday ('such splendid stuff') and, for the first time, to *Salome* on Sunday. He did not find it very digestible, but returned to it a month later. The Busoni circle had by now dispersed and Dent had been accepted in a group of artists. At a party where he had been set down to accompany Brahms' songs (and had refused to attempt 'Meine Liebe ist grün') they were told to select their own ladies to take into supper. Dent solved the difficulty by offering his arm to the old grandmother, who seemed to be quite out in the cold. He was now – for once – looking forward to a month in

London, and hoping to find the regular hours of his mother's establishment conducive to more work. 'I find that if I don't come back to England for a short time at any rate after being long abroad I get the sort of discomfort of mind that the body feels when circumstances have prevented the satisfactory fulfilment of one's after-breakfast obligations.'

In May (1907) he was off again, writing anxiously and thoughtfully from Pavia about the programme for one of Clive's early recitals; his sister had joined him at Milan and after a few days at Bergamo they travelled to Varenna on Lake Como. 'It was supposed to be a quiet little place with a primitive inn, but when we got there it was neither primitive nor quiet . . . The terrace and view were as lovely as any scene in an opera, and we both thought the other people in the hotel seemed to do and say the things that they would in a fashionable modern play. The people in question came there for golf, and we were not smart enough for their acquaintance. In the small hours of the morning we were much bothered by church bells, and also by a dreadful bird which I felt sure must be American, it was so aggressively vulgar. It imitated most other birds in a sort of music-hall way – there was a very charming nightingale which used to sing to us until this creature frightened it away – and it interspersed these numbers with fragments of popular tunes and descending chromatic scales, executed with the energy of a steam merry-go-round.'

From Pavia he went to Florence, then walked to Perugia, managing twenty-five miles a day, and taking a very circuitous route through Impruneta, Greve, Siena, Asciano, Monte Oliveto, Buonconvento, Montepulciano, Citta del Pieve, Orvieto and Todi, with occasional rest days. His comments are idiosyncratic as ever: 'Between Todi and Orvieto there is nowhere to get a decent meal – but I started at 7, and got a drink at Prodo (9.30), at 11 two raw eggs and some water at an osteria of the nature of Five Miles from Anywhere (except that I believe the Cambridgeshire inn is quite good) – and as the place was not attractive enough to rest in and no trees anywhere to lie under (Trees, where I walk, do not crowd into a shade as a rule) there was nothing for it but to trudge on to Todi, with, as usual, a steep hill at the end, where I arrived about 2.' He asked Clive to pass on to the Provost (M. R. James) that he had twice slept in no. 13: at Montepulciano, where the number was undisguised, and at Perugia, where, having refused to pay 3 francs for a room he was offered one for fr.2.50 on the second floor, and found that it was no. 12 bis, the next being 14. 'However, I slept very well last night, and have had no trouble with the sheets.' Readers of James's *Ghost Stories of an Antiquary* will have no difficulty with the allusion.

In August, though he had had plans of breaking new ground by going down through the Abruzzi to Termoli or S. Benedetto di Tronto, he was again at Fano, after a fortnight's work in Rome. In Fano composition would not come, and the excuses were characteristically original. 'I ought to be wrestling with a great work, but the cook has begun his daily *solfeggi*[1] and that stops my composition short . . . He appears to be musical, and while he prepares the food he sings unceasingly – fragments of everything – and I think he must also be or have been a player of some brass instrument in a wind band. I suppose it ought to give me ideas . . . If I could only get my breakfast brought to me by six, I could get a lot of work done, but I can't compose on an empty stomach; and they will not bring me my breakfast before 7.30 at the earliest. At 9.30 the noises begin – and indeed at six the military band practise; then there are church bells and bugles, and after about 9.30 comes what I hate most of all – the rasping loud voice of a woman who appears to be a chambermaid. She appears to be in a chronic bad temper and enceinte; and the local dialect makes her talk additionally disagreeable.'

In Fano there was not much music – an operetta company whose repertoire was Suppé's *Boccaccio*, Strauss's *Eine Nacht in Venedig*, and *The Geisha* – 'I have seen them all once, or at any rate, one act of each and never wish to see them again.' Dent wondered why they didn't do *Véronique*, a favourite of his and Clive's. He did, however, go to their first night, Lecocq's *Ninon de l'Enclos, ou les amours de Cyrano de Bergerac*. 'It is obviously modelled on Rostand's play, but without any of the poetical episodes. I thought the music very attractive, as far as I could grasp it, but it was a process of conjectural restoration from scattered fragments. The band was worse than the Cambridge Theatre at its worst, the basses never knew where they were. The men sang fairly decently; the women were disgusting, and of course there was no ensemble; Italians

[1] For the benefit of the unenlightened it should perhaps be explained that these are vocal exercises, not culinary ones.

can't do it. My recollection of the historical Ninon was that she practised as a prostitute up to the age of 80. This one was only about 40, but there was no doubt of the rest of the resemblance . . .

'The cook has got to his cabaletta movement, when he pours out phrases with terrific energy and rapidity. It is more than I can endure and I must go down to the bathing place.'

Dent returned to King's for the October term of 1907; one of his first initiatives was to ensure that Clive would undertake serious studies in Europe rather than enjoying Mrs Knatchbull's hospitality at Babington or 'the easy laurels of the Cambridge Carnival' – an unkind reference to his successes in the Greek play, in the A.D.C. (Amateur Dramatic Company – notably as Lady Bracknell), with the orchestra, and with the music to Anstey's witty libretto of *The Return of Agamemnon*, some of whose lyrics his brother could still remember some sixty years afterwards.

A major initiative in November 1907 was the formation of the Marlowe (Dramatic) Society. Its founding fathers consisted chiefly of those who had been involved in *The Eumenides* in the previous year, including some of the livelier members of the influential Greek Play Committee. Among the former were Justin Brooke, Rupert Brooke, and Andrew Gow; and among the latter Francis Cornford, A. W. Verrall, and M. R. James. Usually undergraduate drama was staged by the A.D.C., but its energies were devoted solely to comedy. When the proposal was made to put on *Dr Faustus*, a set-book for the Pass degree in 1907 but then very rarely performed, the A.D.C. was not interested in undertaking it, and by staging it the Marlowe Society took its name and origin. Among the early productions with which Dent was associated were *Comus* and Ben Jonson's *Epicoene*. At a rehearsal shortly before the first performance, a prominent Cambridge don described it as 'a group of incompetent amateurs mumbling in the dark', but it continues to flourish with a reputation beyond Cambridge and a number of play recordings to its credit.

At Cambridge there were all the old jobs: lectures, the orchestra, a few students at the Day Training College, and a recital by O'Neil Phillips to promote – 'he appears to expect Perrier-Jouet in a mug after his concert. I have half a mind to provide him with a bottle of Perrier, which is equally fizzy and less exciting.' Dent was anxious to acquire a house of his own rather than remaining in college,

THE TRAGICAL HISTORY OF
DOCTOR FAUSTUS

BY

CHRISTOPHER MARLOWE.

Monday, November 11.
Tuesday, November 12.

The Pope.	*G. H. L. Mallory*
The Cardinal of Lorraine.	*Cosmo Gordon*
Doctor Faustus.	*Brooke*
Valdes } magicians.	*Cosmo Gordon*
Cornelius }	*Chevalier-White*
Wagner, *servant to Faustus.*	*Hugh Otto Baron*
Robin.	*J. P. Robinson*
Ralph.	*G. P. Barker*
Vintner.	*J. R. Salter*
Old man.	
Three Scholars.	*W. Falkner H. J. Sambrook*
Friars.	*H. Coward White G. H. L. Mallory*
Lucifer.	*W. Denis Browne*
Belzebub.	*C. O. Rumsby*
Mephistophilis.	*Rupert Brooke*
Good Angel.	*Charles H. J. Rantley*
Evil Angel.	*Geoffrey Keynes*
The Seven Deadly Sins.	*G. L. M. Barker*
Devils.	*R. E. Hubback*
Helen of Troy.	*A. R. Marshall*

Chorus.

*The audience is reminded that the play
is not over until the chorus has spoken the
concluding lines.*

The Marlowe Society:
programme of the first
performance.

The Marlowe Society's *Epicoene*:
Reginald Pole as Sir John Daws
(top) and W. O. Phillips, of
Corpus, as Epicoene (bottom).

"THE SILENT WOMAN."

BY THE CAMBRIDGE UNIVERSITY MARLOW SOCIETY.

This comparatively young society is to be congratulated on the energy and enterprise which it has displayed in its newest production. Only a nominal subscription of 5s. per annum is imposed, and the committee can thus draw for their cast on a far wider public than is open to the A.D.C. "Epicene; or, the Silent Woman" is by no means widely known, but Dryden characterised it as the best constructed English drama he knew, and the interest on Friday night never flagged, although to a modern audience the plot *does* seem a trifle complicated. Needless to say, a great deal of the play was cut to suit the requirements at once of modern taste and modern patience.

The music was entirely satisfactory, consisting of Old English dances and work by Orlando Gibbons, Dr. Coleman, and others. In particular we enjoyed the song which the page sings in the first act—" Still to be Neat." It is not generally realised that this is a translation of one of the Carmina Priapeia, by Petronius. The music is by Dr. John Wilson. The stage was small but tastefully arranged, and the dresses were those of the period. Names of the cast were not printed on the programme. True-wit possesses by far the longest and most thankless part. His business is not to be farcical himself, but to make others so.

He made the most of his opportunities and acted with dash and verve. Sir John Daws was a convincing character-study, and Mrs. Otter, a purely farcical personage, was both amusing and restrained—a difficult combination. Dauphine was rather too typical of the stagy amateur. Cleremont looked very splendid, but was not very inspiring. My Lady Haughty had the only feminine voice of the female caste, in striking contrast to Epicene, who combined the double-bass and piccolo with rather disheartening effect. Morose looked admirable, and affected the old Irvingesque manner. He gave us the impression of being rather bullied and unable to hold his own. There were times when the voice of the prompter was heard a little too often in the land, but the whole performance reflected the greatest credit on a young society.

where he compared getting his room into shape to re-building San Francisco, destroyed in an earthquake the previous year. Clive was making excuses to postpone his departure – Moszkowski in Paris could not take him till March – but Dent was determined that he must undergo a term of compulsory independence, the sooner the better; his Cambridge friends should make a league to be rude to him and drive him out of England.

By now Rupert Brooke, in his second year as an undergraduate at King's, was beginning to make inroads on the affections of a wide circle of his contemporaries, and most of Dent's letters make some allusion to him. Clive was with a group which included Rupert on holiday at Andermatt at Christmas, and also the following year (1908), when the party composed a burlesque melodrama. He had been driven into exile at last by the generosity of a group of friends, of whom Dent was the foremost, who were paying for him to study, first in Munich. Meanwhile Dent had spent Christmas at King's – he referred to it as 'the successive bank holidays – I am thankful that they are now over' – singing humorous glees and catches with J.E. Nixon and a boy of about eleven who was staying with him. Nixon, a fellow of the college portrayed with affectionate mockery by M. R. James in *Eton and King's* and solely as a figure of fun in E. F. Benson's *David of King's* (under the name of Crowfoot), held glee-parties which he conducted with a paper knife. His tenor voice, however accurate, was scarcely elegant, and he tended to be unkindly deserted by his colleagues on the high notes. However, he was a real and knowledgeable enthusiast, and Dent preferred to take his amateur enthusiasm seriously, as he did also in the case of another well-known fellow of the college, Oscar Browning, whose egotism often masked his finer qualities. On this occasion 'The Alderman's Thumb', by the eighteenth-century Dr Harrington, which describes a City dinner in which in the fight for turtle and other delicacies the alderman's thumb is cut off, was, not surprisingly, the boy's particular favourite.

Letters from Clive became more frequent, partly because he was obliged to request and to acknowledge subsidies, and partly to give Dent news of various friends to whom he had letters of introduction. Dent moved, in a soaking January, to 4 Belvedere Terrace,[1] which was to be

---

[1] Later re-named 77 Panton Street.

his home in Cambridge for thirty years. Mrs Knatchbull was to play in Cambridge 'and I believe I dine with her. Odder programme than ever. She telephoned me the other day and made more din, bawling, than a Holbrooke symphonic poem.' In Munich Clive was going to hear *Die Zauberflöte* for the first time; it was a work very rarely performed in England. He was taking regular German lessons and reading several plays before seeing them performed, and also hearing a great deal of opera, *Carmen*, *Tristan*, Adam's *Der Postillian*[2] and Lortzing's *Undine*.

Dent writes very fully of musical activities in Cambridge, at the centre of which he was tirelessly involved; in 1908 he reached his zenith as a letter writer. One finds him everywhere: playing the tympani at a symphony concert; translating *Sherlock Holmes* at the theatre to a visiting foreign pianist, fortunately on the night of the County Ball when the theatre was almost empty; giving dinner to Rupert Brooke and unable to shake off an infatuated older man who insisted on coming the same day. From their first encounter he was convinced of the talents, as he was also captivated by the character, of W. Denis Browne, little remembered now but as the writer of four exquisite songs and of letters home recounting the death and burial of Rupert Brooke, his contemporary at Rugby, at Cambridge and in the Royal Naval Division. In March, Clive moved on to Paris; Dent had met Moszkowski and Mrs Knatchbull at a recent concert in London where she had been soloist in his pianoforte concerto, which Dent liked. If his orchestration and style were not modern, at least they were skilful and clear, getting great sonority out of the band with small means, mainly because the counterpoint was good. Thus there were hopes that Clive would be in good hands as a student of advanced composition. As soon as he could find rooms (at 48 rue de Clichy), Clive started with Moszkowski, and attended a concert lasting $2\frac{1}{2}$ hours consisting entirely of Debussy; at the Opéra-Comique in *Lakmé* and *Alceste* it was a relief to hear a singer *playing* with his voice, after those horrible tight-throated German men. There was no Debussy in Naples, where Dent was spending most of his vacation working in two libraries; Martucci, director of the Conservatoire told him that it was more important that Naples should get to know Haydn, Mozart and Beethoven.

[2] *Le Postillon de Long jumeau.*

When Dent returned to Cambridge – after a few days in Petersfield, where he saw something of Vaughan Williams, whose music and personality he much admired – he found anxious letters from Clive about the cost of singing lessons; Isnardon was apparently the best and most popular, but also the most expensive, teacher in Paris, and it was doubtful whether the money which Dent and his friends had raised would meet this; there could hardly be a further 'whip round' till autumn, but then there was every prospect of a response generous enough to keep Clive abroad for the winter. The £58 in hand, together with Clive's allowance from home should last four or five months and pay for Isnardon's lessons, as Clive fully agreed.

The musical novelty at Cambridge was a performance of *Comus*, with Henry Lawes' music and contemporary dances arranged by Dent, to be performed in Christ's College garden to celebrate the tercentenary of the birth of John Milton. The initiative came from Rupert and Justin Brooke; Dent was to conduct, but light-heartedly suggested that he might get 'hoofed' by 'Mr Rupert Beerbohm Brooke, who is quite the Actor-Manager. He has got rid of Pole as the attendant spirit because he was not beautiful enough; he has also got rid of Brierley of Christ's (Comus) for the opposite reason . . .'

Isnardon was proving 'quite splendid', trying to get Clive's voice more in front, and to make him sing quite legato and without effort rather than beginning him all over again; Moszkowski on the other hand was hideously strict, no doubt beneficial but scarcely letting a single bar stand of a new violin sonata. At the Opera there was Rameau (*Hippolyte et Aricie*), and from Moscow and St Petersburg the Russians had brought *Boris Godounov*, which Clive saw twice – 'I have scarcely ever been so impressed by anything – oh, such heavenly singers, every one.' He was convinced that Puccini had heard it, as *Butterfly* was chock full of the same tricks. He also saw Rimsky-Korsakov's *Snegourotchka*. Dent later made a number of translations of songs from Borodin, Moussorgsky and Rimsky-Korsakov for a recital of Clive's, and Clive produced *Boris* in the original version at Sadler's Wells in 1935, and *Snegourotchka* (*The Snow Maiden*) in 1933, the first performance in England.

Meanwhile, Rupert and his friends were anxious to lure Clive back to Cambridge on 10 July, chiefly in order to show how much better they acted than he did; there was

42

Edwardian Cambridge
celebrating a 21st birthday.

much scoffing at Clive's 'operatic manner', but Dent told
Rupert not to say his own lines like a Gustave Doré angel.
A holiday at Marlotte with Mrs Knatchbull – inevitably at
this time in Paris – and with Moszkowski had not enabled
him to get to know his teacher better, so Clive returned for
Comus, which was proving so demanding in rehearsal that
Dent had to miss Isadora Duncan. Dent had urged him to
stay on in Marlotte, Barbizon and Moret – 'which last is
famous for its barley sugar. Go there in preference to
Cambridge, which only produces sausages'.

After *Comus* Dent went, as usual in summer, to Italy,
walking from Bologna to Sassoferrato, via Casentino and
Arezzo. He then walked on to Jesi to see the Lotto pictures,
not to worship Pergolesi, whose birthplace it is and about
whom he had written an article in Grove which would not
have ingratiated him with the inhabitants. Thence he went
by train to Bologna, and on to the Veneto for more walking.

43

It had become almost a drug to him, for he did no work and heard no music until he returned to Yorkshire to provide company for his dearest friend, Lawrence Haward, who was recovering from a serious attack of pneumonia. He completed the first movement of a quartet, and had got the main themes for the second and third movements. Haward's very useful bibliography of Dent's writings, compiled and privately printed in 1956, indicates that it was never completed.

In Cambridge taste was changing, and a concert of music entirely devoted to Debussy and Duparc was warmly received, so that Dent thought of asking his friend O'Neil Phillips to give another recital, to be mostly, if not exclusively, modern French. At C.U.M.S. some of Rootham's music was to be performed – 'all in MS which in this case stands for Much Swearing also'. It had been agreed that Clive, who had been giving a number of recitals including Vincent D'Indy folk-songs, should go to Italy early in the New Year (1909), and the usual gracious flood of introductions, with brief pen portraits and addresses, was forthcoming. For example, 'Scontrino is a Sicilian, teacher of composition at the R. Istituto Musicale. He is said to have the evil eye, but he is a dear creature in spite of his very dry quartets. His wife was a prima donna, and married an Egyptian in Cairo who left her all his money.' At Verona stay at 'Quattro Pellegrini (not Pellegrino which is for American tourists, as Byron lived there)'. At Florence Lapi is 'amusing occasionally, as all the Gordon Craig freaks eat there'.

In spite of, or perhaps because of, the surfeit of information, Clive, who went out via Munich where by now the Ewalds were close friends, chose to stay at a pension in Florence kept by a Russian woman and chiefly frequented by Germans. He was hearing the *Ring* in Munich, while Dent was likewise hearing it in London, and *Madame Butterfly*. Dent also braved a thick fog to hear E.W. Naylor's *The Angelus*, which had won the Ricordi prize. Perhaps it would be kinder to refer a reader to Dent's article on it in the *Cambridge Review* than to quote more than a line or two of his letter: 'It was like the Golden Legend dramatized, only without any of the Golden Legend's attractions.' Naylor and Dent were friendly colleagues on the musical faculty at Cambridge for many years, in spite of Dent's inability to appreciate *The Angelus*; Dent's own cursed infertility as a composer probably made him doubly critical of the productions of his Cambridge colleagues at this period.

Clive remained in Florence till June, studying singing with Pavesi, chiefly concerned with mastering the Italian language and taking advantage of the opportunity to speak German with the other guests of Madame de Wiskovatoff. At Cambridge Dent arranged the music for the Marlowe Society's performance of Ben Jonson's *Epicoene*, much more of a landmark then than now, stage-managed by Reginald Pole. At the first performance the prompter had far the biggest part, but on the Saturday it went splendidly; the music came from books at the British Museum, and it was planned to make a suite from this and the *Comus* music. In December Dent, at Hugh Allen's[1] request, had read a paper to the Oxford Musical Discussion Club on *Don Giovanni*, which he repeated to his history class of organ scholars, playing and singing half the opera with them. When Allen asked him to read it at short notice to the Musical Association he was less enthusiastic, for what was written for young men wouldn't do for 'old women of both sexes'. There was yet another Matthew Passion in March, causing him to exclaim that he never wished to hear it again – or the Brahms Requiem. On the personal side he commented that Rupert Brooke was hardly ever visible owing to Socialism, and mentioned a self-abnegation dinner of all the socialists in all the colleges: King's dined in Rupert's room off bread and cheese at 6*d* a head, and deposited the difference between that and the price of Hall to be sent to the Labour candidate at some election. In 1909 such an event merited an exclamation mark. New names that crop up among Dent's friends at this time are George Mallory, later to die on Everest, then an active member of the Marlowe Society, and Theo Bartholomew, Assistant Librarian at the University Library; largely self-educated, he was a man of deep culture with a genius for friendship.

Having played a prominent part in two Greek plays and composed music for Anstey's burlesque *The Return of Agamemnon*, Clive had the ambition to write music for one of Aristophanes' comedies, or at least that Dent should do so. He was thus a little disappointed to hear that Vaughan Williams had been asked to compose the incidental music for *The Wasps* – and feared that his 'churchy' music would be far too ponderous. Dent replied that Vaughan Williams

[1] 1869–1946. Then organist of New College, Oxford; 1918 Professor of Music at Oxford, and 1918–37 also Director of the Royal College of Music.

was reported to be making heavy weather of it, but that he himself would rather set one of Gilbert Murray's translations, and had very little respect for the plan of doing Greek plays in Greek for modern audiences.

In Florence with Pavesi Clive was singing airs from opera – *Dinorah*, *Trovatore*, and *Ernani* – with the most intense passion, and like many English singers having more trouble with the single consonant in Italian than the double one. He chuckled over a performance of the Will o' the Wisps ballet in the *Dannazione*: 'it consisted of about 15 exceedingly tall, bony and ungraceful females more or less in skin tights – none of them really knew the steps – they were all in red with the exception of three at the back, one of whom was especially tall – had *no* idea of what to do and merely waddled about imitating the others, sometimes quite alone and in the middle of the stage, always with the hands hanging like a dog begging in front of the chest and the knees bent. The whole ballet seemed to consist of hops, which took place whenever the cymbals clashed.' He had spoken enough German, and moved to a small pension where only Italian was spoken.

Dent's dislike of the Matthew Passion was further accentuated by the performance in March 1909 which Alan Gray conducted: 'He never grasped at all, I think, that there are two complete orchestras throughout the work and that Bach directs one to accompany some airs and the 2nd others; so he was always 'bowing' to the wrong leader to come in!' The Marlowe Society had contemplated a London performance of *Epicoene* but withdrew in face of difficulties (including, if Dent is to be believed, the fear of Augustine Birrell's son that his father's reputation would be further endangered if he was to act. Birrell as Chief Secretary for Ireland had recently been heavily criticised for an alleged lunch with Marie Lloyd). Now *The Knight of the Burning Pestle*, again with Dent's musical arrangement, was in gestation. Dent had been talked into judging a choral competition at Moreton in Marsh with Allen, who was pleased with his remarks – 'so were the people – not often that my remarks are relished, is it?' But staying in strange places and having to be polite to swarms of strange females was never to Dent's taste, and on such occasions the female and clerical element was always in the majority. He was flattered to receive an invitation to contribute to a Festschrift in honour of Hugo Riemann, Professor of Music at Leipzig and 'the most learned of learned Germans', and proposed to base his essay on a little Jesuit book, the supposed autobiography of a young Italian gentleman in 1680 who went to the opera and carried on with a prima donna. The studies were published at Leipzig in 1909.

In May Dent was in Berlin, writing in Italian about his experiences there. On his arrival he had immediately been taken to d'Albert's *Tiefland*, which had had a great success at Berlin, but he had been so much bored that he would have left after the first act. He was also going to Méhul's *Joseph*, which with *Fra Diavolo* he at that time regarded as the two most beautiful works of all the French operatic repertoire. He thought that to go to *Elektra* would be a duty rather than a pleasure; but to his great astonishment he liked it better than anything he had heard of Strauss – 'It is much more clear and logical than *Salome* – less perverse and more sincere; indeed, it almost approaches nobility, which is saying a great deal for Strauss.' In June they went together to Ethel Smyth's *The Wreckers*, the first London performance, and since it was one of the comparatively rare occasions when he and Clive attended an opera together there is no record of Dent's reaction to it.

There was another musical event in July at which surprisingly Dent was not accompanied either by Clive or by Mrs Knatchbull – a recital by O'Neil Phillips. Dent sent a long and characteristic report, charmed by the perfect control of tone, the precision, the accuracy and the wonderful sense of rhythm, but maddened by the hostility of much of the playing. 'What pleased the audience most was a Bear Dance by one Béla Bartók, in which the pianoforte is treated like a mere tom-tom; one might as well play it in boxing gloves, and indeed it sounds just like that. These silly women were dying to have it a second time; however O'Neil had the decency not to repeat it.' Some ten years later Dent was proposing to Clive that he should translate *Duke Bluebeard's Castle* for Clive to produce at the Old Vic.

Plans for *The Knight of the Burning Pestle* had been given up. Unlike the first Marlowe performance it was to have been performed by a 'bisexual company' and Dent naturally inferred that the ladies were the weak vessels. Rupert had come back 'pink and impenitent as usual' (it was he who had proposed the venture); 'he is living in Arcadian solitude at Grantchester, so I suggested to him that he should write something that we might act in a garden, with music by me for Miss Darwin and Miss Luard to play on the flute and viola, elusive and ethereal, like Rupert's Comus costume'. It did not come to fruition.

Since Clive's return from Italy his throat had gone badly out of order, and he was being treated by an 'electrical doctor'. As he was in no condition for stage work or dramatic singing, he wrote asking Dent whether he should accept the post of organist at Guy's Hospital – two services on a Sunday, a Friday practice and an 'oratorio' choir[1] with one weekly practice – for £75 a year. He also wanted Dent's opinion on Elgar's First Symphony and the 'Ode to Discord' (a new work of Stanford, now forgotten). Dent was a little impatient at being asked the first question, feeling that Clive should make his own mind up and best knew his own circumstances and intentions. The second question is ignored altogether; perhaps he had not troubled to attend a performance or study a score. He had just been at Oxford, where a party of a dozen or so had got together to read Bach cantatas and Palestrina masses. Fortunately (from Dent's point of view) there was also the final act of *Fidelio*, and he had persuaded the others to run through Vecchi's *L'Amfiparnaso* (1594), always a favourite of his. George Butterworth had also been there, and Bevis Ellis, who was later to sponsor the first performance of Butterworth's 'Banks of Green Willow' – he was also responsible for that of Vaughan Williams' 'London Symphony'. On this occasion Dent found them both over exuberant: 'Ellis is a good soul *au fond*, but George Butterworth wants sitting on.' F. S. Kelly, the Australian pianist and composer, like Butterworth to be killed in 1916, was another welcome member of the party.

A Long Vacation could not pass without a few weeks in Italy, but this was not one of the most successful, as Dent picked up a gastric infection in Perugia, 'which odious place I endured for the sake of investigating a picture with a very curious and interesting piece of music painted on it'. There had been some enjoyable walking with E. S. P. Haynes, the King's contemporary to whom he was later to dedicate his book on Mozart's operas. He had been a splendid companion – 'but expects curious things, and is difficult to do things for. The two infallible remedies for all his bad tempers are good wine and an obscene jest, but if

---

[1] It was at a concert with this choir that he gave the first performance of Vaughan Williams' 'Five Mystical Songs'.

I'm tired I can't always think of the latter, and if he refuses to go to my particular humble trattorie, on account of possible fleas, how can I guarantee the former?' Writing from Florence he rallies Clive about his stay there: 'How all the ladies fell at your feet and how some of them tried to go further but failed; how you spoke all languages to perfection; how you composed music for a play of Gurattini and were carried around Florence in triumph on the shoulders of enthusiastic Italians (I foresee you as the successor and eclipser of the Maestro Sidney Jones).' The music, entitled Contradizzioni, remains in manuscript, and led to no such scenes of triumph; Sidney Jones's operetta *The Geisha* was popular in Italy; he was at this time conductor at the Empire Theatre in London.

In the winter term (1909) the main musical interest was naturally Vaughan Williams' music for *The Wasps*; Clive joined Dent for the two performances, his appetite whetted by Dent's November letter, which commented: 'The music is extraordinary and will make a stir. I think it is wonderfully good on the whole. It has a great deal of folksong and quasi-folksong in it, which gives it a definite character, and makes it intelligible, popular without being banal. I have been reading the play and wonder if I have interpreted it and V.W. right: apparently the tiresome old men of the chorus are symbolised by Stanford and Parry – "the men who fought for Athens in the good old days" and now get in the way of the younger men, hostile to any new movement. When Philocleon tries to be modern and gets drunk, he sings the march from The Birds with Josef Holbrooke harmonies or worse. The music is appallingly hard to grasp, and I think it is intended to be a wild nightmare opera. But as far as I can see it is good, and new. There is a great deal of it and it is much more frankly opera than previous Greek plays.'

The performance led to some vigorous correspondence in the *Cambridge Review*; first an anonymous writer attacked the bad stage-management; Dent had written a long article on 2 December saying, 'Those of us who understand music better than Greek feel that a step has been taken in advance; those who are "Grecians" may very probably disagree . . . Our wasps had no sting to speak of; and their only idea of indicating the nature of them was to turn their backs upon the audience and wobble their practicable abdomina.' Walter Durnford, Vice-Provost of King's, was the target, and Dent typically wrote with more than his wonted asperity because Durnford had talked loudly to a pretty undergraduate during the slow movement of a Mozart concerto played at a smoking concert. Clive, less characteristically, joined the campaign to free the Greek plays from the 'traditional' interpretation, and elicited what was his only contact with Lytton Strachey, who wrote to him (21 May 1910), 'I hope you will not think it an impertinence if I write to say how much I admired your article in this week's Review. It was indeed a pleasure to read something at last so thoroughly to the point. You smote the Philistines hip and thigh – and most politely, too! It will be deplorable if the whole thing now simply fizzles out – but that, I suppose is what one must expect. In three years' time we shall be having all the old ineptitudes and hideousness over again, unless there's a miracle. I feel that the one miracle which would be really satisfactory would be your appointment as supreme autocrat over the whole production. And for that, in spite of the old women of Cambridge, I shall humbly pray.'

At this period Dent's friend E. M. Forster had become one of Clive's more regular correspondents. In answer to an inquiry about the description of Beethoven's Fifth Symphony in Chapter Five of *Howard's End* Forster wrote (on 24 October 1910): 'I think I got the "elephants dancing" out of somewhere, but cannot be sure. Je prong mong bieng oo je le trouve; it is perfectly awful.'

In November *Love's Comedy*, a play by Ibsen with incidental music by Clive Carey and Denis Browne, had been moderately well received in Cambridge and enthusiastically by Dent, who commented, 'Your music sounded delightful, though I thought there was a little too much of it.' Some years later, after Browne's death, he was trying to recover the music. Unfortunately, the object for which the tickets were sold was Women's Suffrage, and this fact did not appear on the advertisements, but leaked out and gave offence to many.

In more traditional vein than any of these, at Mrs Jenkinson's they celebrated the centenary of Mendelssohn: 'a nine year old child unveiled a little white china bust of Mendelssohn with a little laurel wreath round his neck, and then we had Songs without words (except apologies) from Mrs Jenkinson . . . I wished my mother could have been there, but I think she would have thought it all a little passé.'

By now Clive was playing a lively part in folk-song and

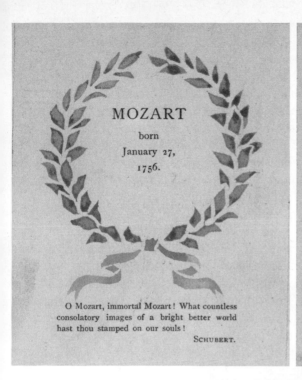

MOZART

born
January 27,
1756.

O Mozart, immortal Mozart! What countless
consolatory images of a bright better world
hast thou stamped on our souls!

SCHUBERT.

PROGRAMME

Concerto in C, no. 8
    Allegro—Andante—Tempo di Menuetto

Köchel 246. Composed at Salzburg in April, 1776.

Songs

Concerto in E flat, no. 9
  Allegro—Andantino—Rondo presto: Menuetto cantabile

Köchel 271. Composed at Salzburg in January,
    1777.
————————

(For Jean)
Twelve Variations on the Air
    'Ah! vous dirais-je, Maman.'

Southmead,
January 27, 1909.

Music at 3 o'clock.
Tea at 4.30.

Music 'at home': Mrs Jenkinson
at her harpsichord.

dance matters, in close association with Mary Neal to whose *Esperance Morris Book* (1912) he contributed both dances and sea-shanties, including a version of 'Shenandoah' which became, and remained, very popular. Thus when Dent asked him to help with the Marlowe's *Dr Faustus*, to be performed before an audience of German students invading Cambridge for a week in August, he demurred at first. The germ of the idea was Dent's; he thought that *Faustus* would appeal to the German mind, on the grounds that if the Society did *Macbeth*, they would say 'Ach, we do that better at our Hoftheater.'

The preliminaries were not altogether harmonious. Clive had no opinion of Rupert Brooke as an actor, but Rupert and some of his friends were determined that Rupert should play Mephistophilis. Clive was to produce, but already he found that all kinds of decisions had been taken which he did not like, and he was inclined to withdraw from it altogether; it seemed to him pure folly that Dent and his Cambridge friends should try to get these things up in about a fortnight. Dent was similarly exasperated, for the band and the music were no light matter, and in the middle of the Long Vacation so many of the people were not there: 'Sins[1] can't be got together till Friday 8.15, so I am not going to waste the band's tempers and time by asking them to play until the Sins learn their steps. We tried the strings last night, minus the viola who didn't turn up. It is curious how long it takes people to grasp the style of Elizabethan music.'

Everyone involved in the 1910 performance seemed to have views of his or her own and to be determined to express them. Prominent among these were Jacques Raverat[2] and Frances Cornford, who looked at things with a painter's eye rather than a musician's, and saw poses and groups as single permanent moments rather than as parts of a movement taking place in time as well as space. In spite

[1] The Seven Deadly Sins are summoned by Lucifer and Mephistophilis 'in their proper shapes' to feed the soul of Faustus.
[2] Jacques Raverat, a graduate of the Sorbonne, had come up as an advanced student in 1906, and was soon a close friend of Justin and Rupert Brooke. He married another member of their circle, Gwen Darwin, the artist and illustrator, whose *Period Piece* delightfully recalls the Cambridge of her youth. Her cousin, Frances Darwin, writer of some memorable poetry, married Francis Cornford, a classical lecturer at Trinity, whose encouragement had been an important factor in the launching of the Marlowe Society. The production of 1910, for which Dent had arranged music and dances, was a more ambitious 'bisexual' affair than the performance with which the Marlowe Society had opened in 1907. Clive had then played the part of the Chorus.

GERMAN STUDENTS IN ENGLAND.

AUGUST-SEPTEMBER, 1910.

Two members of a party of German students who visited England in the early autumn of this year have recorded their impressions of English institutions, writing in courageous English two articles, of which we print the first to-day:

The monuments of English literature were shown German students in London libraries (British Museum, University, Guildhall, Carlyle House), in all important Cambridge and Oxford libraries, in Manchester's Rylands library, in Stratford's Shakespeare Houses, in Lichfield's Dr. Johnson House, in Grasmere's Wordsworth House. On the other hand, no theatre performance of Shakespeare's plays was to be heard equal to the care attributed to him in plenty of German theatres. But Marlowe's "Faust," represented in a small hall by Cambridge students and lady students, hit fascinatingly our hearts, spoken perfectly well, decorated in a genuine Shakespearean manner. In Manchester's Gaiety Theatre quite a modern play, written by Bernard Shaw, England's in Germany most beloved writer of to-day, was represented also most finely. German study of English literature so widely spread, but sometimes misled by judgments of even learned people, needs indeed nearer connexion with the life and the surroundings of English thoughts.

As far as English music is concerned, we will never forget the lovely dances of old masters, selected by a tasteful hand for accompanying Marlowe's "Faust," and the fact that it was English people who extended the immortal sounds of the Continental masters all over the world. From this point of view it does not matter that London's big churches have not got choirs as on the Continent.

Dr Faustus: the bi-sexual
company is noticed.

of his difficulties in producing such a difficult cast, most of whom had been involved in the play before, Clive withdrew his threat to pull out and apologised, for he appreciated that on the musical side Dent had already done much preliminary work and that once he had started anything Dent got through a superhuman amount. Clive's objection was chiefly to the shortage of time for actual rehearsal.

When the performance had eventually gone off well, and was generally acclaimed the best that the Marlowe Society had done, Clive wrote: 'I'm glad things went off so well on Wednesday – after all the play's the thing – and if the whole production is an advance on what has previously been done – if people would only *see* that, I'm satisfied. I know I've got a horrid habit of wanting to get the credit for everything – which is foolish and unnecessary even when one *has* done the things – (which fault please squash when you see it!) – but I suppose I ought to expect that they think it's all their own doing, and won't thank one for one's pains. I suppose they don't grasp that one spends money and time and much nervous energy in doing a thing of the kind. I don't think I can undertake any more Cornfords and Raverats – willing enough material is all very well, but when it's obstinate and opinionated, it's impossible to do anything with it. I can't believe one should choose one's players just because they are good fellows or intelligent. They must have *some* slight talent for acting . . . Good-bye, and many thanks to you for your splendid work. It couldn't possibly have got through without you.'

The Germans were enormously pleased – and especially delighted with the literary quality of the acting and the absence of ranting or sentimentality! In fact they most admired exactly those actors about whom Clive had the strongest misgivings.

4. *The Magic Flute*

Dent's letters in 1911 were almost exclusively concerned with *The Magic Flute*, which was performed in Cambridge at the end of the Michaelmas Term. As with *Dr Faustus* he did most of the preparation himself. Clive appears to have been altogether uncommunicative, but his photograph album reveals him to have been very active elsewhere, especially in matters concerned with folk-music. Besides the work which he did for the *Esperance Morris Book*, in which he wrote the notes on the dances, he collected a

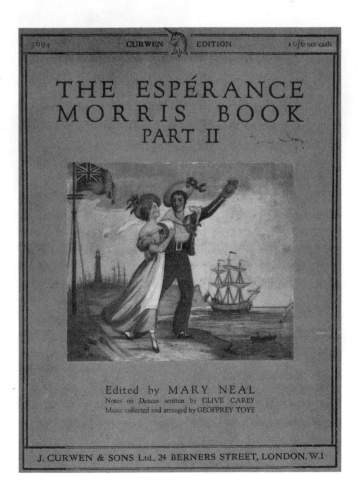

'One midsummer morning':
Mary Neal collecting folk-songs.

'Jockey to the fair'; a rehearsal at
Leith Hill House.

number of folk-songs in Sussex with Dorothy Marshall,[1]
who took down the words. Some of these were eventually
published as *Ten English Folksongs*, which Dent saw
through the press in 1915 when the world of 1911 was
vanishing for ever. Days were spent at Leith Hill with
Vaughan Williams, at Babington with Mrs Knatchbull
(with Moszkowski and Adeline Genée in the party), at
Stratford and Southwell for a special performance of
Comus, and at Brampton for a festival of Morris-dances.

[1] She writes 'Get your dirty old man at Lewes to come and sing to you at the
nearest pub – with a tin of Keatings handy.' Modern readers will need to be told
that 'Keatings' was a proprietary brand of flea-killing powder.

56

'The operatic manner': *Comus* at Southwell.

Clive also arranged the music and dances for Granville Barker's production of *The Winter's Tale*, and did *The Lotus Eaters* (Parry) with his choir at Guy's Hospital.

In the autumn Clive acquired Rupert Brooke, then writing his fellowship dissertation, as a singing pupil. Rupert's ambitions in this direction were not very great; he wrote to Dent (from The Old Vicarage, Grantchester) 'I don't want to sing much; and I don't imagine I should ever be able to. But I want to be able to get hold of the airs; and chiefly I've an idea it might train my dreadfully uneducated ear a little.' Dent suggested Clive, and Rupert wrote to him: 'What I want is somebody intelligent, who understands voices – as one can see these ordinary teachers probably don't. What I am is a very poor, quite sensible, but (at present) almost entirely earless and unmusical prospective pupil; who is working rather harder at other things.'

Clive took him on, and besides giving him lessons brought him into the cast for *The Magic Flute*, about which Rupert wrote to Katherine Cox, 'I've realised that taking part in theatrical performances is the only thing worth doing. And it's so *very* nice being an intelligent subordinate. I'm a very good subordinate – it's such a test. I'm thought not to dance well: but my intelligence and devotion have brought me rapidly to the front. I am now the most important of seven negroes.' A year later Rupert remembered that he had not paid for his lessons and wrote to Clive, 'I that was musical as Apollo's lute am now as harsh as any raven', but circumstances did not bring them together again.

It is hard now to realise what a landmark the Cambridge production was. Performances of the operas of Mozart in England were not nearly as common as today, and were almost invariably done in the original language, the few exceptions being stilted renderings in which the needs of the singer and the vivacity and wit of the librettist received scant attention. *Die Zauberflöte* had very rarely been performed in England, even in the original German, during the century that had elapsed since its first performance at the Haymarket in 1811. It was commonly regarded as a hotchpotch of incomprehensible freemasonry, symbolism and knockabout. The Cambridge production was therefore a leap in the dark: Dent wished to set new standards of translation and was determined that the words and the plot should be understood. To this end he also

Maisie Fletcher who played
Pamina.

prepared an introductory volume, besides the translation,
and with a high seriousness resented by some contemporaries (notably Naylor in the *Cambridge Review*) expected his audience to prepare themselves by studying both
before coming to the performance. Although he hated
'reverence' of any kind, his appreciation of the wisdom of
Sarastro came as near to it as any feeling which he
possessed.

The casting is notoriously difficult for amateurs, requir-
ing an exceptional coloratura soprano for the Queen of the
Night and at the other end of the scale a very deep bass for
Sarastro. On the second night Pamina lost her voice and
her part was sung by Papagena from the wings. Yet the
success was undoubted, and *The Magic Flute* found its way
back into the standard repertory. The translation prepared
the way for Dent's new rôle as the champion of opera sung
in English, while Clive's singing – as Papageno – and
production were to be repeated in the Mozart festival at the
Old Vic ten years later. He too had found himself.

Rootham was to conduct, a sure source of amused
irritation to Dent; already, a year before, the discussions
started: 'I can't help laughing over R. and his knowledge
(!) of the Z. I needn't describe his way of talking. However,
he *will* know a lot about it soon. And his modesty is really
wonderful; do you know he actually admitted (to me,
strictly unter vier Augen) that he had never conducted an
opera in his life. "Well, Rootham," I said, "I may as well
tell you that I have never stage-managed one!" '

It was hard to find anyone who had ever sung in the
opera before; one friend had at least sung in one ensemble
of the Three Genii at the Conservatoire at Vienna, and thus
knew the music in a singer's way. Hal Goodhart Rendel
made some preliminary designs for the scenery, and the
small size of the stage of the New Theatre added to the
difficulties. Albert Rothenstein (later Rutherston) was
consulted, and Marcel Boulestin, then correspondent of a
French musical review, and later to be renowned as a
connoisseur of good food, was drawn into the discussion.
Proofs of the translation were regularly sent to Clive with
orders to *sing* it through, but his replies and amendments
are lost.

In the midst of all this activity news came that O'Neil
Phillips had committed suicide in Montreal where he had
been teaching for the last eighteen months. Dent wrote
regretfully: 'We might all reproach ourselves. But I don't

Clive as Papageno.

see what in the world we could have done, for O'Neil was the most difficult person in the world to help . . . I never knew a man so cruelly treated by nature. I suppose if he had had a proper education he would never have been so good a pianist as he was; and yet it was just that want of education that would always have prevented his becoming a really great pianist, though he had undoubtedly some qualities which gave one the very highest hopes. He would never have been a really good player until he got a success which would make him approach his audience as friends. You and I, I suppose, don't regard suicide as a possibility: we think we could always start fresh whatever happened.'

By April 1911 the translation was complete. Could 'the voice of music', which would be preferable, be sung instead of 'that sound of magic' or was 'music' incompatible with a high A? Unfortunately it was. 'Do you approve of the symbolism in the fire and water scene – "passion's fires" and "sorrow's waters"? That is all me, you know!' Dent was digging into the foundations of Freemasonry, and the translation had to be revised again in the light of his discoveries; the duet of the Armed Men was practically identical with the inscription on the sarcophagus of Hiram which was still part of Masonic ritual in Germany in 1836; there was a definite reason why the men were in armour.

Meanwhile at Oxford Hugh Allen was putting on *Freischütz* – another overdue revival – in June, and Dent wondered whether Cambridge could do anything like it – not least in the harmony between conductor and stage-manager! Shortly before the performance of *The Magic Flute* was to take place, Clive's father died. Dent was sympathetic and revealing: 'It is only later that one begins to realise the sense of loss, and by that time one has begun to idealize the personality that is lost, and in this way feels sometimes more intimate with the person than before death. As you know, I never became really intimate with my father during his lifetime, and I neither wish nor expect a survival of personality after death. But the memory, (probably absurdly idealized) of my father is a very living thing to me, and becomes more and more intensely so to me as I grow older.'

Cambridge University Press printing: the programme of *The Magic Flute*.

THE MAGIC FLUTE

By

WOLFGANG AMADEUS MOZART

Performed in the New Theatre, Cambridge on Friday and Saturday, 1st and 2nd December 1911

The performance took place on 1 and 2 December (1911). When eventually it was over Dent slipped away unnoticed 'so tired that I should merely have been quarrelsome and obscene when everybody else was excited and happy . . . Don't be offended with me – you sang and acted wonderfully . . . and I hope the whole thing will be a good thing for you with the public and engagements etc. – also for the little Hopper[1] and Marchand.[2]

Much of his eventual summary, in a letter written a few days later, can bear with reproduction, for the occasion was a turning-point not only in the lives of Dent and Clive Carey but also perhaps of opera in English, and in England.

[1] Victoria Hopper, Queen of the Night, who later sang professionally as Sylvia Nelis.
[2] Hilda Marchand, Papagena – and Pamina from the wings.

60

'Now that nearly a week has passed I am getting to see results clearer. At the performance I was almost as unconscious of the existence of the audience as the cabdrivers waiting outside. You on the stage and Rootham in the orchestra were practically *among* the audience and in touch with them – feeling what they feel and making them feel what you feel. A stage-manager has no business to feel: and in order to do my work accurately I had to switch off the sense of music altogether, so that the sounds made by the instruments and the voices meant no more to me than the ticking of a chronometer which directed me to do certain things at certain moments. So that when I was tired, I knew it; whereas you other people, who were just as tired as I was really, did not know it, because you had the music to excite you and keep you going, like alcohol. And I did not dare take more than one glass of claret at dinner . . . as I knew I must keep my brain absolutely clear and cool to conduct those choruses. After I had been disagreeable to you I began to see how tired I was and during the last scenes I just sat still and tried to calculate it out whether I had strength left or not to go through with the business to the end. I came to the conclusion that I had not, and so I went home. It had to be done quickly and secretly, because I knew the chorus would never have let me go, and if I had been thwarted I should have lost control of myself for want of strength. There; that's the psychological analysis of it all, as far as I can get it straight now. The trouble all comes from confusing pathology with morals . . .

'As to quarrelling over bouquets etc. it is all such a trivial business that we may as well ignore it in consideration of the real results achieved – the test of which to my mind was that a lot of people came to the theatre thinking themselves unmusical and Philistine, and found that their ears really were opened to them, by Mozart . . . Theo (Bartholomew) told me eventually that I was quite right to go away, as it would only have made Rootham rather uncomfortable. I can see that he is feeling very much annoyed with the Press, because they toss him off in one line as an "efficient conductor" (not always that!) and say a great deal about me. But what opera conductor ever does get more than that, except Richter at Bayreuth? and any conductor would have been reduced to mere efficiency by having to conduct amateurs.

'The explanation of the Press view is simply this: I published a book, and as an author sent it out for review. I

"THE MAGIC FLUTE."

Cambridge Amateurs' Ambitious Undertaking.

MOZARTS OPERA.

Great interest is manifested in the performance of Mozart's opera, "The Magic Flute," which is to be presented by a talented company of local amateurs at the New Theatre to-day and to-morrow.

"The Magic Flute" is practically an unknown work to English audiences of to-day. London has seen it twice only during the last 20 years.

Credit is due to Dr Cyril Rootham and Mr E. J. Dent for initiating the enterprise; whilst the services of Mr Clive Carey were enlisted, and the opera will be produced under that gentleman's direction.

Dr Rootham has recorded enviable triumphs in the musical world, and he is eminently fitted for the duties he has taken up as conductor.

Mr Clive Carey was at one time organist of Clare College, and has gained distinction as a vocalist.

Mr Edward J. Dent has been responsible for an entirely new translation of the German libretto of Giesecke and Schikaneder, and a pamphlet dealing with the history and interpretation of the opera.

The principals have all had a thorough training, and one or two of them are budding professionals. The chorus consists of about 50 voices, and is entirely local. The ladies are drawn from University, town, or Girton; while the men are all either undergraduates or B.A.'s.

The orchestra is partly amateur and partly professional. Rehearsals have been carried out with the greatest possible enthusiasm, and an all-round excellent presentation is confidently anticipated.

MR. DENT'S VOLUMES.

For the benefit of those attending Mozart's "The Magic Flute" at the New Theatre, to-day (Friday) and to-morrow, Mr E. J. Dent has written a very interesting book, which is published by Messrs W. Heffer & Sons, Ltd., at one shilling net, entitled "Mozart's 'The Magic Flute,' its history and interpretation." The same gentleman has also translated "The Magic Flute" (Die Zauberflöte) from the German and Carl Ludwig Giesecke and Emanuel Schikaneder. Both volumes are delightfully entertaining. Students of opera will find the first of great value, whilst a study of the second will give one a very clear idea of the story, and vastly assist in a fuller appreciation of the performance.

Mr. Clive Carey.

Dr. Cyril Rootham.

The Cambridge Chronicle,
December 1911.
Mr Clive Carey.
Dr Cyril Rootham.

also wished to get it reviewed before the performance so that book and performance might advertise each other mutually . . . but the majority of critics were compelled by their editors to notice both book and performance in the same article. Well, if a London paper wants a notice on Saturday morning of a play acted in Cambridge on Friday night, the critic has to write $\frac{3}{4}$ of it before he goes to Cambridge at all, and telegraph the last $\frac{1}{4}$ after the first act of the play. Naturally the quickest and most interesting way to make up the first $\frac{3}{4}$ was to review, or at least to lift from, my book – there was the stuff ready written.

'The pity of it is that the reviews are practically useless to me. Heffer [the Cambridge publisher] says that if I had written a novel, reviews like that would have sold an edition of 5,000 in three days. My book being a book about musical history, I may be thankful if I sell 5,000 in three months. And good press notices would have been of real value to you, the Hopper and the Marchand, towards getting engagements. As to Rootham . . . he says he has had "avalanches" of congratulations, and doesn't know how to answer them – so I was much relieved to be able to say that I had had a few, and those mainly from what one calls unmusical people. I don't myself think that the criticisms of regular opera goers matter very much. The enthusiasm of Vaughan Williams, Donald Tovey, Streatfeild, Robert Bridges and Charles Ricketts really does count.

'What *you* did came out everywhere: you taught Steuart [Wilson] to sing and everybody to act, you designed and carried out the groups at the end of Act I and the beginning of Act II, which seem to have been the things that really moved people most deeply, and the discovery of the three Ladies behind the blue curtain in Act II. I must stop as this is too long.'

Whereas there are numerous photographs of the Greek plays, and even postcards commemorating the performances, presumably because the university was largely involved, there seem to be few records of *The Magic Flute* beyond the programme, a photograph of Clive as Papageno, and Marcel Boulestin's drawings reproduced here.

Two of a trio: Denis Browne and Steuart Wilson, January 1913.

Mr. CLIVE CAREY

Mr. E. DENT, DIRIGEANT LES CHŒURS DANS LA COULISSE

The Magic Flute, Boulestin's caricatures.

5. Enter The Fairy Queen

' I am not saying that one went out, as one might into a garden, and there saw that a rose had flowered, or that a hen had laid an egg. The change was not sudden and definite like that. But a change there was, nevertheless; and since one must be arbitrary, let us date it about 1910.' Virginia Woolf was writing about human relations, and consequently of religion, conduct, politics and literature. In the musical world Vaughan Williams' *Wasps*, the Oxford *Freischütz*, and the Cambridge *Magic Flute* – and perhaps the performance of *Dr Faustus* too – seem to justify her provocative statement. Dent and his friends began to think of other neglected operas suitable for revival. Meanwhile the manager of the Carl Rosa was asking for permission to use Dent's translation of *The Magic Flute*, and received a cordial reply, also suggesting that if he wanted complete stage directions in detail he should write to Clive, and could do worse than engaging him professionally besides. Chatto and Windus agreed to take Dent's as yet unfinished book on Mozart's opera, hoping to bring it out in the autumn of 1912, and Dent proposed to spend the Easter vacation in Vienna to do some more research. The book eventually came out in 1913.

In January (1912) Dent wrote to Clive, 'Rootham is rather keen to do Weber's *Oberon* if possible. It seems to me anything but possible: but it is certainly W.'s best stuff, and is conveniently unknown in England now. The difficulties of stage-management etc. merely incite me to try and conquer them, but I don't see Cambridge amateurs making much effect with the solo parts. I have just been playing through Berlioz' *Troyens à Carthage*,[1] which is glorious – but utterly beyond us and hopeless for any small stage. As to Rameau I wonder whether *Castor and Pollux* would not be better than *Hippolyte and Aricie*.' There was also a suggestion of Cherubini's *Faniska* but Dent thought this

---

[1] Both the *Trojans* and *Castor and Pollux* were eventually performed in Glasgow, Dent making the translation of *The Trojans* used in 1935.

J. B. Trend.

disappointing – 'the arias and things are all too long and all in symphonic form'.

The Cambridge success was bringing Clive more professional engagements as a recitalist, singing Moussorgsky, Debussy, Ravel and Respighi, together with his own new settings of some poems by Mary Coleridge; and in Cambridge Denis Browne was his accompanist. Clive was having some difficulty in translating the Russian, and Dent wrote 'I have got a large dictionary, and have made out some of the places that baffled you. In the Trepak the words which you translate "The chamois leads a dissolute life" mean "The sickles make a noise like fiddles (in the cornfields)".' He helped him too with references to early books and manuscripts in the British Museum for performances in 'Shakespeare's England' and in arranging incidental music for Granville Barker's Shakespeare season. Busoni had been over again to give a recital, and Dent's close friendship with J. B. Trend, later Professor of Spanish at Cambridge and finally his executor, was beginning.

In Vienna in April – 'I rather hate Vienna as it is so appallingly expensive' – Dent was much helped by Goldschmidt, the rival of his Italian journeys in search of Scarlatti, and by Goldschmidt's uncle, who had a great collection of books and pictures of the period of Mozart. He visited the villa near Prague where Mozart wrote *Don Giovanni*. He saw *Rosenkavalier* conducted by Strauss, and enjoyed it very much – 'the play is so clever and the acting wonderful. I think I should loathe the music if I heard it a second time. It is full of waltzes of the most banal type and other tunes of the usual Strauss kind. The mise-en-scène is miraculous.' Reinhardt's *Everyman* – 'all sensations' – he also enjoyed, but *Zauberflöte* was done quite miserably, 'the scenery was expensive and tasteless; the costumes suggested *Parsifal*, and so did all the business of the priests. It was all disgustingly Christian.' 'The best thing I have heard here has been Bruckner's Ninth Symphony. I heard it some six years ago and made nothing of it; this time – under Weingartner (the papers said his rendering was a sacrilege) – it moved me deeply. It is so interesting to get a real symphony that is Wagnerian material with hardly a touch of Brahms. It is the kind of stuff that Elgar ought to write but can't. There is a Haydn-like solemnity about it that is very fine.'

Back at Cambridge in the summer term for Gray's last

Musicians' holiday, September
1913: folk-dancing.

concert before handing over C.U.M.S. to Rootham they
were doing Vaughan Williams' 'Toward the Unknown
Region', and Dent was studying *Idomeneo* with a view to
writing a chapter on it. 'What a pity M. never had the
chance of *Idomeneo* later in life! It is just short of a
masterpiece. I can't make up my mind as to whether we
could attempt it here. Of course we could not have M.'s
"molto amato castrato del Prato" to sing Idamante, but M.
did rearrange the part for a tenor later.'

The decision was taken to try to put on Purcell's *Fairy
Queen* in November 1914, and Novello's agreed to publish
a cheap edition. Dent spent part of the Long Vacation at Le
Puy en Velay, eating his first snails, and sending Clive (who
was now much involved in folk-song collecting, lectures
and recitals) copies of traditional Auvergnat songs. He
was devoting himself to strict counterpoint, and writing
exercises every day. Clive was drawn back to Cambridge
by Walter Durnford to train the chorus for Sheppard's
production of *Oedipus Tyrannus*, as his close friend A. F.
Scholfield, who had been joint stage-manager of *The
Magic Flute*, was off to Calcutta as archivist.

Until late in 1913 there was little correspondence. Clive
overworked and put himself in the hands of a 'suggestion

doctor' and Dent was busy seeing the Mozart book through the press. Beecham, having rescued the Denhof Opera Company (many of whose singers participated in the Beecham Opera Company, 1915–20) was intending to use Dent's translation. Dent's reaction to Clive's nervous troubles was to recommend complete solitude and strict counterpoint. 'You tire yourself unconsciously with talking, and just talking to pass the time, and to be agreeable. I think you could afford to put on some of my boorishness! Also let me recommend strict counterpoint as a substitute for knitting, and as an addition to tobacco. It has the same advantage, I expect, as patience games; it demands a certain attention, with no tremendous intellectual effort, and with no emotional effort. It takes one into the trance-world of music without exciting the nerves; and it is helping one's musical brain all the time. However, if you are doing music all day, I daresay it might not be so useful as a sedative . . . I should hate to go to a "suggestion doctor" myself, for I could not bear to give up my will and personality. Some people like to do so, hence the success of the Catholic religion. But, as our Rector said in his sermon yesterday – "if St Paul had been in the garden of Eden instead of Adam, the history of the world would have been very different!"' Unusually, Dent was writing from his family home in Yorkshire.

Dent was on the whole pleased with Beecham's *Magic Flute* (October 1913) though 'Beecham made a horrid mess of the band, very rough and loud, and all the tempi of the ensemble much too fast. I suppose he was bored.' He realised that the dialogue in the first two scenes needed rewriting, but later editions did not contain many changes.

The break in the correspondence now gives place to much detailed discussion of *The Fairy Queen*, at first very often concerning cuts to try to reduce its length, or suggesting the transfer of songs from one act to another. As the opera is really a succession of masques, this was permissible enough, and since it had last been staged in 1693 and the manuscript, lost in 1700, had only been rediscovered two hundred years later, there was huge scope for initiative but no precedent to follow. Dent had to simplify the orchestral arrangements of J. S. Shedlock, who had discovered the copy at the Royal Academy of Music, and realise the figured basses – in fact to write totally new accompaniments, which he submitted to Clive for criticism. Clive was in Manchester, acting in *The*

Pierrot of the Minute for which he had written the incidental music. Morris-dancing had caught on, and as musical director for Mary Neal's folk-dance club Clive was very much in demand, though in Cambridge Dalcroze eurhythmics were another new craze. It was proving very difficult to obtain concrete plans for the scenery and costumes from Mrs Cockerell,[1] who had designed the sets for the *Magic Flute* with great success.

Originally Mrs Cockerell was to have designed both the scenery and the dresses for the 1914 production of *The Fairy Queen*. On 5 January 1914 Dent commented: 'Needless to say she has made no drawings at all', while at the same time he was delighted with her ideas – 'What she wants is to simplify everything as much as possible, to avoid anything that in the least degree suggests pantomime or a [Beerbohm] Tree production, and to get some sort of unity of idea into the chaotic scheme of Purcell's librettist.' Within a few weeks Dent passed on to Clive the news that 'Mrs C has made a drawing of Juno's group with black slaves as peacock attendants, kneeling in front of her. It will be rather like Monostatos and the Queen, but might be very effective.' In the same letter he mentioned that Sedley Taylor was very much bored by Purcell and feared that it would be all 'anthems and archaeology'.

Nearly six years – and a hundred letters – later the abandoned scenery was to become the province of Lionel Penrose, an undergraduate at King's, and Mrs Cockerell, with her sister Joan Kingsford (Wood), whose drawings are also reproduced here, was chiefly concerned with the dresses. Dent wrote (on 5 January 1920): 'I hear the Chinese chorus are all to wear sulphur-coloured dresses, and we propose to give them head-dresses of various kinds taken from Chinese pictures which Cockerell has ... We are also considering monkeys – slate-coloured tights covered all over with patterns, in long black hair – and one to be reddish. All to have bare patches of different colours on their behinds, and their own faces, made up to a conventional pattern, in tight-fitting all round caps. Will C.B.R. [Rootham] be frightened of the pink and blue buttocks? ... Mrs C. says the ladies all seem to want to have their skirts shortened and the men want to have them lengthened: the opposite of 1911.' Dent was ingenious and

[1] As Florence Kate Kingsford she was already well known as an illuminator of books when she married Sydney Cockerell, Director of the Fitzwilliam Museum, Cambridge, in 1907.

The Fairy Queen: Mrs Cockerell's design for the monkey and peacock attendants.

The Fairy Queen: Joan Kingsford Wood's design for one of Phoebus's attendants, and Mrs Cockerell's design for Winter.

resourceful to a degree that must surprise those who think of him primarily as a 'pure' musician and scholar, sending diagrams of lighting – 'even I know the optical fact that the angle of reflection = the angle of incidence' – discussing methods of drawing curtains, proposing a cheese cloth, which Mrs Cockerell thought too reminiscent of Drury Lane. 'By the time she makes her first drawings you and I shall have had time to change our minds several times!' As with the *Flute*, a model had been constructed, and Dent was becoming expert at chopping cardboard. Mrs Fletcher, who had sung Pamina until her voice gave out, was singing much too much, and Dent was fearful that by the time of the Purcell opera she would again be unfit – 'the devout women will keep her at her works of piety and I should like to wring their devout necks'. As the Marlowe were putting on *The Alchemist*, there were opportunities to pick up actors from that source.

For once Dent had to forgo a vacation on the continent at Easter (1914); not only were there Novello's proofs of *The Fairy Queen* for revision, but there was also 'my neglected book', presumably *Foundations of English Opera*, which made very slow progress, eventually seeing the light of day in 1928. Instead he sent to Clive a long list of hotels where he might stay, and maps, and advice about walking in the Chianti country: 'You will find the hills very cold, and bitter winds would chap the lips horribly – at the same time one gets very hot walking, so take warm underclothes in your rucksack, and hazeline cream. But food is good and beds are warm, especially if you have the "prete" in bed.' *The Fairy Queen* was not forgotten: 'If you go to Milan there is a room in the Castello decorated by Leonardo da Vinci with a design of trees and golden knots of string, which might give Mrs Cockerell ideas for our wood. It is worth looking at, and perhaps you might get some good photographs of it and send them to me.'

Dent reported on Bevis Ellis's concert, at which Geoffrey Toye conducted, and Butterworth's 'The Banks of Green Willow' received its first performance. 'The best items in the whole concert were George Butterworth's – it is all real sincere music, with something of Parry's contempt for mere orchestral effects. Bax is a clever little brat; but what has a born Cockney to do with Celtic twilights? He takes himself too seriously and has no education. His Bohemian overture was like Hampstead people in a Soho restaurant.' Dent never discarded his prejudice against uneducated musicians. At another Bevis Ellis concert he heard Vaughan Williams' new 'London Symphony', and thought it 'really a very great work: rather like the "Sea Symphony" but an advance and not so full of Stanfordisms . . . Of course it has no tricks of orchestration, but I like the solid stuff, and it is all thought and felt.' He again made unfavourable comments on Bax: 'I prefer Ornstein and futurist music. Roseingrave when he heard Scarlatti play at Rome said he thought ten thousand devils had taken possession of the instrument; when I heard Ornstein I thought it was ten thousand apes.'

Eventually, when Clive was on holiday in Sicily, Dent crossed for a week to Compiègne, and solitary walks in the forest. He made a brief excursion to Paris to see Lully's *Psyche*, and found it delightful but less formal than he hoped *The Fairy Queen* would be. Denis Browne's ballet *The Comic Spirit* was to be produced at Bristol, where Clive was in repertory at the Theatre Royal until June. He was playing Dick in Masefield's *Nan*, which he hoped would get rid of the ridiculous self-consciousness he felt among professionals, and was full of engagements, but

Stage sets by Lionel Penrose
Act II (the sleep scene), Act III
(Bottom with the ass's head and
the sleeping lovers) above;
Act V (i) (Juno and attendants),
(ii) (the Chinese scene, the
monkey's dance) below.

determined to do *all* the rehearsing of the company for *The Fairy Queen*. For the time being he could do nothing more than write letters, while Dent as the man on the spot was bound to take the decisions about actors and scenery; with 120 dresses to make they could hardly follow the original production, which probably had a different set of dresses for each act. The acting edition was now in page-proof and still too long; one way to reduce it would be by doing parts in dumb show, possibly with music – Dent had found that these were quite common on the Elizabethan stage. Rootham was becoming impatient, but Clive, struggling now with the part of Finch McComas in *You Never Can Tell*, could still write only about scenery, determined that it should not be mannered or precious in any way – 'it does

72

seem to me that to have a building at the back as well as Corinthian pillars further in front will effectually prevent people even of the most lively imaginations believing that they are in a wood'. Dent mollified him: 'The wood is complete and looks beautiful. It is to be not so much a temple as a sort of semicircular colonnade with a seat, on the top of a step or two, perched on a green hill far away. It seems quite reasonable that there should be a temple or a classical summer-house in an Athenian wood!'

Throughout May letters continued almost daily from Cambridge and Bristol; two perfectionists trying to agree or to agree to differ. One reports it chiefly to recapture something of the enthusiasm of the adventure, and the combination of scholarship and taste which went into each detail, Clive holding firmly to his concept that the architecture should be kept for the front part of the stage and the whole of the scenery behind it should be out-of-floor — trees, hills and sky. Similar controversy, if that is not too strong a word, occurs about exact numbers of attendants for Titania and Oberon (and whether Oberon's can be duplicated with Juno's), Naiads, Dryads, fairies, haymakers, and of course about their dresses. Dent had much the harder part of placating would-be actors while Clive was delayed in Bristol.

Eventually they contrived a play-reading in Rootham's rooms in June before dispersing for the Long Vacation, from which so many of them were not to return for four years, or for ever.

6. The Great War

Dent's letters continue unbroken throughout the Great War, during which he and Clive met only two or three times. Their earlier correspondence indicates that neither of them had any inkling of the forthcoming catastrophe, a state of ignorance not by any means confined to artists as single-minded as themselves.

Still in holiday spirit in 1913: more musicians. Left to right, Iolo Williams, Geoffrey and Francis Toye and Marcel Boulestin.

It is not easy to analyse Dent's standpoint at this time. Medically – presumably because of his extreme short-sightedness – he was exempt from active service, and he was already forty when eventually conscription was introduced, so that he could have escaped notice had he wished. However, he was a pacifist and preferred not to hide behind convenient excuses; he accepted that there must be different opinions about the war, respected those which were sincerely held, and hated the cant that war generates. Rupert Brooke's romantic view seemed to him immature, and he was not afraid to say so at a time when this was unpopular.

To begin with there was a little hesitation about abandoning *The Fairy Queen*, and Clive continued his stage career, helping his friend Bob Maltby[1] in a pastoral

---

[1] He had been a prominent member of the Oxford University Dramatic Society, and had played the part of Pan in Clive Carey and Denis Browne's *The Enchanted Night*.

74

The last holiday abroad, 1914: a formidable combination. Left to right, Miss Pethick, Mrs Pethick Lawrence, Mary Neal and Olive Schreiner.

play and taking part in *Prunella* by Granville Barker and Laurence Housman. In November 1914 he joined up in a non-combatant rôle, and was in France as a ward orderly in the Medical Corps early in 1915. His letters to Dent do not survive, but his letters home more often describe musical and dramatic performances, or abortive attempts to obtain the material needed for them, than the so-called 'horrors' of war. For Clive, once he had been removed from the discomforts of a Casualty Clearing Station to the comparative security of a commission in the Army Ordnance Corps, these were chiefly deprivation of music and the death of friends, of whom Denis Browne and Bob Maltby were probably the closest. Bob Maltby's letters to him, usually pencilled on sheets of a field message book, show how early they both became convinced of the futility of continuing the war and of the need for a negotiated peace. Their link with the political agitation for peace was through Emmeline Pethick-Lawrence and her husband. Miss Pethick had taught singing to Mary Neal's folk-groups and had taken a leading part in the campaign for women's suffrage. Already in November 1915, Maltby, on leave from his battalion of The Rifle Brigade, had entreated

Bob Maltby dancing the part of Puck in Denis Browne's *Spirit of the Future*, 1913.

them to work hard in the cause for peace, and to be quite certain that the time was ripe for it. In December he wrote to Clive: 'A happy (and speedily peaceful) New Year to you. I feel sure you will be the one sensible person who will survive this holocaust – for which all thanks be to that impotent Almighty of ours . . . I wonder what you feel about things – I am so convinced myself that the time for peace has come – and I cannot help believing that terms are being discussed already – anything else seems so ghastly and incredibly criminal as to be beyond belief. Do you agree with me?' He died of wounds as an infantry subaltern on the Somme in 1916.

Throughout the war there is something almost obsessive about Dent's indefatigable letter-writing – to Steuart Wilson, Denis Browne, Maltby and Clive especially. Of course he felt that they must wish to share, even at second hand, such musical life as survived in Cambridge and London. At first it was easy to write of keeping music and the Marlowe Society going as 'the really important things', but as the scope, especially for academic music, contracted and the list of casualties increased it became harder to keep this faith. Visions of rebuilding the shattered fabric of Cambridge music became chimerical. Dent did not feel guilty at being out of the war, though once he reveals some uneasiness about enjoying the peace of a walk to Grantchester, yet one feels that the detail with which he describes some of the musical events at home – Stanford's *Critic*, Elgar's incidental music for *The Starlight Express*, Ethel Smyth's *Boatswain's Mate*, and Holst's *Planets* – was not only to interest his readers but also to reassure himself of their importance.

One wonders if something withered in the non-combatants that remained alive in those who, whatever their hardships, at least enjoyed the *companionship* of war. The little coterie of intellectuals based on King's – Dickinson, Sheppard (seconded for special duties), Pigou, Maynard Keynes and Dent – with their outposts abroad, Forster in Alexandria and Percy Lubbock with International Red Cross, had little to sustain them beyond 'Cambridge values' in philosophy and in music, and after a while they did not even seek one another's company. They were spared the physical conflict, but no less than the combatants they were vulnerable to the loss of friends – perhaps more so, since the soldier was constantly making new friendships. Stoically, when emotion was both starved

Pte Carey, R.A.M.C., here not taking the war very seriously.

and exhausted and intellect alone remained, they sustained or tried to expand the interests that had nourished them before the war.

Dent's letters indicate obliquely rather than directly the increasing strain. Light-heartedly in 1915 he could write of Clive as 'sworn to fomentations and bandages' and wonder whether he might be released to produce opera in London. The lowered standards and ambitions of Cambridge concerts also make a pale reflection of the gravity of events. The description of a concert given in a Cambridge hospital by an incongruous group of singers including G. E. Moore, the philosopher, the historian Holland Rose, a piano-tuner, and a Siamese prince is the more poignant for its deliberate restraint. A reunion in June 1915 at which a group of Dent's young friends revel in *Prince Igor* and *Coq d'Or*, both first performed in London in 1914, and in sea-shanties which Clive had published, seems to strike a little jarringly when communicated to a lance-corporal on duty at a hospital in Flanders.

'The more friends I lose the less I want to sing cantatas about them' Dent wrote; it was becoming impossible to reconcile the two. Dent's reticence breaks down occasion-ally: 'I would gladly destroy all the museums in the world if that would stop the destruction of young life.' In the mouth of a musical antiquary – for this was what Dent feared he was becoming – this means much; the sardonic humour was put aside. It says much too, for the resilience, not only of Dent, and of Clive Carey, but also of the spirit of man, that as hostilities drew to a close their thoughts reverted to *The Fairy Queen*.

The changed tempo of life in August 1914 is reflected in Dent's letters – shorter and less connected paragraphs – a single letter discussing on two sides of paper the fate of *The Fairy Queen*, progress on the opera book, the number of troops in Cambridge, Clive's unfinished music for *The Starlight Express*, and a hurried visit from Rupert Brooke: 'Rupert was here yesterday, interviewing the O.T.C. authorities, who sit and answer questions in Corpus. He says he can't write, and war corresponding being out of the question now, he wants to try for a commission. He had picked up a lot of odd gossip in London – that Kitchener wanted to have Bonar Law as his secretary and couldn't see why the idea was objected to.' In September Dent took a month's holiday with Theo Bartholomew at a solitary inn on the Sedbergh–Kirkby Stephen road – 'We are in a temperance establishment and live on the plainest food, with nothing stronger than tea.' They walked 20 miles a day, wet or fine, and in the evening Dent was making a new score from the parts of Vaughan Williams' 'London Symphony'; the original had been lost at Aix-la-Chapelle when it was overrun. 'Cambridge will be a strange place, and the numbers of the University of Louvain will not compensate for the loss of those who have gone soldiering. I suppose you know that Denis and Rupert have got into some sort of Naval Brigade, but Denis says they will not have to go to sea. Denis is at present at Leamington with Erythema, whatever that may be![1] Well, we shall have to struggle along with Cambridge as best we can, and I mean to devote my energies to keeping music and Marlowe going. Other people will do refugees, relief and Red Cross, and we can't leave the really important things neglected. There must be some people coming up, and a certain number of freshmen; and if Cambridge is entirely depleted of athletes we may find it easier to get hold of the artists.'

Dent was writing round at this inappropriate moment soliciting help from old friends of the Greek play and the Marlowe Society for Reginald Pole, who had bronchial trouble, had spent the previous winter in California and wished to return there for his health. Clive's answer is not extant, but it was friendly; a similar letter received a dusty answer from Rupert Brooke. It is perhaps characteristic not only of Dent's generosity but also of his naïve high-mindedness that he could see nothing incongruous in sending out this appeal at a time when most of Pole's contemporaries were enlisting. He had a scheme for keeping the Marlowe alive by giving a lecture on masques, using material collected for the recalcitrant book on opera origins, and illustrating it with some scenes acted; he asked Clive's opinion. For the Antiquarian Society he was preparing a lecture on 'English Musical Drama during the Commonwealth', and wanted to perform some of Shirley's *Cupid and Death* (1653); the special attraction of this was that its music was composed by Christopher Gibbons and Matthew Locke, who was also involved in D'Avenant's *The Siege of Rhodes*, the first opera heard in England (1656). In March he was able to report that, thanks to J. T. Sheppard's production, it was a huge success, though no particular notice of it was taken in print. One could hardly

[1] A skin disease.

expect to attract attention outside Cambridge in wartime.

Steuart Wilson had been wounded, and Dent went to Netley to see him. Small talk included the appearance at the Music Club of two former members now in the kilts of a Scottish regiment: 'Rootham nearly lifted them in his curiosity, and others professed to be shocked because of his question "Why do you wear the sporran just *there*?" I gave an anthropological explanation, which I now gather was quite correct.'

Clive's 'Ten English Folksongs', published by Curwen, came out in 1915, and had considerable success. It contained several settings whose popularity his own recitals did much to forward, notably 'Lemady' (On Midsummer Morn), with which many will particularly associate him, and 'Scarborough Fair'. Dent took considerable trouble on Clive's behalf, corresponding with Lucy Broadwood and Dorothy Marshall. He also dined as a guest with the Society of English Singers, to which Clive was later to belong, for a discussion of whether the musical phrase should give way to the literary phrase or the reverse. Dent surprised himself by being on the same side (the musical) as Plunket Greene – 'no music, except occasionally a phrase hummed to illustrate a speech, and almost every one of them German . . . They pressed me to speak, and I'm sure I disgraced myself, for I talked of Monteverdi!'

Staccato paragraphs continue throughout 1915, a conscious attempt to divert, and the opinions somewhat exaggerated: he played 'The Lost Chord' on a grumpy pianoforte at an inn in Haslingfield; read an article by Stanford in the *Musical Quarterly* criticising Richard Strauss which developed a Rossini crescendo of scandalisation ending with the fact that he was given a Mus.D. at Oxford!; and 'Do you remember an absurd thing at the Hall called Firbank who tried to look rather like Lord Alfred Douglas of the sonnets? a great adorer of Rupert? He has written a novel and to my amaze-and-amusement sent me a presentation copy. It is very 1890 – incredibly artificial and absurd – and really quite amusing. I read four chapters aloud to Theo who was convulsed with laughter. But it was most charming of him to send the stuff to me, as I haven't seen him for years. He went (in both senses) to Rome, and became "secretary" to a Monsignor; I understand.' In May it was still possible to talk of half a dozen English opera schemes for the autumn, and of the possibility of Clive's release to run one of them – 'I suppose all these operatic managers think the war will be over by then.'

'You can imagine how obsessed we get with Rupert's death' – he had died on 23 April 1915 – 'and the tragedy of it was that it should be just at that moment when the emotionalism of the war and the Winston entourage had carried him completely off his balance. Gilbert Murray writes about his sanity and sincerity etc.; but the fact is, he was always having emotional crises and even nervous breakdowns, not quite like O'Neil, because although self centred, he was not self torturing. The last sonnets were beautiful, however little sympathy one might have with their sentiments; and I had hoped they would later fall into their proper place as part of a big series leading up to deeper realities and a more philosophical conception of the whole horrible business.'

Cambridge was dreadful at times but Dent was rewarded in an intangible way by some of the young people; Forster had come for a day 'elusive as usual'; the Moody Manners Company had been there for a week, but Dent had been able to attend only *Samson and Delilah* – 'the whole thing was without rhythm and continuity, and fell very flat to me. If I could go round the provinces attending every English opera performance everywhere, I should soon find out what's wrong with English opera.' The repertoire was a typical one at that period: besides *Samson* there was *Carmen*, *Martha* (which Dent had never seen), *Faust*, *The Daughter of the Regiment*, *Maritana* and *The Bohemian Girl*. The book about the foundations of English opera was complete and Steuart Wilson had read it through, but his wounds seemed temporarily to have robbed him of his usual readiness to criticise. Though Dent thought it rather good on the whole, he was soon to find new material which involved him in extensive rewriting. The search began at Oxford, which Dent found rather dismal: 'But the New College dons are notoriously gloomy, and they breakfast together in Common Room at 8 a.m. What can you expect?' He had also begun to translate *Figaro*.

In a paragraph Dent describes the receipt of a cheerful letter from Pole in California, trying to collar the artistic drama of state and university and hoping to produce Greek plays there, a refreshing contrast with a long letter from Denis Browne about Rupert's death and burial. 'It was painful reading – though all expressed in beautiful English; but evidently Denis and the others were in a fearfully Byronic state of mind, and no wonder. That is perhaps the most damnable thing about this war, the state of unreason it produces.'

With Cambridge music in decline (though at Clare on the Sunday of May Week they performed the Stabat Mater of Josquin des Prés, and Bach's little Mass in F – and there were criticisms of music by a *German* composer), Dent decided to share rooms also in London, to which he was making frequent journeys. He had just been up twice in a week – for a symphony by Donald Tovey and Arthur Bliss's quartet. He had also been to Saffron Walden to see Vaughan Williams, 'very gloomy and depressed and bored with having nothing to do, after expecting to get a much more exciting job than yours'. Two months later Pte R. V. Williams, 2nd/4th London Field Ambulance, was writing to Clive, 'I do envy you doing something real in this affair. I must tell you that I was sent up to Guy's for a month to try my 'prentice hand on the uncomplaining poor – the attendance at the surgery fell off remarkably – but I learnt a lot in the way of bandages, stitches, fomentations, dissections, operations and the rest'. In France Clive was not always involved in 'doing something real'. Occasionally, increasingly after he was commissioned, he was able to collect a group of friends for a concert – Stanford gladly sent him 'Songs of the Fleet' for one of them. Perhaps the most ambitious was a celebration of Shakespeare's birthday.

In June, on the day of a C.U.M.S. concert, came the news of Denis Browne's death; Steuart Wilson was staying with Dent and they wretchedly kept it to themselves until the concert was over. It was, for Dent, the worst that could have happened. He wrote to Clive, 'Denis' death makes me more than ever convinced of the necessity of going on with as much musical life and academical musical life as we can. It makes me feel horribly lonely – for he was the only person who could educate me, though I mustn't forget you and [Hugh] Allen. I feel as if it was so difficult to do anything with the present young people – they are not very clever – at any rate they haven't the fire inside them. That of course is merely the war . . . Still perhaps I ought not to be too despondent . . . If I only knew how to do for other people what I did for Denis – but one grows old and 40 isn't the same as 30. Stanford still lives, still lives – and I feel a horrible lethargy creeping over us all. I feel as though I want to retire into a library and do research work in the

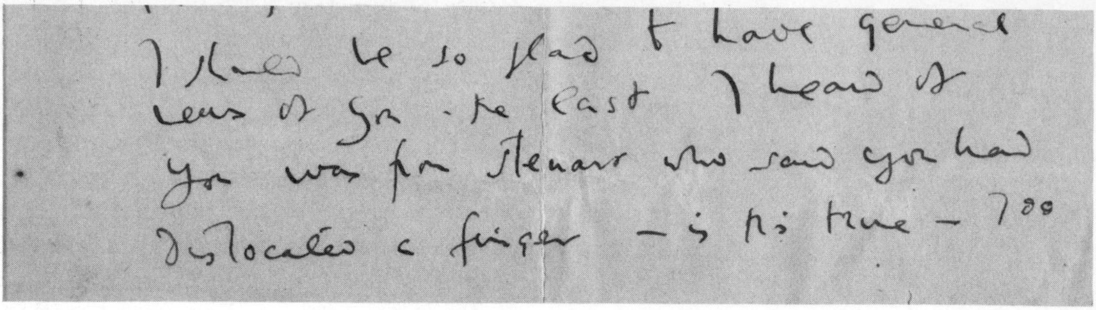

I should be so glad to have general news of you in the East. I heard of you from Stewart who said you had dislocated a finger — is this true —? so

every you doing something real in this affair.

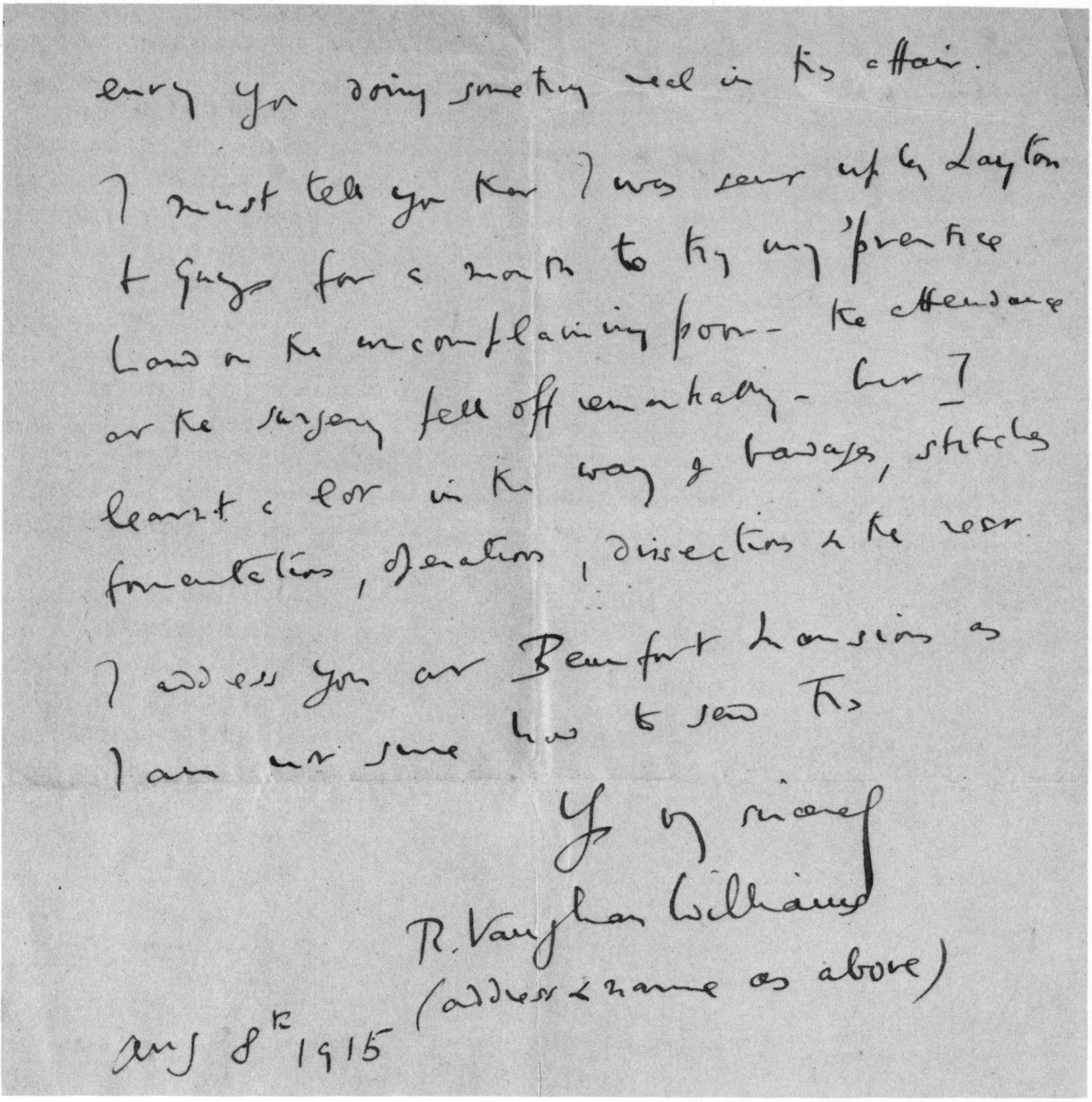

I must tell you how I was sent up by Layton & Gayes for a month to try my 'prentice hand on the uncomplaining poor — the attendance at the surgery fell off remarkably — but I learnt a lot in the way of bandage, stitches, fomentations, operations, dissections & the rest.

I address you at Beaufort Mansions as I am not sure how to send this

Yrs very sincerely
R. Vaughan Williams
(address & name as above)

Aug 8th 1915

Part of the letter from Pte R. V.
Williams.

driest German manner for I am utterly sick of the music I was brought up upon, and there is nobody to give me the new. How I wish I could see "Petrouchka" or "Sacre du Printemps"! All I can do is to plan a lecture performance of La Rappresentazione dell' Anima e del Corpo!'[1]

Altogether it was a discouraging time. The translation of *Figaro* made no progress, the University Press wouldn't touch the book on early opera, and it was evident that Lawrence Haward, to whom Dent had sent it for criticism, was rather bored by it. Haward presumed it was for the brighter students who had also been to the Marlowe performances, but by the time the Press had recovered its nerves Dent feared that they would all be 'dust and a filthy smell'. Steuart Wilson, though he was kind enough to say that Dent 'radiated cheerfulness', had been depressed by the views of other fellows of King's; discussion had shown him how stupid and hopeless the whole business was, whether you followed the ultra-jingo or the ultra-pacifist policy. Amongst the ultra-jingos Dent probably included the Provost, M. R. James, a regular correspondent of Clive and his brother Gordon at this time.

M. R. James.

A local solicitor who sang with C.U.M.S. had had the idea that they should sing the part-songs again (Rootham's 'Highland and Meadow', and 'Stolen Child') at the military hospital, and though Dent thought it a little absurd, he sensed that an objection on his part would be taken amiss both by the solicitor and the composer. They sang them three times over, in three separate spaces between the wards. 'Rootham said we sang very well: I'm sure at any rate that we took extra trouble. The bright spot was just as we began, a window was pushed open – nearly hitting me violently on the head – in the back wall of a ward against which we were standing, a queer head all bandages appeared with a pink patch over one eye and a great twinkle in the other, and joined in, singing bass (not very accurately, I need hardly say) over my shoulder . . . It was the first time I had been into the hospital, and Moule the tuner who brought the pianoforte was also there for the first time. It was rather terrible to hear him say suddenly "But they're all so young!"'

Dent was Denis Browne's musical executor, and within little more than a fortnight of Denis' death had been through all of his manuscripts with Steuart Wilson and

[1] The first oratorio, by Cavalieri, *c*.1550-1602.

83

discussed them with Vaughan Williams. Obeying the instructions that the music was to be criticised with a severe eye and that nothing was to be published that did not represent Denis Browne at his best, Dent destroyed almost everything except the four songs 'Gratiana', 'Arabia', 'Diaphenia' and 'Epitaph on Salathiel Pavy'. Some music could not be recovered; 'The Enchanted Night' in which Denis and Clive had collaborated, and the ballet *The Comic Spirit*, of which Clive had an unfinished manuscript. Dent was later to write, 'When one recalls the world-wide enthusiasm that hailed the works of Rupert Brooke after his romantic death in the Aegean, it is easy to see how a similar excitement could have been worked up for the music of that friend who had buried Rupert Brooke only a few days before he himself was to fall. But Denis Browne was far too honest an artist to have wished for such a reputation. He would have hated such uncritical enthusiasm.' It is a judgement one can both admire and regret.

In fact Dent's resilience was astonishing. He was not callous, but it was his duty to make the most of what opportunities he had and to build for the future. With this in mind he was building up a friendship with T. S. Fairbairn, who ran the London School of Opera. Clive, who had written an appreciative letter to rally Dent after the tragic news of Denis, was anxious that he should not leave Cambridge and immerse himself with a group as amateurish as the London School of Opera. Dent agreed, having recently been to their show: 'Act I of *Bohème* – which is dreadful stuff, I think, musically and dramatically too – and Acts I and II of *Figaro* – which showed up weak points horribly, but was agreeable to see'. He wanted, however, to get work in London, possibly teaching counterpoint, and he was hopeful that Vaughan Williams would send him pupils. He had some hopes too that Beecham and Courtneidge, planning an opera season in the autumn, might use him. Meanwhile at Cambridge he must just endure the return to the musical life of ten years ago or more, in the belief that 'afterwards' one would enjoy another phase of rejuvenation. He was impatient to push modern things, 'Delius or George Butterworth or Rimsky or even Borodin' into these inevitably stereotyped programmes. He was also conducting madrigals for a small group of friends. At a musical evening with the Jenkinsons they had played Chopin's F minor Concerto which he did not know at all well. 'It is glorious stuff – I wish we heard more Chopin. One does hear the Ballades and Nocturnes – but the Concertos almost never.'

Throughout 1915 the letters are so full as to be almost a diary. Dent was also the focus of the diminishing group of friends, passing on to each of them news of the others. The trials of translating *Figaro* provide a constant theme; the trouble was that in a comedy like *Figaro* people don't naturally state their emotions whereas in tragic or semi-tragic opera you can find suitable language. How can one put into English verse platitudinous lines about 'dolce contento' and 'fiero tormento', he complained.

One cannot do more than indicate a few topics, and occasionally provide fuller quotations from what seem to be highlights.

In August Fairbairn was considering a performance of Holst's *Savitri* (first produced in London privately in 1916), but Dent makes no further mention of it. He went to Glastonbury where Rutland Boughton was rehearsing Purcell's *Dido and Aeneas* which Dent had never seen acted; Dent felt that *Dido* was being put on only to please people like himself, but that the real work of the school had been given to Boughton's own operas and Bainton's *Oithona*. About the *Birth of Arthur* Dent was his most caustic, referring to Queen Igraine and Sir Brastian as Migraine and the Blasted Ass, and complaining that people never say anything that matters – 'it's all – "it boots not now, I ween" etc.' – but *The Immortal Hour* was infinitely better. 'Here the words are by Fiona Macleod, so there is some stuff to work on. There is no action to speak of, but there is some character and psychology . . . There was one Irish tune which recurred and kept things together; and I felt that the voices had much more to do. Also a certain Clarence Raybould played the piano and played very well, with a real musical sense. But it is all rather conventionally operatic, you know.'

Dent was sceptical about the value of his *Figaro* translation, and also afraid that the Beecham Company would put on a piecemeal arrangement in which each singer would provide the words he liked best. Although the critics had been kind to *The Magic Flute* he felt that it never occurred to them or to singers that the words in a classical opera mean anything, and they prefer to think that to cultured persons like themselves the memory of the original is too strong to be effaced. Thus to distinguish between Dent and

Lady McFarren was, as Dr Johnson would say, rather like distinguishing between a louse and a flea. He was experimenting with 'secco' dialogue, both spoken and sung, and intended to make further study of it during a holiday on Dartmoor. ('To be obliged to spend a whole year in England is a severe test of patriotism!') He sent Clive his 'rather successful' version of Dove Sono:

I remember days long departed,
  Days when love no end could know,
I remember fond vows and fervent;
  All were broken long ago.

Dent wondered whether there was a suitable opera in English to which children could be taken at Christmas and mentioned *Oberon* and *Cenerentola*. '*Snegourotchka* is a ballet only, isn't it?' he asked. It is unusual for Dent not to know anything. In fact, the *Snow Maiden* is an opera.

There was much diplomatic manoeuvre about the use of Dent's translation of *Figaro*. The Beecham company was interested, but somewhat half-heartedly, and Dent himself was determined that they should not use it until they had paid for the use of *The Magic Flute* two years before. Apparently the singers were totally floored by spoken dialogue and wished to have 'secco' recitatives but Dent's view was that a man who doesn't know how to talk can't sing a 'secco' recitative, but would instead sing them like an angel from Mendelssohn. Dent was finding the musical world in London disgusting when all his own friends and protégés were elsewhere. For once even a work of Vaughan Williams, 'The House of Life', failed to please him: 'It is rather portentous; and I don't care for Rossetti. Those artificial sonnets, so full of "inextricably" poetical words, and always seeming to say to you "you see how saturated I am with the poets of the Trecento", are not very suitable for music.'

Surprisingly, he also went to the Coliseum – the attraction was not 'Barrie's tiresome play about a Second Lieutenant – so antique and false and sentimental after a year of war'; nor even George Robey, whom he saw for the first time and thoroughly enjoyed – 'people like George Robey make me feel patriotic; there's something really English! And he performed his absurdities in front of a drop representing Buckingham Palace and the Queen Victoria monument, with Her Majesty looking over his head with the corners of her mouth turned down.' Dent was drawn by Adeline Genée, performing in a new ballet

86

by Dora Bright (Mrs Knatchbull). He was driven out into the street by sentimental songs, and was able to watch a Zeppelin drop the bomb which hit the Aldwych Theatre – 'the public watched it as if it had been part of the Coliseum show'.

After so many months in London it was hard to settle in Cambridge again; there were only twenty-eight under-graduates in King's; music was more alive than anything else, so plenty of scornful things were said of the effemin-acy of musicians. There was some talk, but it was never more than a rumour, that Dent might be invited to do important diplomatic work because of his knowledge of Italian, and it was also vaguely suggested that he might be used as a translator in the Press department at the Foreign Office. For the time being all that he was translating was the prison scene of *Fidelio* – 'the plot is all right, but the dialogues are wordy and the "lyrics" generally meaning-less: fearful slush. You don't notice how bad it is till you come to translate it, nor how unfailingly good Da Ponte is.'

The row with Beecham over the use of the *Figaro* translation came to a head in November. First Dent threatened legal proceedings if royalties were not paid for *The Magic Flute* (they amounted to £5 4s 10d); the account was settled immediately. Then Beecham asked Dent to come and discuss *Figaro* with him. He was amiability itself, but insisted on using the Krenz re-citatives, and Dent replied that if he proposed to do this he could not use his translation. Beecham replied that he had had a new one made, so they parted in a friendly enough fashion, on the understanding that none of Dent's words would be used. Then the singers protested – they had not time to learn a new version, and in any case preferred Dent's spoken dialogue; Beecham in turn threatened to close the theatre, throwing the singers out of work; then the singers asked Dent to relent and allow his lyrics to be used alongside 'those horrible Krenzitatives'; he yielded provided that the limit of his own involvement was made clear on the programme. Beecham was reported to be furious with Dent for having stood up to him, but at the interview he was altogether amiable. In the throes of these troubles, and reacting from Act I of *Iolanthe* – 'How I hate the "traditionalism" of Gilbert and Sullivan; not of them themselves, but of the companies which perform them' – Dent was looking forward to a new English Opera, run by Granville Barker, Albert Rutherston, the painter, Geoffrey

Toye, Bob Maltby, and Clive, (who had just been commissioned in the Ordnance Corps). Clive's music for *The Starlight Express* was not now to be used; he had been shabbily treated, but Elgar had been invited to do it. Malicious gossip had it, said Dent (who had a fine facility for retailing it), that the author Algernon Blackwood was going about saying that the play was being produced by God! In that case Clive was well out of it, as Dent imagined that He would be as tiresome to collaborate with as Stanford.

For Dent 1915 ended well, though it had been a terrible year. First of all, in December he went to Radley where a former pupil of his was putting on a concert of Purcell's *King Arthur*, which went very well. 'It was enormously encouraging to me to see what my pupils were doing, and to feel that it was in some respects derived from me; and I knew then for certain that it was the best thing for me to go on at Cambridge training musicians.' Also he became interested in coaching a singer, Gladys Moger, and this provided a new outlet for his energies. Not least rewarding was the discovery of how much more at ease she was when singing his words to 'Voi che sapete' than in nervous Italian or an earlier English translation. He was seriously considering taking a studio in London and teaching for one or two days a week, not singing, primarily, but 'counterpoint, composition, ensemble vocal and instrumental, in a word, anything that means *music itself*'. Clive would know what to advise him, and indeed might take it over when he came back, if it were successful.

At Christmas Dent was too ill and too depressed to join the usual party at King's, so he stayed at home reading Casanova's autobiography, sometimes thought to be a complete fiction written by Stendhal. 'I came across a curious allusion to the metronome and the noise it makes – and suspected an anachronism, rushed to Grove, and found that as far as I could gather the loud ticking "chronometer" (and Casanova calls it chronomètre too) was not invented till 1813. Casanova purported to have written his memoirs about 1798. But I can't write to the *Musical Times* about it, because the story in which the metronome comes is so very improper!'

Down in London there was another new activity – reading plays aloud with Harold Monro and others at the Poetry Bookshop. Eventually, having surprised himself by failure as Spirit Ironic and Spirit Sinister, both more appropriate to his character, he read the part of George III in Hardy's *Dynasts* with some success. In Cambridge there was another new task, brought about by the sudden death of Nixon, who had left all his music to Dent (who would probably have had to sort it in any case). Nixon, though lovable and kindly, had been to many a deliciously imitable figure of fun; Dent is more just to him: 'His range was very limited, but he always liked what was best and knew what was good. You never heard him praise a stupid song because the singer had a good voice. I know I learnt an enormous lot from singing glees and madrigals with him.' He had died a few days after the College Musical Society had had to be suspended for lack of performers and listeners.

Even Dent was beginning to yield to the prevailing gloom. Conscription had come in, and it was a weight off his mind that he had been rejected on medical grounds – though he understood that his relations were very indignant at his goings-on. There was always a lot to do at Cambridge, and he was in arrears with a number of articles requested of him, including one on Shakespeare's songs for the *Musical Quarterly*. It had led him to study Chausson and he was fascinated. A Cambridge colleague with enough facility to write attempts at opera which were all empty tags from Wagner and Strauss was introduced to pieces of Erik Satie, and, when he had absorbed them, to Bartók. In answer to a letter of Clive's about Bob Maltby's unhappiness at the futility of the continuation of the war, he replied speaking of his admiration for the conscientious objectors who besides facing tribunals manned by local municipal worthies, not to mention their tutors and their families, yet managed to go into their work and their music quite seriously. When Maltby came on leave, Dent hurried to London to see him, to talk of the future, and to urge him to try to obtain some extension of leave as he was not at all well. This Maltby obtained. It was the last he was to enjoy.

To recount that Dent now for the first time acquired a typewriter may seem a triviality beneath the notice of a biographer or his readers; it must have made a major difference to his friends and publishers: both the German and the English censors had complained that to decipher his handwriting was beyond their palaeographers, and a Kingsman who was a prisoner-of-war[1] had even offered to pay for a shorthand clerk and typist for him. Henceforward

[1] C. E. (later Lord Justice) Harman.

he was rarely away from a typewriter and became extremely skilled with it.

He went twice to Beecham's *Flute* – 'pretty well what one would expect: good singers, but no acting at all, no stage-management, no sense; and as to the *production* I would never have thought it possible to miss so many obvious dramatic points'. It was a wonderful jumble of translations, including some of Dent's, and obnoxious Krenz recitatives, literally translated 'so that all verbs at the end of the sentences themselves find'. He was delighted that they had used his translation of the 'eugenic duet',

> The kindly voice of Mother Nature
> Wakes love in bird and beast and flower.

Quilter showed him some new pianoforte pieces ('rather à la Delius') at a lunch engagement, and Dent thought them a great advance on his songs.

One almost feels that the reduction in the number of Dent's correspondents as the long carnage continued made him even more prolific to the few who remained. Between the June of the Somme and the Armistice in 1918 Clive received another thirty long letters, reporting on practically every concert or contact with an old friend, almost as if Dent was afraid that his friends would be lost to the causes they had at heart unless constantly reminded of them. If ever Clive asks for music for concerts in France or later in Italy, Dent's response is immediate and thorough. Whenever he sees something specially good – like the Stage Society's performance of Congreve's *Double Dealer* or even dancing by children on a Cambridge lawn – there is always a full description, with the repeated lament 'but one wanted one's younger friends there'. Cant and any attempt to victimise conscientious objectors meets his scathing contempt; Pigou, Professor of Economics, was brought up a third time before a tribunal through the malice of colleagues, and again exempted; when Bob Maltby was killed, Dent revealed with admiration that Maltby, a serving officer, had been the author of an anonymous letter in the *Cambridge Magazine* which nearly involved the editors in prosecution. C.U.M.S. carried on, mostly with very conventional programmes – 'Jupiter' Symphony, Beethoven's Seventh, Haydn symphony, overtures to *The Bartered Bride* and *Clemenza di Tito*; there were one or two less familiar numbers – a centenary performance of Sterndale Bennett's Concerto in F minor, and Parry's 'Songs of Farewell'. There is talk of Vaughan Williams' 'new opera' (in 1916) – presumably *Hugh the Drover*, already completed, but not performed till 1924. Dent was examined again by a medical board, but by now there was a definite understanding that university teachers should not be called up unless fit for everything. It was impossible to hear modern music in London, partly because of the expense of the rehearsals, and partly because 'the present public takes music more than ever as a mere narcotic. How ridiculous it is these bishops and people writing to The Times about the degraded stuff to be seen at the theatres, as if the theatre managers were deliberately setting out to corrupt people's minds! They merely supply what they know is certain to pay, and who can blame them in these precarious days?'

Casualties struck hard, none more than the death of Kennard Bliss, the artist brother of Arthur Bliss; but Dent could endorse the feeling that for a man of his sensitivity and integrity instantaneous death was almost better than survival in such awful surroundings. Steuart Wilson was wounded again, seriously, and the letters betray Dent's anxiety for this, almost the last survivor on whom his hopes for the future of English music were placed. He was seeing more of Adrian Boult, whom he liked – 'we must rope him into our schemes' – and contact was maintained with Quilter – 'for years I had wanted to get to know him intimately, so as to be able to criticise his stuff, and point out his errors to him; and now that I am beginning to see something of him I find that he has done most of what I wanted himself'. Quilter too was to be drawn into projects for an opera school; his Blake songs required such simplicity and directness of style that Dent felt that no *professional* singer could sing them. Together they had looked at a new choral work of Percy Grainger's – all climaxes and crescendos, with no real musical themes as the foundation of them. He commented that Vaughan Williams was as bad, but that you don't notice it in works like 'Towards the Unknown Region' because the words are so fine, and your attention is concentrated on 'spitting them out'.

There is hardly a letter without some sidelight on the war, even though Dent's remarkable quality is often his detachment from it. 'It's curious to me how managements face the problem of a male chorus. The Ambassadors dresses up young women to look as much like boys as possible: the Palace employs a chorus about whose being over military age there can be no mistake at all, and emphasises their corpulence, their grey hairs and bald heads: a chorus of "vieux marcheurs". It is singularly repulsive – I mean the general scheme, of elderly dandies and gay females, with nothing else. *Turpe senex miles turpe senilis amor.*'[1]

As the war dragged on, musical novelties, or even good performances, became rare. The Beecham company produced a good *Aida* (always one of Dent's favourites) in the winter of 1916, even if Aida herself looked more like Ethiopia saluting the colours; at a rehearsal for an Admiralty Concert he heard the Sea Symphony scherzo which suddenly took him into a world which was alive, but a concert performance of Glinka's *Life for the Tsar* was 'fearful rubbish – not as good as the *Bohemian Girl*'. Rootham was away ill, and Dent, conducting again, realised that he had settled down too hopelessly to antiquarianism. There were awful rumours that all the old C3 people were to be compelled to join a Veterans' Training Corps, and go and drill; it was only a political move and it came to nothing. Dent had also to sign on at a Labour Exchange, but he was conducting C.U.M.S. for the concert in March 1917 in spite of these omens: 'The absurd thing is that people are all talking about my "reading" of the Haydn (symphony in D), which I really just played through as it was, with extra careful attention to Haydn's own expression marks and no more. I get more and more convinced that in old classics there are always certain places that must be played quite dead level, without any little crescendos or diminuendos and other things; not the whole way through, but an occasional 8 or 16 bars.' In the same month he heard and liked Bantock's 'Hebridean Symphony', though there was 'much too much descriptive business', and he also met John Ireland at William Murdoch's, where with Albert Sammons they were practising Ireland's rhapsody for pianoforte, and his new violin sonata – both magnificent things, Dent thought, though he didn't get very far with Ireland personally.

Beginning the Long Vacation in 1917 Dent was wondering whether the Music Club, which had used all its reserves, could go on in October if the war continued. 'We all thought Russia was inexhaustible, and the British Empire ditto, but they are not, and I don't believe America will be any better. But it may come to an end if a sufficient

[1] A line from Ovid's *Amores*: 'It is a wretched thing for an old man to be a soldier and for an old man to be a lover'.

An unusual combination: Dent,
Jasper Rootham, and the Union
Jack.

number of people realize that it is suicidal to go on – in all
countries.' It was hard to avoid depression: at a new
Galsworthy play at Cambridge – and a really good one, too,
though a failure – 'there were many ghosts – in more senses
than one – for the stalls were full of deadheads, and the pit
was full of those who were not there, but ought to have
been, and would have been'. In London he went to *Boris*,
of which Clive was a passionate advocate ever since seeing
it in Paris, and twice to *Trovatore*. 'Dare I tell you that I am
still more and more convinced that *Trovatore* is much the
greater opera of the two? *Boris* was quite splendidly
done . . . so if I was dissatisfied it was not the fault of the
performance. But I am annoyed by the shapelessness of the
thing, both as play and music. Certain things are always
wonderful – the Coronation scene in spite of its absurdity is
absolutely right: I am not in the least worried, and never
shall be, by Boris stopping dead in the middle of the street
between the two cathedrals to sing his aria. That is all right
in opera. And the chiming clock scene is good; and the
scene at the inn, mostly. The scene in Pimen's cell was cut,

93

and we had the scene between Dmitri and Marina in the garden, but without any Rangoni, or the forests – so it was just a soprano and tenor duet, boring in the extreme. I will blame the performance for this at least, that their cuts made things more shapeless than ever. But a Moussorgsky opera is like a Gluck opera: whatever you do it *has* to be pulled about and cut and tinkered somewhere, and it is all odds and ends. In *Trovatore* there is not a dull moment, it is bursting with guts all through, and everything contributes to the development. I saw it with Beecham conducting – Beecham out for a real Saturday night of it, with the most thrilling results.'

Writing to Clive in Italy in the winter of 1917 – he was with the forces based on Genoa who were propping up the Italians against an Austrian offensive that threatened to overrun the Lombard plain up to the Appennines – Dent was vigorously disapproving of the stuff people were talking about the 'sacred soil of Italy'. After all, Italy had been invaded more often than any other country, and though one would regret the destruction of buildings and frescoes, it was good for us to take Italy's own point of view, that Italy is not a mere museum. Dent realised how antiquarianism had caught him like a cuttle fish and was increasingly enveloping him, so that he no longer knew about music composed after 1800 and could no longer help young composers – though he was still able to help Armstrong Gibbs, who had just had a success with a new quartet. 'I must confess that I am rather overwhelmed by the number of aunts who attend him. They seem to have a curious reproductive power, for there are always more of them at tea afterwards than at lunch before.' He recalled how they used to laugh at an elderly Cambridge friend who would never commit himself to an opinion about new music until he had heard what Denis Browne or Dent had to say about it, but he now felt himself to be coming to the same state: 'I am puzzled and have not grasped the new outlook and its standards, because I have only my intellect to guide me, and have no emotional thrill for these things now, and it does help me and interest me to find out what the judgements of the young people are, because they can still feel the emotion of a thing.' The old man had been right – unlike another of their friends who merely asked in order to know the safe thing to say to the woman he took into dinner after the concert. He began to fear that in ten years' time he would be practising "soulless diplomacy" from force of habit, like Forster's Mrs Herriton. As he himself had served as the model for Philip Herriton in *Where Angels Fear to Tread*, it was a significant transition. In the *Cambridge Magazine* he was writing articles about the invaded country in Italy, using his own drawings as illustrations. He was also serving out buns at the station to soldiers passing through on the last two trains. He commented on yet another visit to *Trovatore* that the first scene should set the romantic atmosphere of the whole opera: 'I want to see the scene centred on an immense fire, with the men-at-arms gathered round it, rather in silhouette, and some of their backs to the audience – a Salvator Rosa kind of effect. And the firelight must be worked so as to heighten the dramatic effect, sometimes sinking to a dull glow, sometimes bursting into a great wild flame that startles everybody.'

The mood of pessimism did not last very long. There was a sudden access of new initiatives. His work with Gladys Moger was bearing fruit in a number of lecture-recitals, of which he made a privately printed synopsis in 1918, and these encouraged him to search widely among new songs, and revived the idea of the London studio; it was good for him to have to tackle accompaniments and play Ravel at sight. Adrian Boult was making his mark as conductor of a series of four concerts at the Queen's Hall, during one of which, at a performance of the 'London Symphony' which, according to Vaughan Williams 'the Boche was determined to make sound like 1812', there was an air raid. Dent greatly admired Boult's conducting, and contributed programme notes which developed into four little papers on modern English music. His attendance at the Society of English Singers convinced him that the public-school patriotic manner, which in the early days had been a real thing with a certain nobility, had now become cheap and could be done by anyone from the R.C.M. Not only was he composing new accompaniments for the song recitals, but he was setting songs too, something he hadn't done since the last of his Shelley songs in 1902. In quite swift succession came 'The Willow Tree Bough' to words by Charles Scott-Moncrieff and two songs from Walter de la Mare.

From the Director of the Zürich Opera came inquiries about the possibility of putting on an English opera, and there was a chance that Dent might go out, with Foreign Office permission, to help them; he thought of doing *The*

Fairy Queen there, since it might be years before the Cambridge performance came off, or *Dido and Aeneas*, or possibly *Dr Faustus* in the Marlowe style. It was to be a propaganda exercise. In London he was offering to help Henry Wood with orchestration, anonymously, and studying Galuppi in the British Museum, as Diaghilev was prepared to be interested in all sorts of things, including the possibility of an 'old English' ballet. As the determined protagonist of the best of Denis Browne, he had not only arranged 'Gratiana' for orchestra in the hope that Henry Wood would do it, but was trying to interest Diaghilev in *The Comic Spirit*. Dent lamented the dearth of university-trained musicians in London, Boult always excepted, and felt his own lack of a strong enough personality to stand on his own; now that the Cambridge group were all destroyed ('one might as well talk of Salamanca or Salerno') he had no link at all, not even with the R.C.M. He was becoming drawn into a new venture in Cromwell Road, the International Conservatoire, about which his younger friends ragged him – 'My dear Dent, it becomes more and more obvious from every sentence of the prospectus that this place is nothing more than a Disorderly House.'

In a letter of 30 September 1918 Dent wrote: 'We had a great excitement yesterday. Von Holst is just going out to Salonika with the Y.M.C.A., so by way of a send-off Balfour Gardiner engaged the Queen's Hall and orchestra to perform his new work, "The Seven Planets". Adrian Boult conducted. Balfour Gardiner was not there himself, but there were a good many old friends: Geoffrey Toye: Norman O'Neill: Henry Wood: Roger Quilter: Arnold Bax and others whom I did not know. They began rehearsing about 10.30 and then after an interval played the whole through about 12.30. Von Holst is a believer in astrology, and the work is a set of pieces dealing with (1) Mars the bringer of war (2) Venus the bringer of peace (3) Mercury the winged messenger (4) Jupiter the bringer of jollity (5) Saturn the bringer of old age (6) Uranus the magician (7) Neptune the mystic.

'The score is enormous: 3 of everything and often four; plus cor anglais, bass clar: double bassoon: 2 tenor tubas: 6 horns: 4 trumpets: 2 drum players: 2 harps etc. xylophone, celesta, gong and the rest. It is bewildering to read, but sounded much less modern than I anticipated. There is no doubt about Von Holst being English! for it is directly descended from Parry, Stanford and V.W. Jupiter is outrageous V.W. – a folk-song that stands out almost too violently. Saturn is more or less Stanford, and a great deal of *Parsifal*. It confirmed me in my long held theory that *Parsifal* was composed not by Wagner but by Stanford. It becomes more and more apparent that all our new school of English music is derived from[1]

and

'Uranus had a good deal of L'Apprenti Sorcier. So you might go on and say Mars=Stainer: Venus=Boito of the notte del sabba classico: Mercury=a scherzo basta: rather Ravelish. Neptune interested me most, for it was really mystical and exploratory with a feeling of posthumous Beethoven, and a sense of getting on to a different plane altogether. But it was extremely queer, and for all the Stanford training Von Holst does produce some very odd discords. But taken altogether the music is very much alive and has long phrases and compelling rhythms. Even admitting its indebtedness it hasn't ever that patchiness and pretence to modernity and ragbag clichés which are characteristic of the Corder school. Partly because the Corder school when you strip off the clichés and the "stunts" have nothing except Mendelssohn and *Rigoletto* at bottom.'

Talking to Adrian Boult, Von Holst and Geoffrey Toye made him feel like a German professor 'bombinans in vacuo' (booming on in emptiness), but Dent was a great deal more lively than that. Letters written during the last two months of the war were much concerned with the appointment of Parry's successor at the R.C.M. One need hardly say that Dent was most anxious that Stanford, already Professor of Music at Cambridge since 1887, should *not* obtain the appointment, which presumably he might have held in double harness, as eventually Hugh Allen was to do with his Oxford professorship. Delay was occasioned not only by Allen's reluctance – although Parry on his death-bed had begged him to take it, Allen went into

[1] Themes from *Die Meistersinger* and *Parsifal*.

the concert hall and played Parry's preludes for an hour before accepting – but also because the council had no president, Prince Christian having died the year before. Dent heard that his own name had been considered, but he truthfully felt that they must be in a pretty bad way if they had come to that. He went to the concert played in Parry's memory at the R.C.M., and sadly found it ineffectual, for he was a devoted believer in Parry's greatness, and was disappointed not to be thrilled and moved – perhaps it was because all the works belonged to the years before 1897 and he had reacted against the music of his student days.

He had another composing fit, combined with participation in the influenza epidemic, and was reminded of A. E. Housman's answer to someone who asked him if he meant to write any more poems: 'Oh, I daresay, if I have influenza again!' Clive, now a Major, was kept in Italy, clearing up after the end of the campaign. Just as obtaining a commission had been largely a matter of 'knowing someone' so was the business of getting out at the end, and Dent was anxious to have him appointed a professor at the International Conservatoire, which would request his demobilisation. Cambridge was livening up, the Music Club had reopened and Dent had acquired a clavichord – 'it's like the influenza, and searches out all one's weak places . . . it's the most curious physical experience to feel the vibration of the strings transmitted directly to your fingertips'. He found himself playing much better with the left hand than with the right, and wondered whether this was because some thirty years before he had studied the violin for a year.

Nevertheless, Dent was thinking of severing his connection with academic Cambridge altogether, giving up lecturing, resigning from committees, and spending most of his time in London. He was always a man who preferred an institution with its back to the wall to a flourishing concern, and the survival of the Conservatoire was very much in the balance. He would keep on his house at Cambridge, and his invaluable housekeeper, and of course he meant to stir people up about *The Fairy Queen*; another ambition was to put on Nicholas Gatty's *The Tempest*, in which he found a wonderful Purcellian beauty. As part of his London venture he took on regular weekly journalism, beginning a series of articles for *The Athenaeum* in April 1919 with an article hopefully entitled 'The Resurrection of Music'. He was also delighted when Delius sent him a pupil for strict counterpoint. By the time Clive was eventually demobilised in the summer of 1919, the International Conservatoire existed no longer. Dent remained at Cambridge, but reduced his commitments there, and their next joint ventures were not only the long postponed *The Fairy Queen*, but the introduction of the operas of Mozart to the audiences of the Old Vic.

A stage performance at a troops' concert in Italy in 1918: Lt Sweet and Major Carey R.A.O.C. in 'drag'.

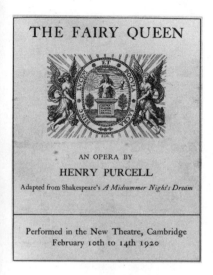

THE FAIRY QUEEN

AN OPERA BY
HENRY PURCELL
Adapted from Shakespeare's *A Midsummer Night's Dream*

Performed in the New Theatre, Cambridge
February 10th to 14th 1920

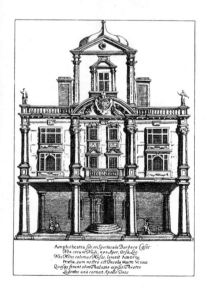

Amphitheatra file en Spectacula Barbara Cæsar.
Non conunt Nudi, non Aper, Ursa, Leo.
Nos Mites colimus Musas, lenient Amores;
Prelia, cum nostro est Incola Marte Venus.
Quafg; ferunt olim Thalamo exposcit Theatro
Lafentes una cernat Apollo Deos.

The war over, *The Fairy Queen*
finally reaches the stage: extracts
from the programme.

The correspondence which covers the years between 1919 and Dent's appointment to the professorship at Cambridge at the end of 1926 is spasmodic; indeed there was a period in 1925–6 when, for the first time in his musical life, Clive was without news of Dent's activities and, feeling very much isolated, was actually writing more letters than he received. This was brought about by the impossibility of their meeting rather than by a lack of common interest. Dent's most whole-hearted involvement was in the International Society for Contemporary Music, of which he was first president, though he disclaimed the credit of being the founder; Clive, partly from disappointment with his lack of apparent progress in the world of professional music in England, accepted the professorship of singing at the Elder Conservatorium in Adelaide University in October 1924, and remained there till 1928. His letters during that period do not concern production of whole operas but of scenes from them; there were few mutual friends of whom he could write, but he was enthusiastic about the performances and progress of his students, and was constantly inquiring after scores and translations virtually unobtainable in Australia.

In some ways Clive's failure was temperamental rather than actual. The years that followed his demobilisation were full of useful work that is now seen to have laid important foundations, but, partly through reluctance to concentrate on one thing and through dissipating his energies, and chiefly through a lack of ruthlessness and an essentially amateur approach that professionals can rarely afford, Clive made no great headway; he felt that he was not appreciated. As Dent wrote: 'You ought to have sung Herbert Hughes's songs; you ought to have flirted with "Ursula the Pig-Woman" (see Ben Jonson); you ought to have sedulously flattered Legge [the *Daily Telegraph* music critic] and Percy Pitt [Artistic Director of the British National Opera Company] and various others – in fact done all the disgusting things which people like ourselves

CHARACTERS

THESEUS, Duke of Athens	HON. CHRISTOPHER TENNANT
EGEUS, Father to Hermia	JOHN STEEGMANN
LYSANDER } in love with Hermia	RODNEY A. GALLOP
DEMETRIUS }	FRED WILKINSON
HIPPOLYTA, Queen of the Amazons	RUTH M. CORDER
HERMIA, in love with Lysander	EILEEN G. B. THOMAS
HELENA, in love with Demetrius	HELEN LEHMANN
OBERON, King of the Fairies	A. H. G. DAVIDSON
TITANIA, Queen of the Fairies	EILA CAREY
PUCK or ROBIN GOODFELLOW	ROBERT MAWDESLEY
A FAIRY	MONICA BEAUMONT
PEASE BLOSSOM	ISOBEL SHIELDS
COBWEB	MARGARET GREEN
MOTH } Fairies	MARY M. TABRUM
MUSTARD SEED	ESTHER CHRISTMAS
QUINCE, a carpenter	G. G. TOMLIN
SNUG, a joiner	WALLIS GOODYEAR
BOTTOM, a weaver	EDWARD HARMAN
FLUTE, a bellows-mender	HUBERT E. RICKS
SNOUT, a tinker	A. B. JEFFRIES
STARVELING, a tailor	W. J. H. SPROTT

Attendants on Theseus   DENNIS ARUNDELL   H. SHEERMAN HAND

Attendants on Oberon   G. R. H. WRIGHT   REGINALD LEWIS
                       J. A. C. ATKINS   ARTHUR WILSON

Attendants on Titania   DORIS SHILLINGTON SCALES
                       A. F. GRANT   CECIL LONGLEY

Indian Boy   JASPER ROOTHAM (Tues., Thur., & Sat. afternoon)
                     FRIDESWIDE STEWART (Wed. & Fri.)
                     MARGARET COCKERELL (Sat. evening)

SCENE—Athens and a wood near it.

There will be intervals only after Act II and Act IV.

Signatures of some participants.

Don Giovanni at the Old Vic, 1920: a sketch of Clive Carey, by Alwyn Scholfield.

can't bring ourselves to do.' In the years before his departure to Adelaide he joined the staff of the R.C.M. as a singing teacher, produced *The Fairy Queen* at Cambridge, and *Figaro*, *The Magic Flute* and *Don Giovanni*[1] at the Old Vic, singing himself in all of them. Some thirty years later Dent still maintained that Clive was the best Don Giovanni he had ever seen, and was delighted when Dennis Arundell rejoined that a man can't sing Don Giovanni unless he has been at a university. Besides this, in 1920 Clive joined the ensemble of the English Singers, touring with them in 1922 to Prague, Berlin, Vienna and in Holland – it was the first visit of English performers to Berlin since the war; his summer vacations were spent from 1920 to 1924 with Jean de Reszke in Nice, first as a student and later as his accompanist and assistant teacher; and in 1924, accompanied by Gerald Cooper, he toured Holland, Berlin and Scandinavia giving solo recitals of English music. He also produced and sang in the first public performance of Holst's *Savitri*, with Arthur Bliss conducting. His other activities included composing the music for *The Blue Lagoon*, *The Wonderful Visit*, and A. A. Milne's *Red Feathers*, and conducting the early performances, besides composing *All Fools' Day*, a fantasy with music which Adrian Boult conducted at the Bristol Opera

[1] An excellent description of the first Mozart season at the Old Vic is to be found in Dent's *A Theatre for Everybody* (London: T. V. Boardman, 1945) pp. 86–7.

Festival in 1926. However, his very versatility (for he also continued to play an active part in folk-song and dance) militated against his obtaining public recognition or financial security.

The Old Vic theatre in the Waterloo Road, on the south bank of the Thames, and its stable-companion Sadler's Wells, on the outskirts of Islington (then unfashionable) were to occupy much of the time and energy of both Dent and Clive Carey for the rest of their lives in their efforts to lay the foundations of English opera, so that their history warrants a brief digression. Their unusual traditions were embodied in the personality of Lilian Baylis, who inherited the lease and management of the Old Vic from her aunt, Emma Cons, in 1912.

Once the Royal Coburg Theatre, the Royal Victoria Coffee Hall had been acquired by Miss Cons, a social worker who probably never realised what she had initiated, for the purpose of providing uplifting entertainment for the poor – under strict conditions of temperance – in 1880. As the Royal Victoria Hall Foundation, a charity registered in 1889, it gradually extended its range, adding to its early

Don Giovanni, 'the *Opera Buffa*' feeling: Clive's 1938 production at Sadler's Wells.

LYRIC THEATRE
HAMMERSMITH
(By permission of the Directors)

June 23 and 24 at 2.30
TWO SPECIAL PERFORMANCES OF

SAVITRI

A Chamber Opera by Holst.   Founded on an episode from the Mahabharata.

(Preceded by Choral Hymn from the 'Rig Veda,' for Female Voices and Harp:
'Hymn of the Travellers')

Scenery and Costumes supervized by C. LOVAT FRASER

SAVITRI - - DOROTHY SILK
SATYAVAN - STEWART WILSON
DEATH - - CLIVE CAREY

AND

LA SERVA PADRONA
(Pergolesi)

Scenery and Costumes designed by C. LOVAT FRASER

SERPINA - - GRACE CRAWFORD
UBERTO - - CLIVE CAREY
VESPONE - - TRISTAN RAWSON

The two Operas produced by Mr. CLIVE CAREY, 'La Serva Padrona' as nearly as possible on the lines
of the original production by Mr. NIGEL PLAYFAIR.

Conductor - - ARTHUR BLISS

PRICES OF ADMISSION (including Tax):

Private Boxes, £2 6s.; Stalls, 8s. 6d.; Dress Circle (Front Row), 5s. 9d.; other Rows, 4s. 9d.; Pit Stalls, 4s. 9d.; Pit, 3s.; Gallery, 1s.

Curwen Press   Plaistow, E.13

Savitri, 1921: poster for the first public performance.

magic lantern lectures, ballad and choral concerts, occasional dramatic and operatic productions and, from 1914, a regular Shakespeare Company. In Miss Cons' day opera was sung in costume and accompanied by illustrated tableaux. Until 1923, when Morley College, which had shared the premises since 1889, found a new home, conditions were cramped and money was always short – tickets cost from twopence to two shillings – so that West End stars hesitated to risk their reputations there. Rehearsals were cut to a minimum, and the opera choruses were usually amateur. However, the theatre was a notable training ground, Charles Corri, the musical director, a devoted and accomplished artist, and its integrity and rising standards gradually gained more notice.

At Sadler's Wells there was an even longer history of entertainment, dating back with certainty to 1683 when Dick Sadler opened his music house in the neighbourhood of the medicinal waters; but since 1906 the theatre has been closed. In 1925 Lilian Baylis acquired the derelict premises, but it was not until 1931 that it could be opened, in double harness with the Old Vic, for drama and opera. These were joined almost immediately by a ballet company. The alternation of different forms of entertainment at the Vic–Wells theatres inevitably caused some stress for players, audiences, and management, and by degrees, notably when Tyrone Guthrie returned as drama director in 1936, Sadler's Wells became the home of opera and ballet, and the Old Vic of drama.

But these developments lay in the future. In the years immediately after the War, at Cambridge and in England Dent felt something of the same frustration as Clive. He continued to lecture, and, though not at first elected a governor, was very lively in the affairs of the Old Vic (and very sceptical of the activities of the British National Opera Company upon whom the mantle of the Beecham Opera Company had descended). His translations required the stimulus of the expectation of an actual performance, and he did some work on *Fidelio* in 1921, and was also anxious to secure an English production of *Duke Bluebeard's Castle*, for which eventually he had to wait more than thirty years. It was not until Clive's return from Australia and the beginning of Sadler's Wells that the impulse to translate reached its zenith. *The Fairy Queen* in February 1920 was both musically and financially a success, yet one feels from the letters – and indeed from the

Scenes from *The Fairy Queen*,
from the *Cambridge Chronicle*
February 1920.

"Fairy Queen" Sketches.
(By Our Own Artist).

PURCELL'S OPERA,

THE FAIRY QUEEN

Will be Performed by Members of the University and others.

Produced by Clive Carey.
Conductor, Dr. Rootham.

Smoking in the Auditorium Strictly Prohibited.

Seats may be Booked in Advance Daily. Box Office (Mr. R. Silk) open 11 a.m. till 4 p.m.

Doors open at 7.15. Commence at 7.45.

Titania and the Indian boy: from the album of Frida Stewart (now Mrs Knight), aged nine at the time of the performance and more properly in bed. The shadowy crowned figure of Titania is Eila Carey, the author's mother.

absence of such a letter as had followed *The Magic Flute* in 1911 – that there was some sense of anti-climax.

The Times celebrated the occasion with a full-column review, somewhat unpromisingly entitled 'The Fairy Queen. Opera or Pantomime?' The writer regretted that the lovers were 'misgraffed in respect of years', so that though Shakespeare and Purcell were made for one another they were kept apart by time and by the failure of the Restoration stage to respect Elizabethan drama. Otherwise, apart from comment on the excessive length of the performance, the reviewer was most enthusiastic, praising the 'vivid and varied vitality' of the production, labelling it 'a thing to be proud of', and with two performances yet to go, already recommending its subsequent revival. 'Mr Clive Carey, singing falsetto in a red wig, was we dare wager every bit as absurd as the original "Mr Pate, in woman's habit" … [he] as producer, Dr Rootham as musical director, Mr E. J. Dent, officially described as one of two stage managers but really literary adviser and arch-inspirer in the background, and all their company too numerous to mention, must be congratulated on having created so much order out of apparent chaos. They have shown us Purcell as a very human creature, with whom one must laugh and cry and dance for joy. And they have shown us where the national opera which he so nearly created would have led us, not indeed to the Grand Opera of Covent Garden, but to a glorified and enriched pantomime over the way.'

So Purcell was launched again, but it was not to Covent Garden or to Drury Lane but to the Old Vic that Dent looked for the revival of the English operatic tradition. Meanwhile the success of *The Fairy Queen* increased Dent's enthusiasm, always latent, for a performance of *Dido and Aeneas*, especially on the Continent, where it was important to restore a respect for the past, as well as recognition for the present, standards of English music. The eventual performance at Münster in 1926 was not very distinguished ('a funny show') but it was a landmark nevertheless; delays had been caused by Dent's determination to have something like a definitive score and this could not be made till a manuscript, rumoured to be contemporary, had been tracked down among the papers of William Cummings (a musical antiquary who had died in 1915) and its validity established. It had been sold to Tokyo. It would have been disappointing if the details which had come to be regarded as 'delightfully Purcellian' had proved to be later accretions: in fact the Tenbury MS of 1720 remains the most authentic source, and Dent's vocal score, published in 1925, with its introduction and bibliography, clarifies the tradition, and reinforced his own understanding of Purcell's style.

Dent's *Foundations of English Opera* (1928), which was to have accompanied *The Fairy Queen* in 1914, could now draw upon a wider experience. Among all the pages of his critical writings there can be few paragraphs more whole-hearted than this. 'No great composer was ever more unfortunate in his surroundings. In spite of his popularity . . . Purcell was never trusted sufficiently to be given a free hand, and between the inevitable jealousy of poets and actors and the disastrous prudence of managers his wonderful genius for the theatre was condemned to a humiliating slavery. When we consider his marvellous power of setting words to music, the massive nobility or the racy humour of his declamation, his unerring perception of a stage picture, his unrivalled fertility of invention and his unsurpassed handling of all technical resources, it is difficult not to believe that he only wanted an equally skilled librettist and the reasonable support of an intelligent public to have become the greatest operatic composer of his time in Europe.' (p. 230)

The book concludes: 'Some of the works described in this book have recently been put on the stage at Cambridge, Glastonbury and elsewhere; their revival was in all cases due to the adventurous enthusiasm of amateurs. They have in no case been adopted into the professional repertory, and it is not likely that they will ever appeal to the professional mind – at any rate in their own country. They must in all probability remain what some of them were in their own day – instruments of education; yet performances of them may serve to educate grown-up composers as well as boys and girls. We must admit that they are dead; but there is at least one place where the dead are of definite use to us – the school of anatomy.'

It was from 'the school of anatomy' that the book emanated. Although he had no sooner taken on regular journalism, chiefly as a source of income, than he was regretting it (in spite of the fact that it provided a regular forum for the discussion of contemporary music), Dent had no strong wish for the Cambridge professorship, when eventually it was vacated by Stanford, at the age of seventy-two, in 1924. By now the International Society for Contemporary Music (I.S.C.M.) was becoming the major interest of his musical life – its first festival had taken place at Salzburg the previous year – and the professorship might limit his freedom of action, even if, with its petty £200 a year, or whatever larger sum the university might find, it would spare him from journalism, and give him the opportunity to write books (*Foundations of English Opera* had already been ten years in gestation).

He had felt, twenty years before, that Cambridge musical education was better than that of the R.C.M.; but since Parry's death he had realised that the R.C.M. was giving all that Cambridge could and what London could give too. This was the result of the 'presence of Allen at the R.C.M., and the absence of Stanford at Cambridge'. Ever since 1892, Stanford had given the R.C.M. his first consideration, and now Allen, who was one of the electors, was in much the same position himself, and would be very reluctant to lose to Cambridge one of the strongest of his London teaching staff, Vaughan Williams or Charles Wood, if they were to devote themselves fully to Cambridge, as Dent believed that at this juncture a professor should do if the university were to recover its position. He reported to Clive, then with the de Reszkes at Nice, the advice he had given to Allen, whom he regarded as the most influential of the electors: 'If you want a distinguished composer who will always be a great inspiring force in Cambridge music, then V.W.; if you want a competent teacher of Mus.B. subjects, Wood; if you want a man who will be energetic and raise money to build a music school and endow it, Rootham.' What Dent feared was that Oxford and Cambridge were increasingly regarded as 'nursery gardens' for the R.C.M.; having no official connections with it, and, having built up a 'Cambridge school' only to see it destroyed by the War, he found such an attitude unacceptable. Equally, he himself did not want to sacrifice the freelance status he had acquired; when he wrote in November 1923 he already had plans for attending an I.S.C.M. Jury in Zürich in February, and hearing Boito's *Nerone* in Milan, and *Don Giovanni* in Nice, where Steuart Wilson was now among de Reszke's pupils, financed as Clive once had been. In March he hoped to be in Prague for the Smetana festival, and to spend the spring in Vienna and perhaps in Italy before the opening of the next I.S.C.M. orchestral concerts in Prague on 1 June. How

Jean de Reszke at Nice, 1923.

could this be reconciled with setting examination papers, holding vivas and lecturing in advanced practical composition? It seemed strange to Dent that he had ever coveted the position, which, as he reported next April amid a welter of news of the I.S.C.M., went to Charles Wood.

When, within two years of his appointment, Wood was mortally sick with cancer, Dent – unless Rootham was appointed – could hardly expect not to be asked to become professor. 'If I was elected unanimously', he wrote to Clive, now in Adelaide, 'I would accept it from a sense of duty; in any case I admit that £500 a year would be a great assistance to me; but I want another £500 a year, and freedom to do all my various activities, not £500 a year and prison, which is what the Professorship would mean. I should have to give up a great many of my interesting activities, and I doubt whether I should find much time for writing learned books. And I feel that I am now completely out of the world of lectures and examinations, and don't want to go back to it. I love teaching, but I am not competent to teach modern composition. I hate lecturing, and I have forgotten all I ever knew about harmony and counterpoint and fugue. And I simply loathe examining. What I want is what you mention in your letter – I want to produce operas and work in a theatre with you and other people of the right sort. But I am growing old, and realize that I am regarded merely as an aged and incompetent amateur with a bee in his bonnet and several grievances as well. I think the best thing would be for me to re-catalogue Scarlatti.'

However, the position was not to be evaded: Vaughan Williams who himself absolutely refused to stand, wrote to Dent strongly about his standing for it, and other influential local figures, such as 'Daddy' Mann at King's, and Alan Gray, made no secret of their preference for him. In spite of the drawbacks he had enumerated, and his particular dislike of being a figurehead at dinners, he began to see that, even if it was a duty, it was an immensely interesting one. What most encouraged him was the sense that the younger generation could still identify with him. 'The people who are now about 20–25 are painfully conscious that the previous generation has been practically wiped out. It is not true, of course, that all those who would now be 30–35 were killed in the war; but they tell me that the survivors don't help the younger people in the way that my generation helped Rupert's. I begin to think it is rather

'Daddy' Mann, organist at King's College, 1876–1929.

a fact that what I may call the war generation, in so far as they have survived, have kept very much to themselves. I think many of them have married and made haste to get settled in the world; also that however anxious they may be to shake off all the influences of war, they cannot do so entirely. With me personally they do seem to return as much as possible to the old relations; but it is a psychological connection based on the recollection of our old pre-war relations, and that connection somehow can't be made with the younger generation, who perhaps seem to them rather feckless and wanting in idealism. I don't think the younger generation *are* wanting in idealism, but they don't look at things in the same way as mine did. It isn't natural that they should; and perhaps people like Sheppard and myself can see a little further into their psychology. At any rate, they tell us that they find us sympathetic where the intermediate generation is not.'

So at fifty Dent accepted the professorship which he was destined to hold for fifteen years. Within months he was reconciled to it, though he found Cambridge 'fearfully full of little things which make no effect'. He encouraged the men who attended the lectures that he gave once a week to two classes (Part I and Part II) to come to him privately for one hour a week, but refused to have fixed hours for them, and though delighted to see them was equally pleased that they did not always come, as this would have imposed on him an extra 14 hours teaching a week. After all, he was not a tutor or supervisor, and it was not his business to see that they worked. He submitted a memorandum on reorganisation, found Rootham very helpful and friendly and a good examiner, and he determined to show his own goodwill by inviting him to the I.S.C.M. Festival (1927) at Frankfurt.

Indeed by now the I.S.C.M. had become Dent's chief end and activity outside Cambridge, and provided a new outlet for the old urge to travel in Europe and to cultivate musical contacts there. It entailed two or three annual meetings, the first of a jury to determine what works should be performed at the summer festival, and then the festival itself, each as far as practicable held in a different member country. From the start Dent was president, and must have been one of very few participants able to speak four major European languages; besides this, since there was no permanent secretariat, he was virtually the secretary also, drawing in a friend, Gerald Cooper, J.B.

Trend (who now shared his London flat, and became Professor of Spanish at Cambridge), or Edwin Evans, to help him with the organisation at the festivals. Inevitably there were jealousies, and allegations that favour had been shown to particular composers or artists, and it required patience, tact, and an intuitive understanding of the motives which underlay the outbursts, to keep the Society together, and to expand its size and range. The breadth of his pre-war contacts, the international respect for his scholarship, and his detachment from the narrow partisanship that had been an almost inevitable concomitant for those more closely involved in the war, gave him a European standing greater perhaps than he enjoyed in Britain, certainly before the professorship set the official seal of approval on his works.

The English Singers, 1923:
Cuthbert Kelly, Steuart Wilson,
Flora Mann, Lillian Berger,
Winifred Whelan, Clive Carey.

Before he went to Australia, while he was travelling Europe with the English Singers or as a solo recitalist, Clive was a useful fugleman for the I.S.C.M. As eighteen countries had joined by 1923 and there were to be only twelve hours of music at Salzburg, there were bound to be disappointments. The new states of Czechoslovakia and Poland were victims of what Dent described as 'narrow nationalist egoism', and the choice of Prague as the venue for the second festival was resented by Germany. The jury met for four days, and Dent, though he hoped that Arthur Bliss's pianoforte concerto with tenor might be entered and chosen, had to be specially careful not to appear to show partiality towards British works. When the first festival took place at Salzburg, a counter-festival was planned ('by that idiot Korngold and that odious person Wilhelm Grosz') to take place immediately afterwards; by the fourth programme Dr Korngold (father of the composer) and Dent were reconciled. 'I didn't listen to the music much, as I was too tired with the conference and general worries, but on the whole I enjoyed it more than I expected. I am coming round to Stravinsky! The Busoni Fantasia was great: Arthur Bliss's Rhapsody a great refreshment for tired ears, and Kodály's violoncello sonata exciting beyond description. The programmes improved as they went on . . . I do feel that in spite of all troubles the International Society is now very firmly established.' There had been trouble between Casella and Scherchen which had even erupted into the Italian press, for which Casella apologised. 'I thought it something of an achievement on my part to make an Italian fascist apologise to a German communist! Like Papageno, I never knew I was so strong! They insist on my going on with the chairmanship, and they gave me much embarrassment by upsetting the business of the Conference every day to pass votes of thanks to me! I had to tell them that they were not in order. This is all rather a bore, as the idea has got about, even among responsible members of the Society, that I was its creator, which I certainly was not . . . One reason why things were in such a muddle this year was because I refused to dominate.'

In April 1924 Dent wrote from Rome; he was trying to persuade the Germans that Clive, who was giving two recitals in Berlin, was also the best man to produce *Dido and Aeneas* at Frankfurt. Meanwhile troubles were again impending with the I.S.C.M., this time with the French. Dent was torn between a number of loyalties, not least by his love of Rome itself; he had half a mind to follow the example of another fellow of King's, Oscar Browning, buy a flat in Rome and settle there for life, except that he had an impression that the English residents already there had by now given up the struggle in despair, and were gradually disintegrating. He had come to realise that the I.S.C.M. could be held together only by personal friendship, and wondered whether it might be his duty to cultivate it in various countries rather than to write books. The orchestral festival was to be held in May at Prague and Peter Warlock's 'The Curlew' and Vaughan Williams' 'Wenlock Edge' were to be sung at Salzburg in September, and Dent

The International Society for Contemporary Music, Salzburg festival, 1922. Left to right, Karl Weigl, Karl Alwin, Wilhelm Gross, Arthur Bliss, Paul Hindemith, Rudolf Réti, Ethel Smyth, Paul Pish, Willem Pijper, Egon Lustgarten, Egon Wellesz, Anton Webern, Karl Horwitz, Hugo Kander.

was hoping that Steuart Wilson would be engaged to sing them; he felt that Vaughan Williams was not very well disposed to the I.S.C.M., believing it to have too much of the 'frivolities of Berners and Poulenc'. This was a point of view with which Dent had some sympathy, though he was very thankful that they 'mitigated the stodginess of the Teutonic composers'.

Eventually the Salzburg festival went off very well in spite of the French: Lionel Tertis played finely. The disappointment was 'Wenlock Edge' – 'one of the most appalling experiences of my life'. Neither John Coates, who was asked first, nor Steuart Wilson, was available to sing, and nothing was done till the last minute when the Swiss provided a very good quartet and pianist; a young American singer resident in Vienna was also engaged 'quite a pleasant young man and I am sure he was doing his best; but he is a thorough bad singer to begin with, a fairly good musician, I think, but with no knowledge of V.W. and certainly with no understanding of English poetry whatever.' Dent wrote that though the Swiss had made the introduction to 'Bredon Hill' really sound as he imagined Vaughan Williams had meant it to sound ('generally it sounds filthy, and these Swiss made it thrilling'), they didn't understand the English nor the general style of the music. For him the best thing was the performance (under Scherchen) of Stravinsky's octet for two flutes, two trumpets, two clarinets and two trombones, which had provided a brilliant end to the festival. The English and Americans played jazz music afterwards with the Zika quartet.

The next year's jury was to be Casella, Wellesz and Kodály; it had been intended to contain a Frenchman. There was some talk of submitting Clive's setting of 'The Ghost' (words by Walter de la Mare), which had been sung by the English Singers, and Dent surprisingly wrote that he would 'feel very nervous about correcting the proofs of anything so modern'. The next song festival (August 1925) was to be held in Venice. Meanwhile Dent was anxious to get the Spanish section going by personal contacts with Turina and Falla. For the Prague (orchestral) section Vaughan Williams' 'Pastoral Symphony' was to be performed, and there was some uncertainty who would conduct; as the orchestra was Czech an easy solution would have been to use its regular conductor, Talich, a great admirer of the work, but Boult, who eventually conducted, was not surprisingly Vaughan Williams' first choice. After the Prague festival, Dent spent ten days in Dresden, hearing Busoni's *Doktor Faust* four times. 'It is a very noble work and grew on me tremendously. But it won't fetch the public: it is too intellectual, and there is not enough in the way of female voices. There is far too much male chorus. I suppose it is Busoni's German side, for the Germans love male choruses. I detest them, and I've little use for female choruses either.'

In London, having given up criticism, he could no longer afford to go to the opera and was painfully conscious that his clothes were in rags. Still, there was nothing that particularly attracted him – 'I don't really much care how Toti dal Monte sings Lucia – though I'd sooner hear *Lucia* than any of the Puccinis.'

It was just as well that the Venice festival was 'a roaring success', for Dent had hardly got over the exhaustion of Prague and Dresden; at Cambridge in the summer he was engaged on writing an article on Madrigals for the new Grove; on seventeenth-century chamber music for Cobbett's Cyclopedia, and on the composition of modern English songs for *Music and Letters*; editing the Mozart Requiem with new English words and a rewritten pianoforte accompaniment. The articles involved much research and thought and brought in little money; they provoked some bad temper, and Dent described them as 'very concentrated in style and occasionally acid'.

The concerts were held at the Fenice, where the stage was so heavily raked that the piano – to Schnabel's anxiety – looked likely to roll down into the orchestra. Casella insisted that Dent must open the festival with a speech – 'I was rather terrified at coming on to that stage and facing that audience to address them in Italian; it was the first time that I had ever made a real speech in Italian to an audience in Italy. At Salzburg last year I spoke in Italian when I made my commemoration of Busoni; but there were not half a dozen Italians in the hall. As a matter of fact the Venice audience was at least 75% foreign, and I should think 40% if not more did not understand a word I said; but there were Italians enough to laugh, which was the main thing.'

This time Steuart Wilson was there to sing Vaughan Williams' 'Three Rondels', the only British work chosen; he had a great success, attributable in part to the training which he had been enabled to have with de Reszke; his singing of the 'Daniel Jazz'[1] – 'a rotten work to my thinking' – especially pleased the Germans.

Dent had what he described as a 'frantic time' with the composers. 'Schönberg was incredibly offensive, and I had to tell him in so many words (in my sweetest tones!) that he was not the only composer at the festival. He replied very malignantly "Ich hatte stets verstanden dass ich überall der einzige Komponist bin!" To see him rehearse is like watching a small boy who has got hold of a live butterfly and is pulling off its legs and wings one by one. Boris Ord happily described the Serenade as the "Serenata delle Zanzare" for it was rather like a tortured night with many mosquitoes and frantic attempts to catch and squash them . . . Schönberg was not the only little tin god whom I had to put in his place; I had to be severe with Dr Herzka and Leopold Schmidt, people of whom every-

---

[1] Composition for tenor vocalist and eight instruments by Gruenberg (1884–1964).

body in Vienna is terrified. But I was not going to have Herzka banging into my box in the middle of the Malipiero songs, even if he *was* bringing Frau Mahler to call on Frau Busoni, who was with me the last night; and I told him to wait till the music was over, and shut the box door in his face . . . Stravinsky was very cordial and friendly, as well he might be; for he got 5,000 French francs fee . . . and also an ovation when he came on to the stage. Schönberg ostentatiously got up and left the theatre. The sonata [Stravinsky's], I admit, was poor stuff, like early Beethoven with a lot of wrong notes.' Clive in his reply echoed these comments on Stravinsky's later music – 'it's so dreadfully dull, and dullness with wrong notes is almost worse than dullness with right'.

After the festival – and the Piazza at Venice stimulated and delighted Dent more than any place in the world –

there was a reception at the Lido 'like something between Wembley and a Turkish bath'; Dent stayed on after the August crowd 'more naughty and more amusing than ever' had broken up, then went on to Ravenna, glad that the frescoes in the dome and round the galleries at S. Vitale 'done by some very indifferent painter of the Luca Giordano–Tiepolo school and quite bad' had been left to give a sense of historical continuity; the other ancient buildings had been restored so perfectly as to look like reconstructions put up yesterday. Thence by way of Florence, which seemed small and noisy after Venice, he went on to his uncle at Nice, with no engagements till the jury meeting at Zürich next January, and time to work. It was this way of life that the professorship at Cambridge would destroy.

From September 1925 to July 1926 Dent wrote no letters to Clive in Adelaide, though they met in Milan for two days when Clive was on short leave. Clive had been in Australia two years and was then planning to return home after the third year, though eventually he stayed for four. The worst of Australia, as his couple of days in Italy reminded him, was being forced to hear only your own language spoken, with no chance of getting a different outlook on things, and all that is implied by a different language. Dent's silence was disappointing, for his own letters from Australia were full of news of productions with his students of scenes from opera on which he was starved of *comment* – *Dido* (witch scene), *Magic Flute* (first scene), *Carmen*, *Figaro* (second act), Charles Wood's *Pickwick*; he also sent requests for the scores of *Iphigenia in Tauris* and *Orfeo*, which were not obtainable in Australia, and for information and advice about furthering the careers of his best students if they came to Europe. It may not have been worth Dent's while to listen to Toti dal Monte in London, but to Clive her taking the trouble when on tour in Australia to sit through a whole concert at which he and his students were singing was an immense encouragement.

When at last the next letter came, with apologies for a misunderstanding about the scores, news of *Dido* at Münster, the I.S.C.M. Festival at Zürich, research on the Guarneri in Cremona, and Wood's illness and the prospects of the professorship, relations were fully restored. The winter months at Nice had been spent in writing *Terpander, or Music and the Future* for Kegan Paul's

Today and Tomorrow series. Dent had also promised them years ago to write a longish book on the psychology of music; Frank Howes had now written rather a good one, but 'I am conceited enough to believe that there is always room for a book by me, whoever else has treated the subject!' It was never written.

The Zürich festival went very well: Falla was there to enjoy a most successful performance of his *Retablo de Maese Pedro* by marionettes, and Dent's impression was that overall the music was far better than in previous years; Walton's 'Portsmouth Point' had its first performance and was widely acclaimed. The next I.S.C.M. Jury was to take place in London; it was a special disappointment to Dent that Henry Wood, whose judgement and musicianship he greatly admired, had had to refuse to serve.

Of the 1925 production at Cambridge by Dennis Arundell of Handel's *Semele* (1744), Dent wrote (on 16 December 1924) 'they are determined to drag me in, but I am equally determined not to be involved' – a favourite word of his. Nevertheless, subsequent letters reveal not only his enthusiasm for this and later revivals of Handel's operas – this was a first stage performance – but also the substantial part he played in it.

Rootham was the conductor, always a source of exasperation to Dent – 'he says he has got a marvellous chorus who sing the whole thing straight off at sight and that he himself dances the rhythms of the more amorous numbers to show them how they ought to go' – but a month later Dent conceded that the chorus was indeed excellent and that it was marvellous how they had learnt all the work by heart, including several big fugues.

Whatever his expressed intention, Dent was soon fully committed. 'Everybody's nerves were rather on edge, as usual, but I found that a few suggestions on my part were welcomed and sometimes adopted. They adopted from the first my surgical operation on most of the arias, which I invented a long long time ago, but had never a chance of trying in practice before – it consists in transplanting the middle section into the middle of the first section, thus avoiding the Da Capo but preserving the outline of its form.

'Original: Tonic to dominant, dominant to tonic; minor keys; tonic to dominant, dominant to tonic.

'My scheme: Tonic to dominant; minor keys; dominant to tonic.

'You will find that in nearly all the big arias of Handel this dodge will work quite happily, though it may want a chord or two altering at the joins . . . "Where'er you walk" was sung uncut, I need hardly say.'

Dent was very wary of 'stunts' unless they were very well done (as Clive was also to be when working with Tyrone Guthrie) and feared that Dennis Arundell might have too many ideas and be in danger of over-producing. In his letter to Clive in Australia he contrived to make 'stunts' appear more ridiculous than they were, although he was full of praise for the more imaginative and effective moments: 'that wonderful air "But hark the heavenly sphere" held us all simply breathless; it was really a most memorable moment every night – one felt the whole audience tense to it'. He also singled out for praise the previous scene, a mountain top; the scene in the cave of Somnus; the putting of Juno's revenge song earlier; and the red baroque draped curtain falling sideways after the death of Semele, with the chorus starting at once behind the scenes with 'Oh terror and astonishment' and gradually coming on to the fugato.

He was not so much pleased when in the opening procession of priests 'Mr Beales of Corpus entered with next to nothing on, carrying a live prize fantail pigeon, and Mr Timberlake of Cat's, in a similar sort of costume, struggled with four champion borzois valued at £500 each.' In the second act 'the shepherds and shepherdesses looked dreadful, for the green skirts and orange scarves suggested boy scouts, especially with the hats and poles that some carried – and also because the fatal shadow of the footlights on the steps was even worse than in the "Fairy Queen", making everybody look as though they had boots on, indeed stockings, at the back . . . During "Where'er you walk" the stage was darkened and the chorus carried the cypresses on – very clumsily, like scene-shifters. Barkworth said that the front trees looked like green polar bears trying to climb the columns; I thought they looked more as if they were making water against them . . .

'I suggested the sort of group in front of the curtain with lanterns on long poles. But I did not suggest – and I simply hated – the plan adopted by Dennis and Douglas Williams (Pembroke – who designed the dresses) of then transferring the whole thing to the 18th century. They came on in black and grey Venetian dominos, looking like dissipated parsons and nuns coming away from a night club. It was all

'Green polar bears': the Arcadian
scene in *Semele*.

so obviously "hommage à Hammersmith" . . . The audiences were not good at first, but the theatre filled up as the
week went on. Lord Balfour [Chancellor of the University]
came to the matinee and scandalized Cambridge by loudly
clapping "Where'er you walk".'

In the Long Vacation before he accepted the professorship, Dent's versatility was heavily taxed: there were
10,000 words on 'Social Aspects of Music in the Middle
Ages' for the Oxford History; a chapter on the musical life
of Cremona (for which Dent had lost the original notes
made on the spot, and repaired the damage, more or less, at
the British Museum); a paper for the *Musical Quarterly* – a
centenary number – on why the younger generation have
no use for Beethoven; and a final revision of *Foundations of
English Opera* which after ten years he found out of date,
not well written, and 'very Cambridge and provincial'.
There was also an article written in German for a Festschrift on the influence of Purcell and English music on
Handel; and there were Busoni's essays to translate. Clive
was meanwhile producing and singing in performances of
Holst's *Savitri* in Sydney and at Melbourne where the
redoubtable Mrs Dyer filled the theatre, seating 800, at a

guinea a seat. The part of Death, which he had played at the first public performance at the Lyric Theatre, Hammersmith, was a particular favourite of his.

One hesitates to include other opinions from the seven years between the end of the war and the professorship at Cambridge which have been covered in this chapter; the main themes were journalism, Cambridge, opera (especially at the Old Vic), scholarship, and, above all, the International Society for Contemporary Music. On the whole what is surprising is how rarely Dent descends to the ephemeral, though long accounts of the Cambridge production of the *Electra* of Sophocles, or of Mascagni's operetta *Si*, or Reinhardt's *Le Malade Imaginaire* (in German) at Salzburg no longer bear reproduction, especially since he played no prominent part in them himself. A few quotations – without comment – complete the chapter.

(May 1922) 'I find the Kindertotenlieder [of Mahler] tedious, though skilfully made: and the Leider eines fahrenden Gesellen odious. But I have a violent prejudice against Des Knaben Wunderhorn and all the old-fashioned nonsense about Blumlein blau. The Blue Flower and the Blue Bird are both a Blue Boar. But I am staying on in Vienna to hear Bruno Walter conduct Mahler's 2nd symphony tomorrow. I hated the symphony when I heard it in Berlin under Furtwängler but Bruno Walter is supposed to be just marvellous in Mahler, so perhaps I may be converted.'

(December 1924) 'By the way Miss Baylis wrote a very funny account of Lucia Young (Mrs Arthur Beamish) as Venus in *Tannhäuser* "the poor child *would* wear her wedding ring and looked much too respectable!"'

(March 1925) 'We had one really glorious experience the other day, and that was Jelly d'Aranyi playing Mozart's Concerto in D with 'Enery [Henry Wood]. I begin to think she is the finest violinist living. To J.B. [Trend] and me it was beautiful and perfect beyond all conception or description from beginning to end; but none of the critics seems to have noticed anything about it.'

(June 1925) 'Last night I had to go to a curious concert of the Savoy Orpheans at the Savoy . . . There was a lecture by an American on "syncopated" music with historical illustrations – Alexander's Ragtime band; a banjo band; a jazz band; some pianoforte duets, some saxophone solos, and lastly the pièce de resistance – a Rhapsody in Blue by

Mr Gershwin for pianoforte and band. It was the last word in dreariness; Mr G. . . . has no great skill as a pianist, and the stuff was a medley of cadenzas remembered from Liszt, Rachmaninoff, Balakireff, Chopin, Weber and tutti quanti – with various grunts and shrieks from the band. All this stuff is based on Liszt and on the solid German Jew sentimental stodge. The saxophone soloist imitated all the worst vices of the sentimental singer; I had no idea you could play so much out of tune on these instruments! It sounds (in the soprano regions) like a bad street singer, or a vox humana stop on an organ.'

Titania.

Eila Carey.

The Beggar's Opera in America
1928–9: Clive Carey as
Macheath.

The years between 1927 and 1939 brought the two friends into closer professional collaboration than they had been at any time since 1920, the year of the eventual performance of *The Fairy Queen* and of the first Mozart operas at the Old Vic. After singing in a number of Melba's farewell concerts in Australia to the extent that friends warned him that he had become Melba's 'white-haired boy', Clive returned in 1928 through the United States, armed with introductions to her managers and an invitation to join her in setting up an opera school in Paris. '*It may be amusing*', she wrote, underlining as many words as Queen Victoria, 'to fight a few erratic Italians – bring a dagger and a gun – *Do come.*' Nothing came of the venture, and the pattern of his life in London resumed very much its earlier shape – teaching at the R.C.M., giving lectures and recitals of lieder and of folk-songs, tours for the Associated Board as an examiner, a long American tour in 1929 playing the lead in *The Beggar's Opera*, and again with the English Folk-Dance and Song Society, and, most important, producing opera for the Vic–Wells Company.

Once Clive was back – he married in 1929 – Dent's letters became increasingly concerned with two main topics, closely inter-related, the affairs of the Old Vic and Sadler's Wells – Dent was a governor now, and on the opera sub-committee – and translations. Every translation was submitted in draft for Clive to comment, not primarily on its accuracy, but on its singability, with discussion of what cuts were likely, how the recitative would be handled, in what way the 'period' of the production would influence the language, and so on. Dent made most of his translations specifically for production at Sadler's Wells, though he was often disappointed and compelled to wait a year or two before the eventual performance – sometimes after being harried by Lilian Baylis to do the work quickly. He made no charge for royalties for several years; when eventually he was persuaded by Dennis Arundell to do so, the money was put into a special fund for the use of the theatre library.

Sylvia Nelis and Audrey Mildmay at Charlottesville and a poster for *The Beggar's Opera*.

The International Musicological Society at Cambridge 1933. Dent the president is seen on the right; Boris Ord, Dr Mann's successor as organist at King's, is seen with his mother in the centre.

The exceptions were *The Trojans* and *Benvenuto Cellini* for Erik Chisholm in Glasgow.

As the I.S.C.M. became more firmly established, Dent, who was succeeded by Edwin Evans as president, played a less conspicuous rôle; he was president also of the International Musicological Society. A Cambridge colleague, Scholfield, who was University Librarian, advised him when he took on the professorship, 'Don't let yourself become an administrator. Leave that to the people who are too stupid to do original work'; but Dent commented that such people are usually too stupid to give a committee any original ideas. 'As you know, my family were all born chairmen – or think so! And I see that my work now is to tell everybody else what they ought to do – horrid responsibility! I have fits of fearful longing for solitude and complete aloofness, to think out my own ideas and write. I am already in rather bad odour at Cambridge because I am not always in the middle of things; but even if I spend the day alone in my house I am always dealing with other people's affairs by letter.' He was also chairman of the Royal Philharmonic Society, striving (often with a reluctant committee and secretary) to ensure that new music did not become the monopoly of the B.B.C., which was willing

enough to let the Society have an option on 'first performances' if only they could make up their collective mind. A
rumour that Henry Wood was to be intrigued out of the
Proms in 1929 and a new orchestra was to take over caused
a characteristic outburst: 'The B.B.C. seems to be a
perfectly impossible body; it is run on the best Viennese
civil service principles – nobody has any authority and no
outside person can ever find out who has the authority to do
anything. The only un-Viennese person is the Director-
General, Sir John Reith, who is a bear and a bully and
knows nothing about music at all; his only idea is to
preserve the moral purity of the institution and turn out
anyone who has ever been near the divorce court, or has
avoided the divorce court when he ought to have gone to it.'

Apart from the translations there was a good deal of
literary work; the Busoni biography was published in
1933, a full-dress affair of nearly 400 pages. Shortly
afterwards came a biography of Handel for the Great Lives
series, and a visit to Krefeld for a Handel festival. Besides a
production of Telemann's comic opera *Socrates*, which
Dent found amusing though he had never seen so much
liquor drunk in an opera before, there was a performance of
Handel's *Orlando*, 'completely misunderstood, and Hans
Joachim Moser, who had produced it at Halle in 1922, was
much annoyed at not having been consulted about it. I
sympathize with him, as you can well imagine!'

'The Germans used to have no use for Handel', he
continues. 'Thirty years ago they always told me that they
regarded Handel as completely English and that he had no
appeal for them. Now he is being painted brown and
boosted as a great German, and as an inspirer of everything
that is national and heroic. Little they know about
Handel's English environment! or about Ariosto, if they
think that *Orlando* is a hero-saga like the Nibelungenlied.
Musically they do not get there at all; it was interesting to
hear the Telemann, which is much more like Bach's secular
music, so that they understood it better. They see everything through Bach and Wagner, and possibly through the
people before Bach. We had some of them at a chamber
concert; it was very interesting but the general impression
was of a stuffy bourgeois atmosphere, and when H[andel]
came along one realised how glad he was to escape from
Germany to Italian palaces and English freedom.'

In 1929 he and J. B. Trend had been the only foreigners
at Celle for a Heinrich Schütz festival, which they

thoroughly enjoyed – 'I must confess that Heinrich Schütz in large doses is a bit monotonous: they could not afford to perform the motets with trumpets and trombones, but we were delighted with a quartet of recorders. The "youth movement" has taken up the viols and recorders with great enthusiasm.'

Not only did Dent give an address in German on the influence of English composers on Handel, later translated into English by another hand, but also he wrote, in Italian, an article on Bellini in England for a collection of papers published by the Italian Government.[1] In 1938 work began on the 6d book on opera published by Penguin and later revised, which to the layman is Dent's chief claim to fame; at the time he wrote of it as 'a considerable labour for nothing much, but it might (like Haskell's charming 6d book on Ballet) help to get people interested in Sadler's Wells.'

The interest in Handel, coming comparatively late, was to remain to the end. He visited Ludwigsburg to see the theatre in the palace where Jommelli had produced operas, and later Erhardt had given a Handel opera by candle-light: 'It must have been very dangerous. It is an interesting place, as there is a lot of old scenery there still, and the curious machinery for changing the wings simultaneously by a winch and roller under the stage. I felt sorry for the stage hands of those days for there was no room to stand upright under the stage.' In Münster he tracked down a lost cantata by Handel: 'It was always said that in Rome he was asked to set some words in praise of himself by Cardinal Pamphili, but as no one could ever find the music, it was said that H. was too modest to set the poem. However, I thought I remembered seeing it here some thirty years ago, when I was on Scarlatti and knew nothing about Handel; so I came here and found it – Handel's autograph, and a fair copy as well by one of Scarlatti's copyists. There are several Handel things here which I fancy have never been printed in the complete edition – one is a cantata for soprano and chorus for the anniversary of the earthquake at Rome in 1702 . . .' In 1955, when Dent was very deaf and partially blind, he was particularly interested in Farncombe's production of *Deidamia* (in his translation) at St Pancras Town Hall – they would have given another performance for him alone if he had been fit

[1] Reissued in Dent, *Selected Essays*, ed. Hugh Taylor (Cambridge University Press, 1978).

Purcell at Cambridge: *King Arthur* in rehearsal, 1933. Dennis Arundell in shirt-sleeves near the piano; Margaret Field-Hyde in the plaid dress; Cyril Franklin (later the well-known opera singer David Franklin) kneeling, gesturing towards the conductor, C. B. Rootham; Ian Parsons (King Arthur) being measured by Mrs Rootham.

to enjoy it – and he was delighted to hear that, thanks to good enunciation and clear and intelligent delivery of the recitatives, the humour of the libretto had come through.

His staunch advocacy of Purcell led to an invitation to Stuttgart in 1927 to rehearse *Dido* with them, where Erhardt, who was shortly leaving Stuttgart for Dresden, had suggested it to Wilhelm Kempff, who was then Director of the Hochschule für Musik: 'They were splendidly keen on it . . . Heaven knows what it would have been like if I hadn't been there! Kempff is about 30 or less, a remarkably fine pianist but no conductor. He loved the work, but what he really wanted to do was to extemporize variations on the pianoforte in the style of Max Reger on all the little dance tunes! The standard of singing at the

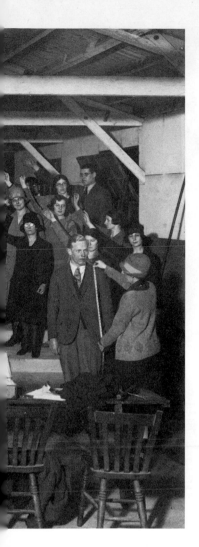

Hochschule is not anything like as high as that of the R.C.M. The chorus was dreadful and the dancing far worse . . . Erhardt pulled things through somehow, and I nagged at Kempff (who took it all in the sweetest way and was most anxious to learn) until I got them to sing in something like time (*tune* was hopeless) and to run the numbers on without pauses. Kempff always wanted to make pauses between the numbers, not to provoke applause, but merely because he wanted time to sigh to himself and murmur "ach! wie wunderschön!" ' Dent was naturally delighted when *King Arthur* was performed in Cambridge in 1928.

Of the events taking place outside Cambridge, the affairs of the Old Vic and Sadler's Wells dominate the decade of the 1930s, indeed they became – with the translations incidental to them – the central concern of Dent's later years. But for a man of so many interests no transition is either sudden or complete, and the I.S.C.M. continued for a while to occupy him. At Frankfurt in 1927 the English composition chosen for performance at the I.S.C.M. Festival, Whittaker's setting of Psalm CXXX, was not a great success, but at least there were a large number of British critics there who had none of them had to listen to so much modern music before, and it was encouraging to hear them proposing a festival in England. Dent still felt that there was too little interest in London and Paris, and that Copenhagen and Amsterdam were not yet ready; Siena was to be the next host. At the Lord Mayor's banquet at Frankfurt, Dent so far broke with protocol as to make a joke in his speech – 'they did not expect it, and it took them a good 30 seconds to see it; but finally they did, and roared with laughter'. There were the usual rows and worries, dealt with in the usual way, culminating in an offer to visit Paris to see Ravel, who was 'rather sore about the International'. In 1931 the jury met at Cambridge and the festival was held at Oxford, and for the next festival it met at Berlin. Jury meetings were becoming very difficult, for Haba and Webern were determined to have as much music as possible by Schönberg, Zemlinsky and composers of their school, against the wishes of Ansermet and Dent: 'Haba chattered and clattered like a machine gun: Webern had outbursts of passionate tirade; Ansermet argued persuasively, Mlle Boulanger and Tiessen sat and smiled and did their best to keep the peace . . . The split between East and West is most remarkable. The Schönbergians

The I.S.C.M. jury at Frankfurt, 1930, the president's head in a noose.

simply cannot bear any music that is amusing and agreeable to listen to; and the Germans are now reacting against all "concert" music, and are going only for a primitive sort of choral music for proletarian choirs, with political words.' In face of that it was surprising that compositions by Arthur Bliss and Walter Leigh were selected. A year later the jury met in Amsterdam – the last occasion mentioned in the correspondence for some years.

Dent attended his first meeting of the Old Vic governors in May 1927, and his immediate reaction was that his colleagues were 'a queer lot'. At that time Sadler's Wells had been bought, but the theatre had to be rebuilt before it could be brought into operation. On this occasion 'Miss Baylis went off into wild hysterics over the telephone shortcomings – apropos of an estimate for electric lighting. The Chairman just let her run on until she had exhausted herself and then proceeded with the business in hand. If she is like that at a Governors' meeting what must she be like behind the scenes!!' From the outset Dent had it in mind that when the first opera season opened at Sadler's Wells Clive should be 'intendant', and others including Geoffrey Toye and Percy Pitt were in accord, but Lilian Baylis (and her 'alter ego', Miss Williams) hoped as usual

130

to defer decisions and retain control in their own hands. Dent insisted that at least there should be a definite decision made publicly that from the time that Sadler's Wells opened there should be opera played every night at one of the two theatres, except on nights when a theatre was closed altogether, for lectures or rehearsals. Lilian Baylis hoped simply to carry on with a producer-in-residence, Sydney Russell, while Charles Corri, who had been at the Old Vic since 1895, conducted the orchestra. Others, notably Lawrance Collingwood and Clive himself, would be used in a supporting rôle, and soon after the opening Clive was producing *The Magic Flute* in Dent's translation, with Joan Cross outstanding as Pamina. From Dent's point of view – and from Clive's – Lilian Baylis's reluctance to appoint someone equal in power to herself, and to find a salary, was very tiresome. While the matter was still in abeyance – and Dent had to be more guarded in his letters than was his custom – Clive, who had his way to make again in the London musical world, did not know whether to accept a voyage on behalf of the Associated Board or not. Conducting intrigues from Cambridge was hopelessly difficult, and in the vacations Dent was increasingly tied down by visits to an elderly uncle in Nice. It was to Java, where Clive was in the midst of a world tour as an

Lilian Baylis with Clive and Doris Carey, 1935.

examiner for the Associated Board, that Dent addressed a letter in December 1931 which described some of the early troubles.

'The Old Vic has been an anxiety too; Sadler's Wells has lost money. We have evolved a new system by which Sadler's Wells gets a larger proportion of opera, as that public seems to like opera better than Shakespeare. What it does love is Ballet, and thanks to Ninette de Valois and Constant Lambert the ballet shows have been very good. But the Baylis can't be brought to see that she ought to put on more ballet nights . . . Constant made quite a good show of *Dido* with Sydney Russell. It wasn't as good as it ought to have been, but it was the best performance of *Dido* that I have yet seen. *The Times* was very sniffy about it; I fancy that on the first night the chorus rather forgot their music in their anxiety to make their movements . . . Ethel Smyth saw *Dido* for the first time in her life and was wild with enthusiasm about it; I expect that she had got the impression that Dido was the composer.

'Dear Lilian always wants things in a hurry; she announced *Ballo in Maschera* the other day, so I asked her what she was doing about a translation. She said Mrs Philips of Carl Rosa was lending her all the material, and that perhaps it would be a good thing if I could revise the translation. She then sent me the Boosey edition, with a wonderful Victorian translation – you can imagine what it was like! and thought I could settle the hash in three days. I wrote and said that it was impossible to tinker at; she must either take it as it stood or give me time to make an entirely new version. She did much the same about *Hoffman*; but there the translation by Agate was not so bad, and it only wanted a few lines revised, to get the story clear at the outset, to get the people's names properly accentuated (Hoffmánn, Antoniá, Schlémihl were all too frequent) and once or twice to correct utter mistranslations:

Spallanzani: Plus de vers, plus de musique

which Agate had translated "you must give her more poetry, more music", when it means exactly the opposite: Hoffmann must not waste his time on poetry and music but must attend to his scientific studies.

'Baylis now suggests that I should re-translate *Carmen* – not because the old translation is bad, but because she thinks she would not have to pay royalties to the heirs of Meilhac and Halévy! I bought the libretto in Nice yesterday, so as to have the original Opéra Comique version. As I expect you know it has spoken dialogue; the Carl Rosa version has all that set as recitative, whether by Bizet or not I forget; I rather fancy the recitatives are by Guiraud. I should like to keep the spoken dialogue . . .'

Six months later Dent was translating *Barbiere* and sent Clive his new version of 'Largo al Factotum'. He wrote (from a village hotel near Bolzano): 'I find Rossini much harder to translate than Mozart, because he has no respect for the words, unless it is just some funny little phrase that stands out; and the funny little phrases aren't really funny in themselves, but only funny in the way they are sung by a traditional buffo. I know there will be trouble over this new translation − not that anybody knows Natalia's [Lady Macfarren's] − but because the *Barber* is full of arias that are "holy" and untouchable because of Lablache and Patti.' He was, as with the *Figaro* that he had translated and Clive had produced some ten years before, hoping that the recitatives would be *spoken*; it would be a tedious business to translate them, 'Indeed, I sometimes think the *Barber* is a dreadfully tedious opera altogether; all the arias are so long, and so mechanical in their repetitions and flourishes, and the performers all do such a terrible lot of traditional business. Yet there always remains the extraordinary vitality of the whole work, for the mechanical repetitions carry you on like an express train; and then there are the scraps of irresistible melody − the bits that everybody knows. What a lot Sullivan took from him! and that annoys me too, for any English translation that is better than Natalia's is certain to be called "Gilbertian" by the critics − and I am sick of Gilbert and not in the least desirous of imitating him.'

In four weeks time, when Clive had sent back his comments on what he had received, there was the whole of Act I ready. Sometimes, rather than face the maddening eternal repetition in the ensembles, he had written new words; he admitted to having stolen a line or two from Lady Macfarren − 'but I think most of my stuff is more singable, if equally silly. She loves such lines as "Be your transport still assuaged".' A week later the rest of the opera was sent for criticism, except for Bartolo's aria in Act I, because there were two versions; at a rough glance Dent found Rossini's the better music but thought Romani's might be more effective and dramatic on the stage.

As so often, after being urgently pressed to make the translation Dent was disappointed to hear that the *Barber* was not to come on that season 'but that of course is the usual way the Vic does things'. It was produced the following year with Barbirolli conducting. In spite, or perhaps because, of these frustrations, Dent wrote that September (1932): 'What I should really like to do more than anything would be to chuck *everything* except the Vic Opera, and devote myself solely to that; but I couldn't live on it, so I fear I must go on with Cambridge; and that ties me to the other things, though you may not at first sight see the connection.'

By the time that Bartolo's aria followed, Dent had seen a performance of the opera in Basle, and wrote at length about it. He had a very keen eye for detail, for example: 'Double staircase out of the orchestra pit to a little landing in front of the prompter's box. Fiorello and the musicians come up the stairs; the musicians were four of them in livery, as the Count's servants, the other four various, and very comically made up and individualized. All carried *real* instruments, but did not play them really, though they pretended to in very good time to the music. Yellow flutes and clarinets, a trumpet, a bassoon, and a full size double bass, which the man carried on his back. All this looked very effective, especially in the musicians' chorus "Mille grazie" in which they pushed each other round and round, so that the double bass and bassoon (an old man) showed up very comically.' It was by dint of such detailed observation and discussion that the Dent–Carey partnership achieved its results.

Meanwhile at the Vic they were tackling *Così*, well but without success, and Dent sent a new translation of 'Mi tradì' in readiness for Clive's production of *Don Giovanni*, suggesting that it should come in at the very beginning of Act II, before the duet for Don Giovanni and Leporello – 'that is the only possible place for it: the idea is not my own, but some German writer's'.

Lilian Baylis was easily upset by criticism, and Dent was determined that she should not lose confidence in those who were working at the Vic. A visit from Lady Cunard with a party – 'they would never have dreamt of putting their noses inside the theatre twelve years ago' – who said that the orchestra was shocking and the conductor had no idea of the opera, upset her dreadfully. To Dent, Beecham's interest – and he worked in close association with Lady Cunard – was always unwelcome to the point of unreason: 'T.B. thinks it would amuse him to play with as a toy; and we can't have him smashing it.' Ten days later he was writing 'I will come to the *Flute* on Thursday; it attracts me more than the Beecham Philharmonic programme, though I should like to have heard Debussy's Rondes de Printemps which I don't know. But if I *must* hear 18th century classics I prefer opera to symphonies.'

In the winter of 1932 *Idomeneo* was in the air: Clive wanted to know Dent's views on it for the Vic, Rootham was planning it for Cambridge in February 1934, and Miss (Maisie) Radford was planning a performance at Falmouth. At the Vic, after the comparative failure of *Così* they had to think in terms of *popular* success; Dent thought of *Oberon* or just possibly *Euryanthe*, but his hopes of drawing the public rested especially on *Norma*, which had not yet been done, or *Fidelio*, which he started to translate. He was full of hopes and ideas: the Vic opera had been invited to Germany, and Dent was very anxious that they should accept the invitation – 'the only sound argument against our going to Darmstadt seems to me that we aren't *quite* good enough'. They should take the ballet too. *Dido* was indispensable for a German visit. What else? *Così* would be safe; *Figaro* would not do with spoken recitatives, nor could *Don Giovanni* be done until the recitatives were perfect. *Carmen* was a possibility, or *Hänsel und Gretel*, of which he had recently seen Prince Reuss's production in Germany. 'I think a German audience might be simply horrified at ours . . . What at once struck me at Prince R.'s was the extreme leisurelyness of *all* the tempi, even of the duet in Act I (Hänsel, come and dance with me). Everything, all the way through, seemed to be much slower than I expected. With English words you *have* to go quicker, as you do in Mozart and Bach, but it would upset a German audience I fear, especially a H. and G. audience.' When the opportunity was missed, Dent wondered whether word had come down from on high that the tour should not take place till Beecham could take charge of it.

He recurred to *Oberon* – 'Do consider it seriously . . . it really is wonderful stuff . . . It is English to start with, and written for an English audience (which must have been in those days rather like a Vic audience of ten or twenty years ago); it is a mixture of Mids. N. Dream and Magic Flute, with all the absurdities of both and the seriousness of neither. One would simply treat it as a huge joke, with absurd exaggerations of the melodramatic and operatic manner both in the dialogue and arias – and discover that the music was ravishing. There is a great deal of stuff in it which is intended to be comic.'

Commenting on Act I of *Fidelio* which he began in January 1933 – musical numbers first as he was 'in the vein of poetry!' – he noted that Marcellina's aria was rather after the manner of the later English ballad operas, but that the German was also like that, and that the whole play insisted very much on the respectability of marriage and especially in humble life (French Revolution period!). The first performance at Sadler's Wells had to wait four years – the gallery most enthusiastic but the financial results disappointing. Urging that it should be revived another year, Dent commented, 'It always happens that some operas fill the gallery and others fill the stalls, and you can't always have it both ways.'

Next, during an enforced sojourn with his aged uncle in Nice, he turned to *Fra Diavolo*, the translation of which occupied little more than a fortnight. The method by which Dent tackled the work is shown in three letters, quoted more fully than usual.

5 April 1933. 'Here is a first instalment of *Fra Diavolo*;[1] please criticize it. I have made the soldiers' chorus at the beginning a sort of conventional drinking song, imagining it to be something soldiers always sing when they drink – not bearing on the play, except when they ask about the bandit.

'In the ensembles I have tried to keep everybody singing the same words as far as possible; the ensembles are devils to translate because they are purely instrumental and would sound much better to *la la la*.

'As we can't make Lord and Lady A. talk bad French I have treated them quite freely (and the music too, in places) so as to make Lord A. extremely pompous, and Lady A. very silly and romantic.

'Note that at the end of No. 1 Lorenzo takes the soldiers out; this seems better for the stage, and saves some dialogue.

'Please advise me about No. 5 (Trio) which I have begun; it is most awkward to translate. I shall try if I can to write an appropriate verse for the barcarolle the second time, but it doesn't very much matter. What am I to do about the 6/8 part? The French verse goes thus

[1] *Opéra-comique* by Auber (1830); text by Scribe. The dialogue is spoken.

etc.

and I can do it that way if you wish, but I think it would be
very awkward; and for the English it would go more easily
and naturally thus

" ' tis really too bad of you, really too bad of you
I shall be mad with you, I shall be mad with you."
more or less like that. Is this doing too much violence to
Auber? Please send me a postcard soon, as I don't want to
do it one way and then be told to do it all over again!

'I should like to see the Marquis got up as a complete
imitation of Beecham, especially in the dialogue with
Beppo and Giacomo. You will note a free suggestion of
mine – is it too monstrous?'

6 April 1933. 'I forgot an important question yesterday –
Fra Diavolo. Novello edition, page 80 (Finale of Act I)
begins

Lady A. ⎫
Lord A. ⎭ Ecoutez!

Marquis   Quelle est donc cette marche guerrière?
I suggest that these two sentences should be *sung*, but that
the next lines (Beppo and Giacomo with Marquis) should
be translated freely and *spoken* (up to entrance of chorus).

p. 92–93. Note that Novello prints the wrong names
against various tunes.

p. 95. Marquis, Beppo and Giacomo ("Tout nous sou-
rit" to "pour nous surprendre") I suggest *spoken*. [Note in
Clive's handwriting "Yes"]

Lorenzo *must sing* "Partons" etc.

Marquis "ils s'éloignent et nous restons"? spoken. All
the rest *sung*.

136 Act II Zerlina's song before mirror No. 10. Beppo
"Elle est jolie" etc. Spoken or sung? Here I think *sung*
["Yes"]

139 Recit. Zerlina "Je crois qu'on vient de rire"? spoken
["No"]

No 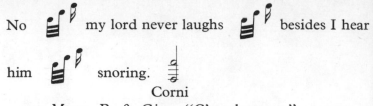 my lord never laughs besides I hear him snoring.

Corni

140 Marq. B. & Giac. "C'est heureux" – sung or spoken?

146–7 Allegro 2/4

etc. spoken or sung? ["semi"]' and so on, up to p. 232.

20 April 1933. 'Thanks for your letter. I think I have managed things as you want them. I send the rest of *Fra Diavolo* – with the exception of the Marquis' big song at the beginning of Act III. I find these things very difficult, and I left some numbers aside for the moment, but I have now finished all except that. I have worked out the ensembles and the repetitions, so if you don't understand the way they go I can let you have the music and words later on. The ensembles have been a horrid nuisance but I think I have got them to go pretty well now. I hope you will like my development of Lord and Lady Allcash!

'The other day I tried to get a French libretto, but the local music shop hadn't got it, as it had not been put on at Nice for fifty years. I haven't written in the stage directions in my MS, but whoever produces it will see to that. In one or two cases I think my translation will necessitate slight changes of directions – but you can easily understand.

'I can't make out what happens at the end! When I saw *Fra Diavolo* at Dresden, and at the Surrey too (I think), *Fra Diavolo* was shot by Lorenzo and fell down behind scenery. But I always thought that was rather unsportsmanlike! On the other hand if he is taken prisoner and hustled off it makes a less effective end for *him*! I leave it to you and Jack [Gordon] to settle!'

So much for the method of translation. As a member of the opera sub-committee Dent was, as has been shown, in constant touch with Clive about the choice of operas (and delighted with Clive's success with the first English production of the *Snow Maiden* that April) and many of their letters concern this. But on the Vic–Wells Board the present and future of the two theatres, and the relationship with Covent Garden, and more especially with Beecham, was in constant debate, with Lilian Baylis – in this instance

138

Clive's production of the *Snow Maiden* at Sadler's Wells, 1934.

strongly supported by Dent – strongly resisting any tendency towards a take-over by which the company performing to an audience in cheap seats in unfashionable parts of London might tour the provinces with a new ethos, perhaps under Beecham's management, under another name. Rightly or wrongly, Dent felt rather bitterly that he was being frustrated at every turn by Beecham and by those who wished to stand well with him, though friends told him that he was being unjust; and when Percy Pitt died he felt himself to be the only member of the sub-committee who had *seen* opera abroad, understood the new developments and really knew the standard repertory. He was most anxious that Vic–Wells should be allowed to build up its own style, and not have foisted on it operas such as *Salome* and *Siegfried*, which were unsuitable both for the audiences and for the theatrical resources. 'T.B. has no understanding of our style, I fear; he sees opera first as an orchestral conductor, and second as a "grand opera" social affair, I think.' Dent resented the success that his 'grand seigneur' way of behaving had recently had on the continent, telling a German inquirer that 'in England we do not regard T.B.'s style as being quite the genuine article'. With some malice he wrote to Clive that at a recent performance of *Rosenkavalier* which Beecham had conducted (to great popular and press acclaim) in Hamburg the Marschallin was some bars out for a long time 'without his appearing to be in the least aware of it'.

Writing of Lilian Baylis he put it this way: 'I have always the fear that Lilian might any day throw me over completely, if it came to a choice between me and T.B. She has a genuine affection for all of us, but no ability to estimate our artistic value to the theatre – and the great value of ourselves to the theatre is our corporate value as a group of personal friends with the same ideals, helping each other. She can only value us separately as individuals, if at all; and having a strong sense of personal affection, she naturally expects the same from us. She gets it, at present, I think; but I fear that at any moment she may expect us, out of personal loyalty to her, to sacrifice all our artistic ideals on the altar of Tommy . . . How characteristic of Lilian to say that *Fra Diavolo* was a failure! Poor dear, she has no imagination of what any opera *might* be, if only it was put on properly. I wonder what she really thought of *Traviata*. I am sure she could never realize that that performance was really epoch-making: yes, I really felt that it was that – it was a really good show, and the first time that *Traviata* has ever been done in England (possibly anywhere) *from that point of view* – as a serious and beautiful work, and a deeply moving play, instead of just a Melba night out and a hopelessly vulgar and ridiculous opera.'

The other point on which Dent had lost to Beecham was the Philharmonic, from whose committee he resigned – not because of the confrontation but because he had fulfilled his statutory term. 'I retire rather gladly, for we have had to surrender to T.B. after all the years of struggle against it. He makes a success of the concerts, I dare say, but he has no interest in modern music, and although I was chairman I had no power whatever in suggesting works to be performed.'

Though he felt the ground shifting beneath his feet in the summer of 1933, Dent was fertile of new ideas. In May he writes, 'I have just been considering *Don Pasquale*, as I found unexpectedly that I had it in the house. It is fascinating musically, I think, and should be much easier to produce (and possibly to sing) than *Barber*; on the other hand, the story (and three acts of it!) is so incredibly fatuously silly that *Così fan tutte* is Ibsen by the side of it! It would make a delightful opera for marionettes. If we did it at the Vic it would have to be staged in some peculiarly fantastic way and I wonder (1) if that could be carried out (2) if the audience would take it. But a serious "straight" performance of it would be dreadful.' Four years later Lilian Baylis asked him to translate it for the following season – 'it is tiresome stuff: the comic dialogue and recitative good fun to translate, but the arias devilish. Have you noticed how in all Italian comic operas the *arias* are all perfectly serious, unless definitely buffo? That entirely excludes the Gilbert style of translation (for which I'm not sorry) – though I frankly adopt the plan of making the arias "operatic" in literary style, with occasional deliberate lapses (Malatesta's Romanza for instance – after all, Malatesta is half *buffo*).' The eventual production had to wait till 1953.

'Stands Scotland where it did?': Lawrance Collingwood's *Macbeth*. Left to right, Dan Morgan Jones, Arthur Cox, Clive Carey (Macduff).

The Marriage of Figaro at
Sadler's Wells: Rex Whistler's
set.

It was possible now to introduce occasional new ventures at Sadler's Wells, though Lilian Baylis was careful to dilute them with popular favourites; thus Lawrance Collingwood's *Macbeth* had its stage première in April 1934. For Clive's production of *Figaro* in October – the translation made for January 1920 was still in manuscript – Dent reminds him of an earlier version of *Figaro* in the Donaueschingen library with a recitative and air for Marcellina, apparently genuine, in place of the Duet (no. 5). 'It is deliberately old-fashioned, like Elvira's air in *D.G.* It is quite short. If you would like to have it I can copy it out for you ... the duet is undoubtedly better; and the aria would be merely a historical curiosity.' For this production Rex Whistler designed the scenery; Herbert Hughes called it 'probably the nearest approach to the Mozart pattern ever seen in England'. Such successes were becoming more frequent – a standard and a style were emerging.

Before leaving for the Long Vacation, spent at Strasbourg, where for three days he lectured for Scherchen to a class for conductors, and in northern Italy, Dent had presided over the Cambridge Congress and Festival of the International Musicological Society, 'terribly strenuous work, but everything went without a single hitch, and there were no rows, even at the Congress! We had glorious weather, about 40 foreigners, mostly Professors, and all enchanted with Cambridge, lost in admiration of the old English music and our performances of it. Everybody was tremendously on their mettle and rehearsed things more than anything has ever been rehearsed in Cambridge before. Really I was quite amazed at it myself; I never in all my life heard such technical excellence of playing and singing in Cambridge before. It will have a wonderful reverberation on the Continent and in America ... Our learned foreigners realized the unique character of the programmes chosen, and that was the combined effort of some six or seven learned people here – Rootham, Boris Ord, Middleton, Radcliffe, Turner etc. I omit myself, for Boris says I am the world's worst programme maker and have no sense of an audience at all!' Dent failed to point the contrast with *Dr Faustus* in 1910 when he had refused to waste the band's time and tempers until the Sins learnt their steps. The credit was largely his.

Joan Cross as the Countess and Sumner Austin as the Count.

For his 'holiday task' he took *Orpheus*[1] to translate, taking the French and Italian versions with him; it was curious to compare the two, the Italian words having eighteenth-century Italian classicality and the French the eighteenth-century affectation of gallantry. Of one translation he was certain. 'I am firm that Mrs Orpheus is to be called Eurýdice in the usual English way, and not Euridíce (Yoory-deechy? Euridice à la francaise? or Oirideekay? or Yoory-dicey to rhyme with Professor Dicey?) But Geoffrey Toye disagrees equally firmly, as he says that "people" are accustomed to the continental pronunciation. At Covent Garden, naturally. I needn't explain *my* point of view; and I am going to use all my ingenuity to call her You-riddy-see. I think it can be dodged, with skill.' Mary Jarred, who was to sing the part, was not enthusiastic to sing it Dent's (English) way, but as she also came from Yorkshire he hoped to persuade her. The Italian version was much lower in *tessitura* than the French, more lyrical and less dramatic, and though the *feeling* of the Italian version appealed to him, he used the French version as the more effective on the stage, while sometimes translating more from the Italian than the French. Though he made a few alterations in the music they were far fewer than Gluck had made in adapting the opera to French words.

In sending Act I Dent wrote, 'You will note: (1) Eurýdice in all cases, as in Shakespeare, Milton and Pope. (2) I think Cupid is intended (both in the Italian and French librettos) to be rather a skittish little person, with a humorous view of the situation, and no doubt extremely pleased with himself as being sent as messenger of the Gods. (3) I soon found I was almost writing *Magic Flute* over again, but the situation led to it subconsciously, and I don't think it will do any harm. (4) I have avoided 'husband' and 'wife' as being rather prosaic (if I may dare say such a thing to *you*!) though in *Fidelio* they are just the words one must emphasise. I have also avoided allusions to classical names such as Styx, Tartarus, etc. in the main, as being unfamiliar to a Vic audience; however, I have put in just one or two, especially where the music was rather of the Handel–Pope period at the end.'

Dent was aware that to very many people his obduracy

---

[1] Opera by Gluck. The first version is in Italian, with text by Calzabigi, produced in Vienna in 1762; the French version, with the title rôle transposed to tenor, was translated by Moline and produced in Paris in 1774. Gluck rewrote the opera completely.

An established favourite, *The Magic Flute*, 1937. The Three Genii and Tamino: Sybil Hambledon, Rose Morris, Valetta Jacopi, and Francis Russel.

might seem mere pedantry, and to others to be pushing too far his single-minded enthusiasm for *English* opera. To Clive he wrote, defending his position, 'I hope you will conjure Sumner Austin [who was to produce] by all his gods to stand out for Eurýdice! I admit that I am a "visionary" as our all too solid Lilian calls me! But *you* at least will understand that to adopt Eurýdice in this opera (for the first time!) means that we present the work in English as a great work for the English public to enjoy; whereas to go on with Euridíce means going on with the old Covent Garden tradition, and putting the opera in (with a sort of implied shame-faced apology for doing it in English at all) merely as a show-piece for a famous contralto . . . To sing Euridíce encourages all the Covent Garden snobs who talk about their memories of Madame Viardot and Giulia Ravogli etc. (whom they probably never heard).'

The manner in which he rode nationalism and inter-nationalism, snobbery and anti-snobbery, in double harness is part of the fascination of Edward Dent. Like Don Giovanni, he claimed 'no head for mathematics'; but if he was a visionary, as Lilian Baylis said, he was a remarkably hard-headed one, and in any case he felt that the Old Vic was the one theatre where visionaries could be of real use. But the fact that he lived in Cambridge and thus could see too little of the practical difficulties of the theatres in London made it easier to dispose of him as well-meaning and his ideas as impracticable. Vic–Wells disappointed him often; a visionary sees a little further ahead than other people – 'that is why I am translating the *Troyens* for Chisholm at Glasgow'. He went to every performance.

In 1936, on board the *Georgic* for the Harvard Tercentenary Conference, he translated *Rigoletto* for Sadler's Wells, sending the result to Clive as usual; at the same time he was translating Busoni's *Dr Faust* for the B.B.C. With Act III of *Rigoletto* came typical comments: 'The main thing is to have your criticism on this last instalment. I hope you will not object to the deliberate brutality of Sparafucile and Maddalena, and the places where the audience may laugh – legitimately, I think, as they do in Shakespeare. I am not afraid of laughs in tragedy; I have seen enough Shakespeare, Marlowe and Webster to know that with reasonably good acting you can recover the tragic feeling and the audience's response in a moment.

'I think the "Bella figlia dell'amor" is intended to be almost a parody of the exaggerated and affected style of love-making, as Maddalena makes fun of it quite brutally. Gilda's "prayerfulness" makes me vomit.'

The advent of Hitler brought a steady stream of refugees, whether Jewish or political (most commonly both) to London. In a sense so English an organisation as Vic–Wells was not a natural market for their talents, nor did the Home Office regulations make it easy to employ them unless it could be said that they were indispensable persons such as could not be otherwise found in England. One solution initially was to take them on as unpaid volunteers while appealing to a refugee organisation to find £2. or so a week. It was not always easy to elucidate whether those who recommended them did so out of genuine conviction or out of kindness. Dent's position was ambivalent; he was most anxious that the team spirit which had been built up should not be dissipated by some unfortunate appointment of a refugee who wished from the outset to assert himself, yet his strong connections with German opera houses made it natural that appeals should be made to him by or on behalf of refugees, and he did not underrate their ability.

One of them, anxious to work at the Old Vic, was especially keen to produce Bizet's *Pêcheurs de Perles*, which had been a great success at a number of German opera houses, and asked Dent to translate it. As Clive had toured Ceylon for the Associated Board and had also sung there, he was the obvious producer, but Dent urged him to consider it as a whole, on the Sadler's Wells stage with their singers, in English, and not to be too much fascinated by the one lovely and celebrated Romanza for the tenor. He must also imagine the Sadler's Wells principals in loin-cloths! Dent was afraid that out of kindness to the luckless refugee – urged on perhaps by Beecham or Albert Coates – Lilian Baylis might swallow it at one gulp.

His own views were expressed with customary incisiveness. 'I have looked at the vocal score and have consulted D. C. Parker's life of Bizet. I agree with Parker that it is a weak work, and an almost comic imitation of early Verdi, as Bizet himself apparently recognized . . . It has some charming numbers and some "effective" ones in the full-throated Verdi manner. But I don't think it would suit us, though I could well imagine Beecham going off the deep end about it (By the way, didn't he produce it once in London?) . . . And I can understand German theatres taking it on; they are short of attractive popular operas, and a "new" Bizet would be a stunt; I expect they are tired now of the old French repertory – Auber and Boieldieu, who were constantly played everywhere in my "Dresden" days.

'The music is certainly attractive, but distinctly cheap, though not downright vulgar; it seems to me that the only way to get it across nowadays would be to have perfect singers in the French or Italian style, a good ballet and strikingly clever dresses and scenery. (As the scene is laid in Ceylon at the seaside the costumes would not be expensive, I imagine!) The four soloists have a fearful lot to do, and I wonder if our people could stand the strain and not get tired of them. The plot is thin but hardly thinner than many other operas.'

In the event Dent was not asked to translate the *Pêcheurs*, which was put on a year or two before his death. He warned

Lilian Baylis that he would like to see some of his translations *used* – notably *Fra Diavolo* and *Fidelio* – before
embarking on a new one.

In 1934 he wanted Clive to consider Moniuszko's *Halka*
– an enthusiasm to which he was to revert many times.
Though he had a vague idea that the Carl Rosa or some
other company had done it in the seventies – the *Concise
Oxford Dictionary of Opera* does not bear this out – he
thought that no one would remember it, and it might be
rather a sensation. 'It is *much* better than *Bo.Girl* or *Life for
the Tsar*; has splendid ballets which are very definitely
Polish. The story is *very* thin, but there are good parts for
the soloist with great opportunities for emotion and, I
fancy, subtleties of psychology – ditto chorus . . . Do
consider it seriously, as it seemed to me to have great
possibilities – with some cuts – in spite of a good deal of
conventional Bo-girlishness!'

It was the finesse of the psychology (and 'the fact that
Tchaikovsky's music often means nothing at all – often just
a monotone against a waltz background') that was making
the translation of *Eugene Onegin* horribly difficult. 'It is
curiously hard for a singer to make words sound ironical
when singing, if the composer hasn't helped him with the
shape of the phrase.'

Clive was looking for a novelty, perhaps a short opera by
Haydn, but Dent gave no encouragement: 'They all seem
to me to be dreadfully tedious and conventional, more like
Galuppi than Haydn.' When he had seen Haydn's
Apotheker in Vienna in 1909 (it was boiled down to one act
– the original is to a libretto by Goldoni entitled *Lo
Speziale*) it had compared very unfavourably with *Serva
Padrona*, even though that had been re-scored for a
Mozartian orchestra and the characters presented as
Dresden China figures in a cupboard, intentionally unreal
– 'this is exactly the opposite of what Pergolesi meant: S.P.
was an *intermezzo* played probably on the apron entirely:
and what made the success of S.P. in Paris in 1752 was its
broad realism and humour, as compared with the stiff gods
and goddesses of Rameau's operas.'

Though he thought Clive's production 'marvellously
clever' and admitted that he and a young guest had laughed
like children over the comic business, he disliked *Fledermaus* – 'that dreadful Viennese vulgar music – so bad after
Offenbach . . . I hope you won't allow Miss B. to do more of
these "operettas" as it is undignified for our theatre. The

old Hoftheater would never have touched them, except that *Fledermaus* was always done *once a year* (only) for the Pension Charity and it was a great joke to see the Brünnhildes and Siegfrieds and Wotans in these parts.' In 1954 he contemplated resigning from his office as Vice-President of Sadler's Wells when Christopher Hassall told him that he was translating *The Merry Widow* for performance there. His enjoyment of *Fledermaus* had not been increased by the fact that 'Miss B. (in her delightfully characteristic way) was spontaneously offensive to me about *Fra Diavolo*! She burst out – "*Fra Diavolo* won't be half as amusing as this!".' Dent thought it would, for even if Auber was a little faded, the tunes are far better than Strauss.

Early in 1935, Clive and Muriel Gough, who had sung at the Old Vic in the Mozart productions of the twenties, a staunch ally, and now a governor, sang a number of excerpts to accompany Dent's lecture to the Musical Association on 'The Translation of Operas', an opportunity for a first hearing of parts of *The Trojans* which Dent regarded as one of his best efforts. From this he embarked

An unusually lavish production: *Boris Godounov*, 1935.

" Boris Godunov "

The Pushkin-Moussorgsky Revival at Sadler's Wells

*Edith Coates as the hostess
of the inn on the frontier*

*Above: Ronald
Stear as Boris*

*Top, right: John Wright as
the novice pretender, Gregory*

This season's first performance of *Boris Godunov* at Sadler's Wells was arranged for the death centenary of its author, Pushkin, newest hero of the Soviets. Moussorgsky's music, which interprets the story and characters so excellently that the poet's share in the opera is often ignored, is played in the original scoring, with one important and effective exception: the revolutionary scene from the second edition has been substituted for the crowd scene in the first. A great deal of thought has obviously been expended on the ensemble, which is again decorated by Doboujinsky's striking scenery, and laurels go to conductor Lawrance Collingwood, especially in his handling of the choruses, and to producer Clive Carey, especially in his handling of the crowds. Principals and small parts are all capitally interpreted—as well as the three on this page are Morgan Jones's Shuiski, Arnold Matters' Varlaam, Henry Gill's Pimen —and the whole of the sombre episodic drama leaves, as it should, a strong taste of this colourful, half-wild page from Russian history

Boris Godounov revived and reviewed, 1937.

immediately on *Benvenuto Cellini* for Glasgow; Adrian Boult had been asking about Stanford's *Lorenze*, written to an Italian libretto, but no more was heard of it. Clive's major enterprise this year was the first production in England of the original version of *Boris Godounov*.

Where opera and translation are concerned the letters of the next three years revert very largely to Mozart, partly because Clive was producing *Don Giovanni* again, and this always fascinated Dent. He was sure that it could be better done at Sadler's Wells than at Glyndebourne or Covent Garden, and took endless trouble about revising the whole translation. He admitted that his version only suited the Vic production, with special features that made some pundits very indignant. To explain the three instrumental items, and the playing of 'Non più andrai' at the supper party, he made Don Giovanni enter with three women and tell them to choose what tunes they would like the band to play; he was always very much aware that a large part of the Sadler's Wells audience would be seeing the opera for the first time. *Figaro* was published in 1937 and *Don Giovanni* in 1938, and the manuscripts of the various numbers, which had passed through various hands since they were first made some fifteen years before, had to be traced, revised and rewritten. In April 1937 Dent sent no fewer than six separate versions of the first stanza of 'Voi che sapete' to Clive, who was himself extremely busy with teaching, recitals and production. John Christie wished to use Dent's translations in booklets to be sold at Glyndebourne – though of course, they would not be sung there – and Dent thought it would be fun to hire touts to sell the translations on the platform at Victoria Station.

In 1936 he made his début as a broadcaster, talking about Busoni's pianoforte music, discovering, when he heard the record, that he probably ought to have an operation on his nose, and that he made very queer noises due to internal obstructions; this was something of a comedown, for four years previously he had written that he was almost the only person able to make himself adequately heard at an international congress at the Palazzo Vecchio in Florence – 'a glorious room, decorated with tapestries representing the story of Joseph; his flight from Mrs Potiphar being just behind the Presidential table!'

The old habit of taking holidays on the Continent had now usually to give place to lectures or congresses; an exception was a trip with J. B. Trend to Seville and

Barcelona, staying in Paris for a few days on the return journey, more bored and irritated by Paris than ever in cold wet weather after the attractive climate of Spain. The Opera too, was poor, *Castor and Pollux* and *Ariane et Barbe-bleue* – 'a dull opera, though it has much beautiful music'. At Seville he had seen the little boys dance in front of the altar (four times) and was charmed with music that reminded him of 'the duet between Frasquita and Mercedes in *Carmen*'.[1] The Sardana, which he saw danced in Barcelona with a rustic band and screaming oboes, fascinated him. 'I told Anton von Webern that it was very like Schubert – an allegretto rhythm on │ ♩ ♫ │ ♩ ♫ │ and changes from major to minor etc. Webern hated it . . . and thought it blasphemous to compare such a thing with Schubert. All that comes from Vienna is holy unto him: anything else is just not music at all. And you know that if there is one thing in the whole world that puts up all my bristles it is "holiness"! The Sardanas were ravishing, and the dance too.' (Letter of 11 January 1936.) He preferred the habit of Barcelona, where concerts began at 10 p.m. (or thereabouts!) and ended possibly at 2 a.m., to Germany, where they sometimes began at 10 a.m.

In 1937 Dent made a lecture tour in America, finding it lucrative, though by the time he had finished, without being over-worked he rather felt that he never wished to see the inside of a lecture room again. He owned that if he felt 'Heimweh' it was for Sadler's Wells rather than for Cambridge. He much enjoyed Cuba, with its clipped hedges of bougainvillea, all flowering thickly on top, like a thick fall of magenta snow, with J. B. Trend as his companion. In Santiago, at the south-east end of the island, there was a wonderful hotel where one could stay for a long while and write a book or a symphony; there seemed to be a professional pianist there practising on a very ancient and rather out of tune pianoforte 'virtuoso music of the wildest, I should imagine by Italian composers of the 1870's like Fumagelli and Golinelli – the sort of stuff Busoni used to play as a boy!'

The tour of America and the holiday in Cuba gave Dent unwonted opportunity to take stock. 'The American outlook on music is often odd: or is it ours that is odd? *Yours and mine*? Have you seen the last "Music and Letters" with a very interesting article by an American [J.

---

[1] So described; probably he refers to the Card trio in Act III.

Murray Barbour] on "just intonation"? I think he is probably sound. But incidentally he mentions that *vibrato* is universally agreed to be *essential* to both singers and violinists; and he mentions, as exceptional, certain University Glee Clubs whose male voice harmony is produced agreeably by voices which have no vibrato and no real "singer's" quality. It read, to me, as if the author just accepted the "Metropolitan" type of singing as the only possible one. That, I think, is a fundamental difference of outlook; in England there are people like ourselves who question all that, and take it for granted that, as educated and sensitive people, we have a duty to *question* it all.'

Lilian Baylis died on 25 November 1937. Just before this she told Doris Carey that she wanted Clive to take over the opera side, but with his customary lack of confidence in his power to lead his equals, and his dislike of the business side he had refused. Dent felt that, provided what was called the 'Soviet' (of producers and conductors) would start at once making plans for the next year and not wait for a new head to be appointed, it could and would do a great deal, but his old fear that 'the Covent Garden set' or the B.B.C. might collar it revived. 'The only hope for the successful development of the Opera lies in going on steadily on the lines that *you and I* really laid down (with Miss Gough and Jack Gordon and the others – I don't want to moderate their share at all). It all comes to what Decius Taylor the American asks for: singers who can *act* (and speak English decently); good translations; ensembles rather than stars; and *cleverness* rather than sumptuousness in production, scenery and costumes etc. It means training up audiences (and even critics!) as well as singers and conductors, but we arc gradually training our audiences to be alert for small points and to appreciate the humour of *D.G.* and *Figaro* etc. In some ways Miss B.'s death ought to remove a certain hindrance, for as you know we have had (since 1920) to waste an immense amount of energy in trying to persuade her to let us do things which time has proved to be immensely successful: financially successful. The younger generation of theatrical people . . . will always understand our ideals: the hindrance will come from "the experienced opera people" – the old Cov. Gard., B.N.O.C., Carl Rosa types etc.'

Dent ended the long letter from Cuba by asking Clive to think of other operas he could translate; it was the best sort of help he could give, and, given long notice, he ought to do at least one a year. 'Each new translation of mine gets slightly damned or patronisingly complimented by the critics, but the gradual *accumulation* of my translations – when there are (say) a dozen in the regular repertory – will ultimately contribute something to the *style* of our performances, though the public won't understand it, and very few critics will either.'

To this gradual accumulation *Il Trovatore* was the next to be added, proving as hard a task as *Rigoletto* had been. With the first instalment Dent wrote that Clive might think it rather crude, but that he envisaged it as rather 'rough stuff' and incredibly superstitious. Attaching no value to the particular words that he had written, apart from the fact that they were reasonably easy to sing, he was chiefly concerned to discuss the distribution of syllables: 'You may perhaps feel that one syllable to each note is a little "comic" and makes it sound like Offenbach. Or do you feel that every note of Verdi is sacred, and that all the translator can do is to make his words sound as much like Italian as possible? . . . Verdi in the arias almost always treats the words as nonsense on which to compose a clarinet or cornet tune. These early Verdi operas are incredibly difficult to translate – I spent hours over "Tacea la notte",[1] but the dramatic recitatives are rewarding; and anyway after doing *Rigoletto* I know that the task is not absolutely impossible, and it's dogged as does it!' As always he was not content simply to translate, but also consulted the Spanish play by Guttierrez on which Cammarano's libretto was based, and found that it threw considerable light on the characters. 'A civil war is going on: Manrico supports the rebel Count of Urgel, Luna is C-in-C to the King, Luna has therefore a political reason as well as a personal one for hating Manrico. Manrico is his *elder* brother, aged 2 when carried off by Azucena. I have deliberately conceived the soldiers in Acts I and III as a horribly rough lot. (Medieval soldiers were: and even as late as Dryden's *King Arthur* looting was regarded as their main affair. Or it may be in *Dioclesian* "To the plunder we run" – Yes). Luna is always in a violent state of "heat" for Leonora: Manrico is more sentimental. But the proposed marriage in the chapel is all

[1] The first stanza goes as follows:
In silence and in calm serene
The world one night was lying:
A full moon in the heaven was bright
No cloud o'erhead was flying.
Suddenly through the trembling air
That for the sound had waited,
Touch'd by an unseen hand, a harp
With sweet, sad note vibrated.
And then a voice uplifted sang,
As through my heart the music rang,
A song of faithful love.

154

Cammarano's idea: M. & L. in the Spanish quite obviously live in sin, and the whole point of the Spanish play was quite obviously its "romantic" and to the Spanish critics still shocking idea that love was more important than family honour or religion or anything . . . The Spanish is much more individualized than the Italian: more violent and passionate. It also has some very beautiful love scenes in verse between Manrico and Leonora, which Verdi left out altogether. Verdi also leaves out Leonora's brother, a proud hidalgo of the old Spanish sort.'

Dent felt that the general 'blugginess'' of his version was much more faithful to the opera than the nice sentimental way in which it is usually portrayed. The translation would indeed dictate the style. It had been a considerable labour, and confirmed his invariable experience that where a composer is really dramatic and concerned to express the sense of words, translation is always possible and often easy; where he ignores the words it is difficult – and Verdi more difficult than anyone.

'Bach composed everything for the organ', he wrote, 'Beethoven for the violin, or the string quartet; Verdi for the euphonium, or the brass band . . . The problem for the translator is made worse because generally the phrasing of the words is contrary to the natural phrasing of the music . . . I had hell over the Trio at the end of Act I. And when I came to the Count's even crotchets I felt inclined to chuck the whole thing! Partly because I was so morally disgusted with the "euphonium" treatment of the voice – a further degradation of Weber's way of treating the voice like a violoncello'.

I Quattro Rusteghi followed immediately; it did not take Dent long to become rather bored with it, for the more he studied it the less Venetian and the more Viennese it became – it was really not unlike *Lilac Time*.

Another instance in which he hoped that the translation would set the style was in Clive's production of *Don Giovanni* in 1938. 'The new dresses are all rather funny and suitable for Scarlatti's *Trionfo dell' Onore* which is practically *D.G.* without the supernatural part. They will give the "opera buffa" feeling all through, I hope. I do want to convey the impression that rape, murder, adultery and especially sacrilege are all great fun.' Without traps – there were none at Sadler's Wells – it was hard to manage the devils in the cemetery scene. Dent wrote a very detailed letter about the production, delighted with Joan Cross's

Donna Anna both for its coloratura and its dramatic force.

There was much else to discuss during the two difficult years between Lilian Baylis's death and the outbreak of war. In spite of the criticisms that he often voiced Dent appreciated that her leadership had held a team together that became increasingly uncomfortable when no new appointment was made. He had always hoped that Clive would be intendant; Vaughan Williams hoped that Dent himself would undertake this, but he could not afford to do so – it would have meant forgoing his pension which he would receive only if he held his Cambridge professorship until 1941. In any case he felt that he was too old, and not a good enough administrator and business man. In private correspondence they discussed other possibilities, both falling back on their old friend Steuart Wilson – who very likely would have been acceptable to no one but themselves. Summing up his own position, after a frank discussion of the strengths and weaknesses of his colleagues, Clive wrote, 'I think I have the imagination and the technique, but I took years to develop any confidence, and now that I have more, my drive is beginning to diminish with increasing age, and I feel that I can't carry on the unequal contest for much longer, but must soon settle down to do what I can to help the singers vocally when they want it. I certainly think I have the right sort of artistic vision for intendant, but not enough business sense, or hardness (for one must have that).' Typically Dent, in discussing the possibilities, was sure that it must be 'a man of culture with a University outlook on life'.

Although fifty-four operas were produced in the nine years before the war, and some of these it was known in advance could not be box office successes, hardly a month passed in which Dent was not exploring new possibilities. In the correspondence in 1938–9 there is mention of Haydn's *Il Mondo nella Luna* – 'very poor stuff; very poor as compared with Mozart, though much about the level of Anfossi or Martini &c.' The libretto by Goldoni had been written for Galuppi, and Dent thought that if Glyndebourne took up the Haydn (they didn't) it might be amusing for Sadler's Wells to do the Galuppi. 'I fancy it is at Brussels – most of them are. It might turn out to be better than Haydn, just as Offenbach is generally better than Sullivan.' Of short pieces – Mozart's *Impresario* having been successfully produced – they discussed Weber's *Abu Hassan* ('amusing, but very flimsy stuff as music') and *Savitri*. Clive had produced *Riders to the Sea* in Australia (and was later to do it at Sadler's Wells in 1952–3). Dent saw it twice in Cambridge in 1938 – 'It is a depressing and dreary work, though I have always known the play to be beautiful, and I admit the beauty of V.W.'s music. It owes much to *Pelléas* – rather as if Rossini had composed *Cavalleria Rusticana*. But the fact is that it falls between aria and recitative; you can hardly ever hear the words, and the music in itself is not interesting enough to move one, except at certain moments.' Dent also believed that some day they might attempt one of Schubert's operas, 'but *not* that stupid *Faithful Sentinel*'.

He was saddened by the choice of *Rosenkavalier*, which Clive produced, because it showed that Sadler's Wells was tending towards 'heavy-weight opera', which he believed should be left to Covent Garden. In any case he liked it less each time he heard it. He suggested, if they wanted another fairly modern opera, Janáček's *Jenufa*, which he had heard at Prague in 1935. He had liked it then, and it would sing well in English, because Czech moves so much quicker than German. Hearing a concert performance of Ravel's *L'Enfant et les Sortilèges* in Paris in 1938 he thought it very

'Heavy-weight opera', *Der Rosenkavalier*, 1939. Left to right, Ronald Stear, Joan Cross, Ruth Naylor and Joy McArden.

charming, and wondered if it couldn't be done at Sadler's Wells.

His views on the overall policy are summed up in a long letter whose theme he was to repeat several times in the next ten years. To quote it extensively here will spare much repetition.

'I am much concerned about the future policy of S.W. Not that I think the "Soviet" is going on the wrong lines, but I fear the "Soviet" are planning only for 1938–9 and not for a longer future. It looks to me as if they were too much guided by the newspapers and the casual chatter of the day. I hate to see S.W. humbly following in the wake of the "famous" opera houses, or in the wake of Salzburg and Glyndebourne. We ought to *lead* public opinion. I suspect that *you* were for *Euryanthe* rather than *Oberon* because Salzburg had just begun to make *Euryanthe* talked about. (Salzburg did *Oberon*, I know, but not with the old English dialogue; and one reason why I wanted *Oberon* was because in its original English form it would have led us a step nearer *King Arthur*) . . .

'I think the *first* thing we ought to consider is the desirability of bringing out *at least one* new native British opera every season. I don't mean that it must be a brand new one, though I hope we shall in the future be a place where new operas are performed for the *very* first time. In this category I include the old operas such as *Dido*, *Fairy Queen*, *King Arthur*, *Bo. Girl*, *Maritana*, *Lily* too, as well as those of V.W. or Gatty and the unwritten ones of Willie Walton! A revival of *Bo. Girl* would be a *novelty* now! But for political reasons we must keep native opera in the limelight, as long as we can keep the accounts level by what we make on *Faust* and *Carmen*.

'I don't at all want to abandon the old safe draws – *Faust*, *Carmen*, *Trovatore* etc. – and I know that no opera house in the world can do without *Cav.* and *Pag.*!

'I am not much in favour of big Wagner, but there is one argument in favour of it which weighs *very* strongly with me, and that is that at S.W. you can see *Meistersinger* and *Walküre* for sixpence, which you can't anywhere else in the world, I fancy! Wagner at any rate, is a real "classic" who ought to be accessible, whether I happen to like him or not. (My own feelings are divided – I adore the *Ring* and *Tristan*, but am bored with *Meistersinger* and *Parsifal*: I like a good deal of *Lohengrin* and detest most of *Tannhäuser*! But this is merely my own private affair!) . . .

158

'As a general policy I think we ought in principle to prepare

1. British opera – at least one "new" work each year and keep up old ones as far as practicable.
2. "Classics" i.e. Mozart, Gluck, Beethoven, Weber, Wagner, Rossini etc. etc. taking care to make a success of such "classics" as are generally a failure elsewhere e.g. *Fidelio*, *Cosi fan Tutte*.
3. Indispensables – *Faust*, *Carmen*, *Cav*. and *Pag*. etc. in due proportion.
4. Later foreign operas – perhaps one a season, but alternating with unusual classical revivals – or rather one "new" opera each season to be *either* a new classical revival such as *Oberon* or a modern opera such as *Jenufa* or a halfway such as *Halka* (Moniuszko).

'I suppose that however many people we turn away from the doors at S.W. we may expect to stay at S.W. for another five years, possibly ten. If we ever moved (under a national subsidy) to a big theatre in the centre, like C.G. or Drury Lane, or His Majesty's, we should have to reconsider the whole system. The ideal would be a pair of houses, large and small, perhaps sharing with drama, as in Munich and Stuttgart of old, but I fear there might be technical difficulties.

'Has the "Soviet" given any serious thought to the question of touring companies going out from Sadler's Wells? We do a little, but very little, and only in the weeks just following the normal season (May). Couldn't a scheme be organised *from S.W.* and including *some* of our best people? I don't want to damage the Carl Rosa, but isn't there room for both? Or if not, couldn't we make an Anschluss? possibly buy up the Carl Rosa and run the whole thing from S.W. What I do want to get rid of are those sporadic Beecham-Coates-heavyweights – B.N.O.C. – undertakings in English in the provinces and suburbs.'

All this found a ready enough appreciation from Clive, but at the Board meetings – and Dent was often absent – with increasingly elderly colleagues ('It might be the Bach choir') he made depressingly little headway. 'And you know what — is like, and her polite but firm method of refusing to discuss anything, like a very efficient Victorian mother with obstreperous children who want to know how babies are born.'

9. *The War Years – the Battle of Sadler's Wells*

The opening months of the 1939–45 war provide one of the rare intermissions in the long series of letters. After representing England as vocal adjudicator at the International Competitive Festival in Vienna, Clive went to Australia with his wife on a personal visit, hoping to complete this before the outbreak of hostilities. There had been some doubt whether the British Council would pay the necessary expenses and compensations for Vienna, about which Dent felt strongly. 'If they don't pay I suppose there will be no British on the Jury at all, and that will merely confirm the Continental belief that England is "das Land ohne Musik". I want to destroy that belief if I can; but it is very difficult, and the Central European Press keeps it up because Germany, Austria and Czechoslovakia all want to make money out of music, as tourist countries, and as exporters of music, and as places to go and study music in. So that it is greatly to their own disadvantage to praise any sort of music in England.' After some lecturing in America, Dent went on with his friend, J. B. Trend, to Mexico.

Professors at the R.C.M. before being dispersed during the War. Left to right, Hermann Grünebaum, Clive Carey, Vaughan Williams, Stanford Robinson.

'I did not like Mexico City, which has all the drawbacks of South Italy in old days, filth and beggars and crowded streets, with very dangerous crossings and noise that is worse than even Florence! But the smaller towns of Mexico – except Morelia, famous (say the guide books) for its fleas – are fascinating: mostly ancient Spanish, but unlike anything I ever saw in Spain, and in spite of uniform town planning as regular as Mannheim or Turin each seems to have a decided individuality of its own.' He would happily have spent the whole winter there, or in New Orleans, but Trend was beginning to get nervous about the imminence of war and his return to Cambridge – it seems not to have affected Dent – and they went on to Charleston. This they found 'adorable, especially out of the smart season; it has all the beauty of Bath and other Queen Anne places, but with a difference, for it has St Martin in the Fields copied from memory in wood and painted dazzling white, beautiful old mansions with great porticoes, and magnificent gardens full of "Riviera" plants and flowers; and a waterfront that you can stroll about on.' It was there that they had news of the outbreak of war, but as they could do nothing, they stayed on in Virginia, visiting Williamsburg: 'It is interesting, but palpably a fake, and all looks like scenery for the *Beggar's Opera*, the more so as there are "hostesses" dressed like Jenny Diver and Mrs Trapes and men in breeches looking after a brand new jail and shops for pewter and olde furniture. But I heard afterwards that there is a certain amount of life there, and they go in, as they should, for what I call Dolmetschery – harpsichords and all that.'

In New York there had been a Congress of Musicology, at which there were some half a dozen European visitors, and hordes of refugees. Dent found himself becoming increasingly fond of the United States and was beginning to take an interest in negroes. 'I loathed them at first, because I could never get away from childish associations with "niggers on the sands" at Scarborough etc. and "plantation songs" (by Alfred Scott Gatty, mostly!); and the Jamaica type of nigger in Cuba, with his Cockney offensiveness, rather put my back up. But latterly I have come to realize the enchanting kindness of coloured people in the States – railway porters, dining car waiters, hotel servants etc. and though I never got to Harlem I began to see that I should be much interested in negroes of the artistic type, and if I got the chance of lecturing or

A rehearsal of the *Rappresentazione* at Girton.

Late thirties Cambridge captured by another Cambridge musicologist, Charles Cudworth: Trumpington Street.

teaching at a negro University in the South I should certainly jump at it.'

While in Mexico he had been translating Cavalieri's *Rappresentazione dell' Anima e del Corpo* for an 'Italian Festival' in Cambridge in March; naturally this had to be abandoned, and it did not eventually see the light till 1949 when Girton College Musical Society performed it. Back in Cambridge after an unadventurous crossing at the end of September Dent found some two-thirds of the undergraduates coming into residence, and two London schoolmistresses who had been evacuated before the declaration of war living in his house. Luckily they were 'pleasant women'.

In November, on a visit to London, Dent had a severe internal haemorrhage, and 'must have bled nearly to death; I certainly felt that I had got nothing left but a sense of humour!' Hearing about it, Clive had recommended 'slippery elm', but the doctors would have none of it; nor would Dent: 'it seems to be a food for the worst stages of illness, like [a proprietary brand]. That by the way, is my *bête noire*: I always associate it with my two old aunts at Nice; I think it must be made from reserved sacrament – it is food only for holy women.' Under the care of an elderly night nurse with a macabre taste in reminiscences of other patients – boys at Eton who had overworked and aged nuns at Clewer dying of their austerities – Dent recovered sufficiently to return home to Cambridge in January; at least the life of an invalid spared him funerals and college meetings, and he was able to take a few pupils for composition. He read the proofs of the Penguin sixpenny on opera, 'an odd mixture of learning and frivolity', and was particularly pleased with Kay Ambrose's amusing pictures and with the illustrations, about which he had fearful trouble, eventually getting all he wanted and more.

For some unaccountable reason, whenever he was seriously ill in bed with a temperature he always reverted to composition, and in London he wrote three motets for unaccompanied chorus, 'all very full of canons and fugues', to words from the Psalms set with a fierce intensity. These were published immediately by the Oxford University Press; there followed a further three motets composed in Cambridge, the first to two verses of Wesley's hymn 'O, Thou who camest from above', quoted in a university sermon printed in the *Cambridge Review*. 'I thought the words rather good, and set them as a canon five in one with a little fugue as a coda – the canon very emotional and the fugato purposely very stiff and formal.' Later letters show how pleased he was with their success when they were performed by Boris Ord and C.U.M.S. and by T. B. Lawrence and the Fleet Street Choir. An earlier song, a setting of Thomas Hardy's 'The Oxen', composed in 1920, he had refused to publish in case it was taken up at carol concerts at Christmas at the Albert Hall, with organ accompaniment. The last lines of the poem[1] probably struck a response from Dent, especially in time of illness.

Other news was of the completion of the translation of *Rusteghi* (which had become *The School for Fathers*) and of attempts to wrestle with the songs in Kodály's *Háry János* with the aid of a Hungarian dictionary – 'they are all nonsense, like all folksongs!' The director of the Florence Conservatoire had written to ask if he might translate the Busoni biography (it was not for Dent to give the permission, but for an Italian publisher to make a contract with the Oxford University Press), and in his letter had requested that he might make certain 'rectificazioni sull' Italianità di Busoni'; Dent drily observed that this meant that everything in the book unfriendly to the Italians must be taken out and Busoni turned into a fascist. He had encountered similar problems when in 1935 he had quoted criticisms of Bellini in the London Press of 1833, and had

Silver Street.

[1]   . . . . Yet I feel
    If someone said on Christmas Eve
      'Come; see the oxen kneel.

'In the lonely barton by yonder coomb
  Our childhood used to know',
I should go with him in the gloom,
  Hoping it might be so.

excused himself by explaining that the English language did not admit of the panegyric style of the daily front page of the *Corriere della Sera*. News that *Dido* was being performed in Florence in double-harness with *Cavaliere della Rosa* led Dent to imagine an over-sexed German propounding that Dido was really the prototype of the Marschallin. The *Cambridge Review* was having to cut down an article of his, and he was interested to discover whether he was to be allowed to have his sentence about its being evident that there were no Missions to Seamen at the harbour at Carthage.

Illness and freedom from engagements were a convenient escape from the war. 'From what I read in the papers the general state of war nerves all round seems to be much the same as it was in 1916 or so. I suppose we shall soon be a totalitarian country, that is, one in which everything that is not compulsory is forbidden.'

Clive in Adelaide was not on the staff of the Conservatorium, as he had been fifteen years before, but was doing some teaching, some adjudication, and some recital work. Leisure and practice enabled him, to his delighted surprise, to believe that at 56 he was singing better and with a bigger voice than he had ever done. Both Sadler's Wells and the College had told him to stay out in Australia in the event of war, and he felt that this was the end of his connection with opera. 'I always hoped I would make some bigger mark on opera in England, but perhaps my little mark has been of use. Anyway there are plenty of people to carry on the production of opera now, and when we started there was really no one who had any intelligent ideas on it.'

After a relapse in May, Dent was writing much more cheerfully in September 1940 – 'I cannot think that a real invasion is in the least degree possible with any success' – with news of the second group of motets, and a calculation, based on the average of all his grandparents, parents, uncles and aunts, that his expectation of life was eighty-one years, six months, which he thought pretty good (in the event, he was five months out). He had translated Flotow's *Martha* and was revising *Orpheus*, hoping that Sadler's Wells would improve on their previous production, and reminding Clive of their visit to a performance at the Savoy with Marie Brema (looking like Queen Victoria) as Orpheus, and Viola Tree, a mile high, towering over her as Euridice, and the gates of Euston as the Temple of Love at the end.

Voice production: Clive Carey
with a student at the R.C.M.

Altogether Dent wrote twenty-five letters to Clive or to
Doris Carey in Australia during the six years of the war.
Inevitably, a great part of them was about the affairs of
Sadler's Wells, in London, in Burnley, where for a time the
opera was based, or on tour in the provinces, and with
plans for the future – especially in relation to Covent
Garden. Throughout the war he kept Clive's replies.
Naturally there are frequent expressions of opinion about
the merits of conductors and producers and singers, about
the real or imagined ambitions of various people closely
connected with the Old Vic and Sadler's Wells, and with
the wider scene of opera: Tyrone Guthrie, David Webster,
John Christie (whom Dent now cast somewhat in the rôle
he had earlier allocated to Beecham). The 'Soviet' was
gradually dispersed until the opera was kept going largely
by the efforts of Joan Cross, who gave up singing, except in
emergency, in order to direct its affairs, and Lawrance
Collingwood, who continued indefatigably to conduct as
long as he retained the health and vigour to do so.

Reduction of staff is always painful, and hurt feelings, now best forgotten, are often reflected in Dent's descriptions of what, although Clive little expected ever to produce at Sadler's Wells again, remained a major common enthusiasm. As the years passed, Dent's need for Clive, both for the familiar consultations about operas and translations and, as he saw it, to play a major rôle in the immediate post-war situation, intensified, so that the leisurely correspondence of the first four years of the war – a letter (often taking three or four months in transit) written every three or four months – gives place to monthly letters providing an urgent commentary on the future of opera. As always, Dent was on every committee, including Covent Garden, but *not* Glyndebourne (if it had one), which he always saw as a potential danger to English singers and to the style of opera and the approach to it which he and his friends had striven for so long to promote. The combination of various factors – their inability to keep up regular discussion, increasing age, the frustration by war of many earlier plans, a sense of isolation and occasionally of hopelessness – adds to the asperity on both parts, but Clive's letters are also full of enthusiasm for the voices he was training and the achievements of his opera classes, and Dent could look beyond the discouragement of falling standards to work in which, once he had retired from his professorship in 1941 and moved to London, he hoped to play a more central part. When an answer cannot be expected for some six months much of the give-and-take, which had been a feature of earlier letters, gives place to a summary of many months of activity.

Only rarely did Dent fail to complete a piece of writing that he set out to do, but one project of September 1940 was still-born – 'I want to seize the opportunity and write a little book, quite popular and for everybody, about "National Opera" ... People will say "this is not the time": I say it IS the time, with Covent Garden *and* Glyndebourne dead, while Sadler's Wells is going comparatively strong.' The Oxford University Press would publish it, and on the strength of the fact that over 20,000 copies of his Penguin book had been sold already he was confident of his market. What had encouraged him was the number of letters he had received from unknown people keen to establish opera houses in Hull, Glasgow and other places. The book was frustrated chiefly by recurrence of illness; he regretted the necessity to renounce theatres and

166

concerts less than his inability to play the part that he had hoped to assume as 'Tyrone Guthrie's confidential adviser on all operatic affairs'. Eventually, in 1945, it was absorbed into *A Theatre for Everybody*.

However, there was plenty of opportunity to do the reading for the book, even if 'National Opera, what it has been and what it might be' never appeared. He read all sorts of old memoirs and old operas too, and found himself revising earlier opinions. 'I find my admiration for Stanford always increasing. He was like Handel, who cared more about opera than anything else in music, even when he had the oratorio festivals at his feet. I very much want the Wells to revive *Much Ado*, which I think is full of good things and most effective, though I never saw it on the stage. Other revivals I should suggest are Macfarren's *Robin Hood* (1860) which is very full of good fun and on the way to Sullivan; Wallace's *Love's Triumph* and the *Amber Witch*; Goring Thomas's *Esmeralda* and *The Golden Web*: and I expect I shall find others. I had hoped to find something useful in Shield, Dibdin, Bishop, but there is nothing there to fill an evening, though possibly one might fake a one-act or two-act out of them each. The plays are so old-fashioned and absurd, and they are nearer to melodrama as plays with music. It's a great pity for their single ballads are often adorable.' He realised that other members of the Sadler's Wells 'Soviet' would think him perfectly crazy if they read this, 'just a funny old Cambridge antiquary with dozens of bees in his bonnet'.

Among the bees was an entirely new libretto in English for Auber's *Ballo in Maschera*, based on Scribe's text *Gustave III ou le bal masqué* of 1833. He had been studying Swedish history under a King's colleague's guidance, and was sure that the opera could be made far more interesting if one tried to stick closer to what actually happened. 'Complete historical truth would be quite impossible, for actually Gustave III was (feminine) homosexual and Madame Anckarström (Amelia) conspicuously masculine in temperament.' Dent's researches have influenced a number of recent productions.

About *The Girl of the Golden West* which a colleague wanted to produce because 'it was such a good story' he was less enthusiastic: 'I find it poor stuff, full of impossible "local colour" like a bad film, and the climax at the end almost impossible without horses. It ought to have been done by Astley's company at the old Cobourg theatre!'

Clive endorsed this view: 'Curiously enough the first scene in spite of its rather absurd local colour is far the most moving and, as I seem to remember, the best musically. Most of the rest of it is full of the particularly annoying type of Puccini aria, where the orchestra walks about in triads in 8ves with the voice – a very easy way of writing, I think!' He shared Dent's enthusiasm for *Ballo* but thought the existing libretto hopeless; having seen Stanford's *Much Ado* five times he had always thought it a charming work. By the time Clive's reply had come, several months later ('We seem to be living in the days of Captain Cook'), Dent had reconsidered Balfe's operas but thought Benedict's *Lily of Killarney* better, though he disliked the final waltz; the later Wallaces were the pick of the bunch.

In July (1941) there was an opportunity to see 'National Opera', as the Wells Opera brought to Cambridge Arne's *Thomas and Sally*, followed by *Dido and Aeneas*, which was played without any intervals at all, thereby gaining much. Already, with clothes rationing recently introduced, the dresses were suffering. This was especially noticeable in *Thomas and Sally*, in which the costumes were very mixed, and the Squire, in a green velvet dress coat, and with a large moustache, looked as though he had come out of a burlesque production of *Lady Audley's Secret*. During the visit Guthrie and Joan Cross discussed with Dent his new version of *The Beggar's Opera*, as Frederick Austin had withdrawn permission for the Wells to use his version, which had had such a long run at Hammersmith after the First World War. Now that the work, instigated at Guthrie's suggestion, had been completed, they had somewhat shamefacedly to admit that Sadler's Wells could not possibly tackle it till after the war, as the provinces had already had more than enough of it in Austin's version, not very well performed. A London production, with plenty of publicity, was the only chance, and this was nowadays impossible; otherwise there was a possibility that the B.B.C. might broadcast it. Dent had been very much interested in the work, which he had set for the small orchestra with which Sadler's Wells was now touring. Needless to say, he approached *The Beggar's Opera* from scratch, and from his researches he soon began to see that the conventional notions that it was a parody of Handelian Italian Opera and that it contained a collection of folksongs were largely untrue, but that many of the airs were theatre-songs of the seventeenth century by Purcell and his contemporaries, very much in the popular taste, with very little novelty about them. In harmonising the tunes and in orchestration Dent was not rigorously archaeological, as he could so well have been, but preferred 'to write perhaps what Purcell might have written if he had lived as long as Verdi'; he deliberately avoided all 'dramatic effects à la Puccini', such as he felt that Frederick Austin had indulged in. In writing for the wind instruments he received encouragement and advice from Roberto Gerhard.

Already Tyrone Guthrie was envisaging that the Vic company should be acknowledged after the war as 'The National Theatre', but it was unlikely that it would ever return to the Old Vic whose roof was badly damaged. He was also resolutely determined on the complete divorce of the Wells from the Vic, and was convinced that as soon as the war was over there would be a huge demand for music and for opera. Dent quoted the prayer of Judas Maccabaeus, not in relation to the nation but merely for Wells Opera, 'O grant a leader bold and brave, if not to conquer, yet to save.' In writing this, he had no wish to disparage Joan Cross, whose management he admired. As always, he was pinning exaggerated hopes on Clive – 'and of course I should like nothing better than to work under you as far as health permitted . . . I have a dreadful fear . . . that on the very first opportunity Glyndebourne and/or Covent Garden will pop up again with a ready-made scheme for foreign opera. I am sure the refugees are all secretly working for it, and once an armistice is signed there will not be the slightest prejudice against any German or Italian musicians.'

When Dent gave up the professorship in 1941 he was still much of an invalid, but the absence of any duties or responsibilities of any kind gave him some relief which communicated itself to his physical condition. His pension was only £220 a year paid half-yearly; to begin with, he made only a few journeys to London, one of which was for Walton's new violin concerto, which he liked enormously as far as he could hear it, for in spite of new screens and a sounding board the Albert Hall acoustics were as bad as ever: 'the music sounded as if in the open air; strings lost, flute and cor anglais sometimes coming through, brass noisy and side drums shattering'.

For the time being there was plenty to be done in Cambridge: characteristically Dent's dormant interest in C.U.M.S. revived now that it was facing war conditions.

Photo] **A MASS ATTACK!** [Cambridge Daily News

Large tracks of kerbing have quickly become whitened in the centre of the town during the last day or so—and this is how it was done. This should provide a useful guide for travellers in the black-out, and will last a long time if pedestrians are careful not to walk on the paint before it hardens.

There were those amateurs who loved rehearsing and playing in an orchestra but were indifferent to concerts and would happily play in a college hall informally, but there were also those who believed in relying on professional help and undertaking big works. Paddy Hadley was now in charge, and belonged to the second category. Dent, whose sympathies were divided, volunteered to reduce Delius' 'Appalachia' – scored for an 'Edwardian' orchestra with all sorts of extras – to normal orchestral requirements. Though it proved to be a formidable task it led him to look again at Delius's operas, and in due course to a recommendation that, with some editing and reducing, *Koanga* would be very possible for Sadler's Wells – attractive music and effective on the stage. *Fenimore and Gerda* he reckoned quite hopeless, even with Berlin's resources, especially as regards scenery and shifting; every scene was static and it got nowhere. Two years later he similarly reduced the 'Song of the High Hills', which he had found more difficult but more rewarding, for it was more imaginatively scored – the greatest work apart from the operas. Altogether during the war years he found himself gaining in appreciation of Delius. Writing in 1944 of 'Brigg Fair', played at Cambridge by Constant Lambert and the B.B.C. orchestra, he commented: 'In 1904 or thereabouts I heard it somewhere in Germany and hated it, being then soaked in Stanford with all the prejudices of the academic mind . . . Yesterday I thoroughly enjoyed it. I am glad I have been through so many musical experiences in the course of my life and have learned to enjoy such a lot of different things. Vaughan Williams can't bear Delius, nor Berlioz either.'

In the same letter Dent made some reference to orchestras and conductors. 'Paddy Hadley wants to have the fun of standing up before a first-class professional orchestra and hearing them do the work while he waves a stick and thinks he is doing it. Nobody except Henry Wood, Scherchen and Busch and possibly a few others abroad is really competent to tell an orchestra what to do: play that in the nth position, or take a breath after the third crotchet in the trombone . . . An orchestra of today has a general style which is suited to Elgar, Rachmaninoff and all sorts of not quite modern music – style based rather on Viennese fiddling and Italian brass-playing; there is no breadth, no cantabile, no sostenuto, but a great deal of brilliance.'

Although he had been let down three times in quick succession, over *Rusteghi*, *Martha* and the *Beggar's Opera*, Dent now undertook to translate Rimsky's *Mozart and Salieri*, armed with a vocal score with German and Russian words, a literal English translation and an American omnibus edition of Pushkin in English. With the aid of a Russian dictionary the task was finished in two days – and likewise not used, but he was philosophical about this – 'these things will come out some day, I expect'. Of more immediate concern was a plan to celebrate the 150th anniversary of *The Magic Flute* at Cambridge at the Arts Theatre; naturally Dent was very much involved, and worked very closely with Kurt Jooss when eventually he was chosen as producer; John Armstrong was the designer. There were numerous conferences at Dent's bedside (he was ill again) and Jooss was armed with Dent's interleaved copy full of notes as to positions and movements adopted in 1911. One problem was that the opera as produced in

Cambridge must also be taken on tour, with strange stage-hands every week, whereas at the Arts Theatre they would have a week's rehearsal and familiarisation. At Cambridge it was sold out every night, but it did not do well in the provinces.

London meanwhile was full of what Dent described as 'refugee opera' – as a propaganda exercise there had even been a proposal to bring over the whole Russian opera and ballet early in 1942 but shipping was not available. This led Dent – quite unexpectedly – to an awareness of how gradual was the impact of his own translations and Proctor-Gregg's, which he acknowledged to be sometimes better than his own. 'I am beginning to realise *now*, from letters and criticisms, that we are only just beginning, after 20 years work and more, to get opera audiences converted to the idea of *expecting* and *wanting* to hear the words of an opera and understand them. It is astonishing how the old doctrine still goes on, fostered of course by gramophone companies, that English is no language for opera, and that if people must sing in English, they must mispronounce their words and make big noises like foreigners . . . Not until now had I realised how *surprised* people are when they do hear *Figaro* in my version (*Figaro* which I made in 1915!): it seems to give them an entirely new outlook on opera, even if they have been accustomed to hearing opera in "English". I suppose it has taken all this time because after all the total number of performances can't be more than about a dozen all told, and *Rig* and *Trov* and *Barber* are only just beginning to get through.' It was a topic to which he recurred on hearing that in New York the Metropolitan put on *Flute* in English (?) in a new version by an Austrian refugee, and that in Philadelphia the local opera management had set up a 'translation bureau': 'I expect that sort of Brooklynese really *is* more intelligible to America's mixed populations than my Cambridge English, which is not always intelligible to the Sadler's Welsh!'

Guthrie, who had just produced the opera (with décor and costumes by Sophie Fedorovitch, which delighted Dent) now asked Dent to translate *Traviata*. As usual, references to the original (Dumas' *La Dame aux Camélias*) indicated nuances of character which Dent hoped that a new translation would bring out. 'In Dumas they are all very individual, but in the opera negligible (except perhaps the Doctor) and nobody realises what they stand for, especially as Verdi's librettist changed all the names, probably owing to copyright difficulties. In the opera you generally see Flora merely as the inevitable *seconda donna*, like Inez in *Trovatore*, and the same singer takes both Flora and Annina the maid. Flora is really Olympe, who is the demi-mondaine on the most expansive scale, kept by the old gentleman, and there ought to be a complete contrast between the party in Act I, which is quite impromptu (a supper for six in the play), and the party in Act II scene 2, which is a huge and extravagant crush, with all Paris there.'

In his translation he did his best to stress the gaiety and light-heartedness of the 'demimonde' atmosphere – quite contrary to the traditions of the Scala or Covent Garden, 'where the stage must look expensive, and the opera must be rendered with all that reverent solemnity which is due to the Real Presence of Patti or Melba'. He suggested that in the Gipsy and Matador episode of Flora's party it should be very obvious that they are all just ladies and gentlemen dressed up, like charades, and the words should be frivolous and absurd, with a syllable to each quaver as in a patter song. Guthrie very naturally pointed out that the Sadler's Wells chorus already found it hard enough to look like gipsies and matadors in the first place, and that the double pretence would be impossibly beyond them. At any rate Dent was dealing with an opera he knew really well, whereas when he translated *Martha* he had never seen it. When next he saw *Traviata* done by the Wells company, a year later, they were still using Lady Macfarren's translation, because Joan Cross very properly felt that to change would mean withdrawing it from the repertory for at least three months, and studying it again, perhaps with a new cast. Meanwhile it was too great a draw to take it off. Dent was charmed by the rendering of Alfredo by Peter Pears, 'the new tenor', whom Clive remembered from operas at the R.C.M.

The letters continued to maintain the pre-war theme: Dent writes at length about cuts in *Don Giovanni*, which must be reduced to three hours, as if he could expect an immediate response: 'I suggested (among the longer cuts) cutting almost all of Anna's story of her attempted rape, especially as a modern audience always takes it as funny (which *I* never intended, in spite of all my other blasphemies!), more especially Ottavio's comments', and so on, concluding with . . . 'on no account whatever cut the *final* sextet, or the secco recitatives belonging to Don G., Leporello, and Elvira, which are most amusing and most necessary to explain their characters, and the story of the play, as well as bringing out what I consider its most essential characteristic – CYNICISM'.

It was encouraging that Arthur Bliss, who had just taken over the directorship of B.B.C. music, when Dent wrote to him about the *Beggar's Opera*, should suggest that it would be ideal for the reopening of the Bristol Theatre Royal when it was properly restored – there was talk of the National Theatre securing it. Though Dent did not for a moment think this would happen, he was delighted to find Bliss looking ahead. Even in the summer of 1942 one must be planning for the improbable future.

The present was grim; not only was the war going badly, but it seemed probable that Dent could not survive it. Nearly all music, especially orchestras and loud singing, upset his stomach completely, and led to vomiting attacks from nervous exhaustion. He had to renounce practically all concerts, and go only to one or two where modern works were played; though he enjoyed these most, they were generally just the sort of music that upset his stomach. 'A Mozart quartet would probably be quite harmless and digestible, but I don't want to waste my time listening to classics any more.' He was alarmed to find that he could not

The first Cambridge air raid: damage in Vicarage Terrace.

rise to his best level, even when he had less pain. To add to these troubles, he had 'Ethel Smyth' deafness in his right ear, hearing most notes a semitone or more too high, while his left ear continued normal. He knew that nothing could be done about it. Though to type for an hour brought on warning pains, his letters, though rare, were longer than ever, devoting a whole page to a discussion of the whereabouts of Rossini's cadenzas as sung in the 1830s. He considered collecting those sung by Malibran and her sister, Viardot-Garcia, by Jenny Lind, Grisi and Patti and wrote at length (and, Clive thought, inaccurately) about Rosina in the *Barber*. During the winter he collapsed altogether, was brought from Cambridge to Manchester by his friends the Hawards, underwent a gastroenterostomy – the surgeon was amazed that he had survived so long and done regular work as well – and made a good recovery, convalescing in a hotel at Grange-over-Sands. For once he did no work, merely reading all the books he could lay his hands on, from *Swiss Family Robinson*, which he had never read as a child, to Coulton's *Medieval Panorama*. 'I never spoke to anyone if I could help it, and rather avoided the "drawing-room", where all the ladies smoked and the men didn't; at the canonical hours the wireless news was turned on, and really when one heard [the B.B.C. news-reader] Hibberd or someone like him intoning, and saw the reverent rapture of the congregation, it was all exactly like family prayers.'

Once he began to recover, Joan Cross suggested to him that he should translate *Freischütz*, though as usual he remonstrated in favour of *Oberon* instead, and lamented that *Don Giovanni* was not in the repertory. She replied that it needed a double cast, with understudies for every part, and sadly these were not available. He was not very fond of *Freischütz* though he admitted the genius of the Wolf's Glen scene; but he conceded that the British public might take to it as cordially as had their ancestors in 1824. He thought it would be the very devil to translate. In the event it took him ten days, dialogue and all, and it was not Sadler's Wells that wanted it, but the B.B.C. – 'imagine Act II (Wolf's Glen) performed by the B.B.C. with unlimited noises off and Dennis Arundell carrying on a running descriptive commentary as if it was a football match'. He hoped through Peter Gellhorn, who knew the opera well, to persuade Sadler's Wells to try it after all, in spite of the amount of scenery that would have to tour with it. There was a chance of returning to the theatre in the autumn (1943) now that the bombing had abated. Meanwhile they had occasional 'seasons' at the New Theatre.

'The future is rather depressing, I think. People say the war is going on very well, but the defeat of Germany is postponed every year – at present it may be in 1945; next year it will be 1946 and so on. Japan will go on till the crack of doom; and even if the war does come to an end in our lifetime there will be a long period during which taxation will be just as heavy as now, or heavier, and most of the young people still held fast in the Forces, if only to be armies of occupation etc. so I don't see when we are going to get back to a normal life of peace. I am not worried about revolutions or social changes; they will come of themselves, and in this country quite quietly and easily as they have always done. But I confess that after a whole lifetime of economy (for although I have never been really "poor" I have never really been well off) I should like to see a period of gaiety before I die; I don't want to go on for ever with "plain living and high thinking". I enjoy high thinking, to some extent, at least what *I* should call high thinking – the life of the "intelligentsia" of which I am never ashamed; but I do detest and loathe plain living! And all the more now I am nearly 70!'

By September 1943 Dent was fit enough to be able to enjoy London again, and began to search for a flat – 'it seems to be generally held by those who think themselves in the know that we shall not be bombed again, at least not seriously, and that it is reasonably safe to take a flat or house, and desirable to take one now, and not wait'. The trouble was that one could get flats but not servants; but he felt that if an elderly bachelor like himself could not get a servant, nobody in the world could. He wanted a man housekeeper to cook and do everything. He translated *Don Pasquale* for the B.B.C., and found it a hateful piece of drudgery; on the more hopeful side, Jooss spoke of producing *Freischütz* with lantern slides – he had already done it in Essen – but for the time being Dent had lost touch with Sadler's Wells.

However, he had plenty of work on the stocks: rewriting his *Mozart's Operas* for a second edition that the Oxford University Press wished to publish; and writing papers on the nomenclature of opera; the Castrati, 'quite frank and open – time someone did write openly about them'; and on the disappearances of the Castrati and the rise of the

German Romantic heroine. Besides that he wanted to write about a collection of librettos in the possession of Florence Nightingale when she was about sixteen, including copious pencil notes of hers on the dresses and actions.

Aided by a niece Dent found a flat (at 17 Cromwell Place); during the last month, as he told his musician friends, his life had been like a fugue in which the subject is always answered in the subdominant, for it modulates from flat to flat until it has made the complete round of the Inner Circle, and ends where it began, in the key of SW. He wrote twice about Crozier's production of *The Bartered Bride*; he had constantly warned against attempting it unless there was an absolutely first class ballet, and the Czech Government in London released from the army Sacha Machow, their best ballet-master, to help the back row from the Wells ballet; the result had been thrilling. Less thrilling were a couple of visits to the revived Carl Rosa in Hammersmith, struggling along with 'ancients' singing in the grand old Italian manner. They reminded Dent of an old Italian friend reading Rupert Brooke's 'Grantchester' to him 'Justa now de lilac is in bloomah / All aroundah my little aroomah.' The inserted 'ah's' make an additional semiquaver in each bar, so that the singer is inevitably behind the conductor. But even these faults could not prevent his enjoyment of *Trovatore*. His hearing was troubling him; the orchestra in the Albert Hall playing 'Elgar's dreadful dreary violin concerto' sounded like a harmonium, but he hugely enjoyed Walton's *Belshazzar's Feast* which followed it – 'a magnificent work and well sung'.

Clive's replies took up many of Dent's points: he had moved from Adelaide to Melbourne and had formed a School of Opera at the Conservatorium with enough success to think now chiefly in terms of teaching rather than production. Like Dent he was sure of the need to start an opera school, starting with the elements of stage technique, attached to Sadler's Wells like the Old Vic dramatic school. The advantages would be incalculable, and the saving of producers' time now spent in training novices how to act would be enormous. He was delighted with the news of Eric Crozier's success.

Another advantage of being in London was that Dent could get to the Sadler's Wells' Board again, even if its lack of long-term policies drove him to distraction. During the war years on tour the opera had been making huge profits while the drama had often lost heavily, but he found it hard to drum up enthusiasm. The great question was whether to stick to the ghost of Miss Cons and 'settlement opera' and return to Sadler's Wells, or to abandon Sadler's Wells, at any rate for the time being, and try to become now the Royal and National ENGLISH Opera, taking a lease of the best West End theatre they could find – not an easy task, as the commercial syndicates could get much larger rents from musical comedies and shows of the *Chu-Chin-Chow* type, an inevitable result of war. The latter course would require a government subsidy, and if successful might stir up the jealousy of commercial managers. Unfortunately, just when the opportunity was there, singers and designers to take advantage of it were in short supply, and in spite of the success of the *Bartered Bride*, after four years of war the management was inevitably beginning to lose the resilience that had sustained the long exile from London. One result of the *Bartered Bride* had been a letter from the Czech Legation to the British Council, duly relayed to the Vic–Wells Board, expressing the hope that when Czechoslovakia was liberated the Sadler's Wells company might perform 'English Operas' there; Dent 'lay low and said nuffin'' having arranged the whole intrigue himself through one of the secretaries at the Legation. He longed for the day when Sadler's Wells might perform *Hugh the Drover* or Stanford's *Travelling Companion* at Prague.

As the prospects for peace improved, Dent's letters became more frequent, and the future of opera in English increasingly the dominant theme. He was furious to find how utterly indifferent people seemed – 'the mandarins have no use for it whatever; they are stuck in the mud of *Gerontius*'. In the midst of a paragraph on this theme he could not resist another swipe at Elgar: 'Did I tell you my suggestions that we should follow the example of old Pietro Raimondi of Naples – about 1830 – who composed three oratorios, *Joseph*, *Potiphar* and I forget the other, to be performed first separately and then all together simultaneously in counterpoint – and perform *Gerontius*, *The Apostles* and *The Kingdom* simultaneously in the Albert Hall with the Three Choirs from Hereford, Worcester and Gloucester? Charles Wood always used to say that there were no tunes in the world that wouldn't combine contrapuntally *with a little coaxing*.'

A factor in the prospects for opera was the increasing remoteness of the Sadler's Wells theatre itself, since the wartime rubber shortage accentuated by the loss of

Malaya, meant a shortage of tyres, and therefore of buses. Another problem was that there was no food to be had there. Dent suggested approaching a family of restauranteurs and asking them to consider opening a branch at Sadler's Wells, running a cheap lunch for people rehearsing, and dinner, interval meals, and supper afterwards, for the audience. It was an idea he had thought of years ago, but the governors were quite horrified at such an idea – 'I might have suggested opening a brothel there! "Quite impossible" – just because they had never thought of it before.'

To keep the achievements and concerns of the Vic–Wells in the public mind, Tyrone Guthrie persuaded Dent to write what was to be mainly a picture book about it. Dent was anxious to get the archives of the early Miss Cons period, 1880–1914; when he asked Miss Williams, the clerk to the governors and for a long while Lilian Baylis's confidante, about them, she replied that there weren't any, for, as long as Morley College was occupying half the building of the Old Vic, there was no space to store archives. Miss Cons had started the whole thing as a sideshow, and never realised that she was creating a National Theatre. 'Miss Baylis's private office was about the size of a W.C. – just room enough to kneel down to her roll-top desk and ask God to send her a tenor! and besides that Sybil Thorndike and a few other ladies had to dress in it, while the rest dressed in the saloon.'

In fact, such archives as there were were in the private possession of Sir Reginald Rowe, the chairman, whom Dent discovered also to be writing a book, dealing mainly (and justly) with his own contribution to both theatres. 'Well, I leave all that willingly to him, and I am going to make the book an excuse for talking about what *you* did for the opera, and the beginnings of Sadler's Wells and especially about all that has happened since the death of Miss B. and since the start of the war; with some considerations about the future.' The book *A Theatre for Everybody*, was finished within three months, though there were delays in publication; Kay Ambrose was given a free hand with the illustrations, but Dent refused altogether to be vetted and censored by the Vic–Wells office (including Miss Williams) with the result that the book retains the liveliness of an expression of opinion, besides attractive historical sidelights.

In the summer of 1944, with theatres closing again

The Royal Opera House, Covent
Garden, in its Mecca days.

because of the renewed bombing, discussions of the future
became more urgent. It was not simply a matter for the
governors of the Vic–Wells, but also for Covent Garden,
then leased to the Mecca Cafe Company. Dent went with
Guthrie to look at the house: 'I wish you could see it as it
now is – "a waltz dream" – my deafness and blindness no
doubt helped, but it really looked like a sort of dream film
in technicolour and sounded like that too; all quite unreal
like a thing on a screen or music by wireless. And the boxes
have been removed completely except the Royal Box and

the Duke of Bedford's, so that upstairs there is a clear space between the edge of the parapet and the back of the wall . . . This gives a huge width and sense of spaciousness. The columns are there still, but being iron they are quite thin and not much in the way. There is a dance floor covering the whole of the pit and stage at stage level. The proscenium is left quite clear, without any hanging border, so that it looks an enormous height. Round the sides and back of the stage there is a classical colonnade, very dignified and grand, with buffet-tables behind: right at the back I could just see a sort of balcony, perhaps for a band, but at that moment in darkness. In the circles there were tea-tables. The dance band (in scarlet) were on a sort of floral rostrum, not very high, in the centre of the stage. The whole place was bathed in pink light from floodlights above, turned on and off at odd times, but the general effect very appropriately chocolate-box, but all in the worst of good taste or the best of bad, as you like. Anyway, everything better and more dignified than one could expect; and most decorous and proper . . .

'I was really rather thrilled, and shall I say slightly intoxicated by the strange effect of the light and the sound of saxophones etc. through amplifiers and distorted ears. I saw at once that, as it is now, the house is just right for its decoration, for what it is functioning as now. And I recalled the old interior on an opera night, and knew that that green and gold style of 1856 was right *only for the Victorian era*. Apart from its perfect acoustics, C.G. is an anachronism, and was as soon as Victoria died, if not before. If you recollect such interiors as the Berlin Opera, even the Paris Opera, the theatres at Bologna, Parma and Genoa, and the Fenice – I purposely do not name the Scala or the San Carlo, or Palermo, which are vast, but not really beautiful – you will understand what I mean when I say that these are theatres for all periods, beautiful and dignified for ever. But the Scala always suggests the 1880's to me, and the Vienna house the 1860's, the Dresden opera another view of the 60's, and Covent Garden yet another. It is in the same category as the Victorian lustre candlesticks and stuffed fruits and humming birds under glass *cloches* – what I call Sitwelliana – now for a moment in fashion, if not already forgotten again. That old Covent Garden was out of date when you and I went to hear the de Reszkes etc. 1895–1905 or so. And I said to Webster, I wished he could scrap the whole thing and make an entirely new interior out of it, without boxes, on modern democratic lines, with all seating planned on rising inclines, so that everybody should have a good view of the stage.'

While Dent was expressing this opinion he became aware of other possibilities: 'I think the L.C.C. will also try to do something; they have got a scheme for the region between Waterloo and London Bridge on the Surrey side and want to make a great embankment with gardens etc., and a "welfare centre" with theatres, concert halls, libraries, swimming baths etc. But of course, whatever they do build, the theatre will be the last thing, and I fear they have little idea of building a theatre on a really generous scale . . . I expect the Old Vic will never be rebuilt. It will probably be sold to the L.C.C.; or exchanged for a site elsewhere in the region, and that region might be the right site for it! But what is absolutely urgent is that the New Vic should be close, *really* close, to an important station like Waterloo, and accessible *all the way* by subway or covered passage, so that people could arrive at the theatre dry on a wet night. One must always reckon with bad weather in this country.'

These schemes belonged to the indefinite future; there was much that in mid-1944 was of immediate concern.

Though Dent was reluctant to agree to it, and was in a strong position to obstruct, he assumed that the 'break-up' of the Vic–Wells empire was probable, and that Tyrone Guthrie's intention to divorce his two wives, opera and ballet, would be fulfilled, with drama proclaiming itself to be the National Theatre at the Old Vic with himself at the head of it. In that case ballet and opera 'haunted by the ghost of Aunt Emma' could stick to the bricks and mortar of Sadler's Wells, or they could try to fill another bigger and more accessible theatre, as they were confident that they could do. For the time being – but this was only a wartime expedient – this was effected by the drama staying at the New Theatre while opera and ballet, normally alternating on tour, moved to Prince's, using Sadler's Wells as a rehearsal theatre and store. What augured well for the future was the youth of their enthusiastic audiences.

There was of course an opposition which wanted international stars singing in foreign languages. Dent characterised these as 'merely elderly people, who remembered the glorious days of Grisi and Mario, and elderly singers who did not want to learn new translations or to rehearse actions under the new young producers', such as Eric Crozier and

Kurt Jooss, to whom he was giving encouragement. Also many people did not like the Opéra-Comique style with spoken dialogue (and probably failed to realise that *Carmen* has always been given in Paris in that way.) Dent felt that the real cause of this anxiety was that spoken dialogue made opera too *realistic*, so that the audience became aware how fat and ungainly the singers were, whereas if they sang all the time, this was less apparent. Beecham in his autobiography (*A Mingled Chime*, which Dent thought very good-natured, containing many wise observations) had said much the same. In any event, as we have seen, Dent felt that Covent Garden was not a suitable house for opera treated in this manner.

A new Covent Garden Board had been formed; it represented Boosey and Hawkes, the old syndicate, and the Council for Encouragement of Music and the Arts (C.E.M.A.) through which the government had operated during the war; Samuel Courtauld, William Walton and Dent were also members, though Dent was not representing the Sadler's Wells governors, who felt that their Trust articles under the Charity Commissioners precluded their official participation. The company was to be non-profit-making. There was also, as general manager, 'a Mr Webster from Liverpool'.

From the outset Dent found David Webster amenable and practical; he was glad to find that he too disapproved of 'the old C.G. system of miscellaneous foreign stars all singing in German or Italian, with English singers allowed to do small parts; no proper rehearsal or production'. But while they agreed about the desirability of building up a really first-rate opera to sing in English, Dent was bound to concede that by this stage of the war Sadler's Wells was at a low ebb, unable to fill the breach, and that it would take some time to build up. Meanwhile, Webster put forward the suggestion of an Anglo-American Company at Covent Garden to sing in English, with the best *American* singers from New York, and Dent proposed that they should occasionally bring over from the Continent a complete ensemble, with singers, scenery and everything (except the orchestra, which the Musicians' Union would never allow). This would avoid the old tradition of 'mixed stars'. Needless to say, Dent put forward the suggestion that Clive would be a marvellous producer with an English or mainly English company, who would like him personally and be willing to do anything for love of him; on the other

David Webster seen with Peter Pears.

hand he doubted Clive's ability to cope with temperamental foreign stars accustomed to go into all sorts of tantrums. Webster knew something of Clive, but reserved his position; he was sure that Christie and Glyndebourne should remain completely separate; for the rôle of artistic director he could name no obvious candidate – certainly not Beecham. Dent would happily have seen Sir Kenneth Clark in this position, if he would have been prised away from the National Gallery. He was hoping, as usual, that the committee would become an informal gathering of friends, and the expectation that when Maynard Keynes returned from America he would become chairman pointed towards this.

He gave Clive a pen portrait of Webster at this time: 'He is rather fat and prosperous looking, not unlike John Christie, but whereas Christie has the "powdery" pink and white surface of a Raeburn, and looks so Victorian that you almost think he's got mutton-chop whiskers, Webster is pink with a high polish, and ought to be Lord Mayor of some big provincial town.'

At any rate it was refreshing to hear Webster express a conviction that there were voices in England just as good as anywhere, although some people say that fine voices only develop in southern climates. They agreed too, to think in terms of three or four years before a first-class company could be assembled. Dent was assiduous in cultivating Webster's friendship, soon appreciating his potential. He told Clive, 'I am encouraging his self-confidence and love of power, because I want to be one of the experts whose advice he takes.' With him he rode his various hobbyhorses – a National School of Opera (which Sir George Dyson, Director of the R.C.M. opposed, 'hoping to keep all the vocal cords in his hand'); an agreement between the companies and colleges to standardise certain translations; state subsidy to keep down prices for sixpenny galleries but not to support luxury opera at millionaire prices, and a warning against the German Jews (not least the translators!).

Discussions (and long letters to Australia) continued apace. If one accepted that Sadler's Wells had few, if any, voices that could fill Covent Garden, sing the kind of opera that the huge stage demands, and dominate an orchestra of 80, then, as Clive said in 1920, they must inevitably stick to an Opéra-Comique repertory. With the best will in the world collaboration with Covent Garden was impossible.

Clive denied that 'big' voices were necessary there – after all, Melba's voice had not been big, but had carried perfectly, and he cited others. Tyrone Guthrie was pushing his own ideals – opera more really dramatic; better translations of foreign operas and better librettos for native composers; co-operation with real poets for opera; singers young enough to look their parts, with good figures, speaking the King's English, and acting like the best actors. There was nothing new in that: Monteverdi had wanted it in 1600 just as Dent and his friends had wanted it in 1920; for the time being they must lower their musical standards, but there was no virtue in telling everyone that they were doing so.

William Walton put forward a reasoned memorandum for co-operation between the two theatres, but Dent found himself siding with Guthrie, not least because of his misgivings about the suitability of Covent Garden for any modern production. One of the planks in Guthrie's platform that Dent most strongly favoured was his plan of encouraging young poets to take opera seriously and collaborate with composers; he felt that if this was to be effective, the experiments would have to be on a modest scale appropriate to Sadler's Wells and he hoped that, from a number of new English works, two or three would survive out of the litter. He knew that Walton was writing an opera for resources much larger than Sadler's Wells could manage – a 'Strauss' orchestra – but he also recalled that Strauss had shown in *Ariadne* that 'you could make a perfect hell of a row with 14 instruments'; it would be much cheaper and wiser to reserve 'experimental' opera for Sadler's Wells.

So, with much difficulty, Dent and Guthrie, (with whom Dent got on well, 'though I have to allow for his Irish impulsiveness, and for his entire lack of the critical habit') put forward a memorandum setting out their proposed opera policy. In a nutshell, it was that Sadler's Wells should be the Opéra-Comique and Covent Garden the grand opera. Dent of course did not mean 'normal opera' by grand opera any more than he meant Edward German and Audran by Opéra-Comique, and inevitably there must be some common ground. He volunteered to put forward a list, so as to explain his thoughts to those who might misunderstand him otherwise. Webster also produced a list of grand opera that he would like to produce – with the help of Sadler's Wells singers – at latest in the autumn of

Tyrone Guthrie.

1945, with names of possible artists and conductors. Dent naturally had his own views on these, and especially on the teachers to whom Webster suggested sending English singers for training. In the first instance they were not English, and included Elena Gerhardt. Clive had commented in an earlier letter that not one woman in a thousand could teach a man to sing, and neither of them, rightly or wrongly, believed that Gerhardt was the thousandth.

It was becoming clear that, though Webster was well disposed towards opera in English, for practical reasons Sadler's Wells would continue as before, and so for a few years would Covent Garden – 'American and foreign stars from all sorts of places with English singers in small parts, all singing Covent Garden Italian' – but something had been achieved, and now, though no formal treaty had been drawn up – or would be if Dent had his way – the question of frontiers had to be faced. At least there was an acknowledgement that grand opera in English sung by English singers, trained if possible in a National School of Opera, was an ideal to strive for. For the present it was unattainable; there simply were not enough singers and conductors to go round, even with the Americans, and it was futile from the outset for the two theatres to run opera in English against each other. Dent, as the sole member of both boards, was used very much as an ambassador, and when a very friendly conference took place in Liverpool he found to his horror that Webster had capitulated to other interests and would be bringing in 'all sorts of German–Jew producers and conductors' and was also asking for a large subsidy from C.E.M.A. since Covent Garden was so much the larger undertaking. Dent had no fear that Sadler's Wells would find its grant reduced, but there was no mistaking that it was to be the 'pedigree herd' (Courtauld's phrase) at Covent Garden again; for the time being Covent Garden wanted the goodwill and the name of Sadler's Wells, but it might scrap most of the company and silence the theatre by turning it into an opera school, not under its own management. Dent was afraid that within a short while it would be an absorption like *The New Statesman* (*& Nation*); he urged that there should be further conferences to see if any sort of co-operation could be planned.

But if Covent Garden was going to borrow for their pedigree herd a few of Sadler's Wells' singers and staff in a combined operation, the Vic–Wells governors needed reassurance. They were very naturally and rightly concerned not only with their legal obligations to the Charity Commissioners and towards their supposedly proletarian audiences, but also their moral responsibilities towards various members of their staff who would *not* be taken over by Covent Garden. With a foot in both camps Dent found that the Covent Garden authorities took a somewhat frivolous view of the close ties between the opera and the Trust. A joint committee to implement any 'treaty' must ensure that Sadler's Wells was not submerged. The governors too came under heavy fire from local interests in Finsbury when it became clear that Covent Garden – in spite of a proposal to keep 250 cheap seats – might be removing the best singers or leaving behind only an opera school giving student performances in a theatre rebuilt by Finsbury for Finsbury, as they maintained.

In the midst of this stalemate Dent drew up his various lists. First, two long lists of fifty operas in each, one for a large theatre and one for a small; this was somewhat academic. Then a list of operas from which the first season's repertory at Covent Garden should be chosen; this omitted Wagner deliberately, as Webster did not wish to consider this the first year. He also knew that Webster hoped to use the ballet as much as possible, though he pointed out that apart from some of the Russian operas, the operas demanding big ballets were composed before about 1850. For the present he wanted to avoid 'museum' operas. He purposely put down a number of British operas so as to show what a lot there were.

He divided the list into categories, not very strictly defined, and marked with (B) those that required ballet, and (BB) much ballet:

(1) CLASSICS *Magic Flute*; *? Così fan Tutte*; *Orpheus* (BB); *Armida* (BB); *Oberon* (BB); *William Tell* (B).

(2) POPULAR FAVOURITES *Trovatore*; *Aida* (B); *Otello*; *Falstaff*; *Carmen* (B); *Faust* (BB); *Boheme*; *Tosca*; *Butterfly*; *Turandot*; *Tab and Schich.* (which will probably take the place of *Cav & Pag* in future); *Rosenkavalier*.

(3) MODERN *Boris Godunov*; *Eugene Onegin*; *Snow Maiden*; *Tsar Saltan*; *Golden Cockerel* (B); *Pelléas & Melisande*.

(4) NOVELTIES *Kitesh* (–B); *Queen of Spades* (B); *Quattro Rusteghi*; Busoni's *Turandot* and *Arlecchino*; Respighi's *Fiamma* (very spectacular); R. Strauss's *Intermezzo* (very amusing).

(5) BRITISH *King Arthur* (BB and drama company as well); *Fairy Queen* (ditto); *Much Ado about Nothing* (B); *Travelling Companion* (B); *Wreckers*; *Macbeth* (Collingwood); Goossens' *Judith* and *Don Juan*; Gatty's *Tempest*; *Hugh the Drover*; *Sir John in Love*; Britten's *Peter Grimes*; Walton ?; Tovey's *Bride of Dionysus*; Boughton's *Alkestis*; Delius's *Koanga, Village Romeo and Juliet* and *Fenimore and Gerda*.

Dent reserved *Figaro* and *Don Giovanni* for the smaller house, and since *Così* had been a great success when recently performed by Sadler's Wells he would have liked to have reserved that too.

He made a special note of *William Tell*, which he had seen in Dresden and Florence, though he didn't suppose a dozen people in England had seen it; (Clive had seen it in Berlin, 'very Nazified'). One of his regrets was that he could never induce any of the important people to play or read thoroughly through it. Indeed, whereas a German intendant would regard it as part of his normal daily work to do this, or to have it played to him by a pianist, nobody in England would do it. He recalled that Lilian Baylis simply hadn't had the time to ask Lawrance Collingwood to play *Fidelio* through to her: 'It was less trouble and quicker to kneel down and ask God what HE thought.'

With bombs still falling in March 1945, and legal delays over the lease (and release) of Covent Garden, all this preliminary work was in danger of being still-born, and the treaty remained unsigned. But Dent was still hopeful that Sadler's Wells Opera, then on tour in Liverpool, would be able to give a short season at the King's Theatre, Hammersmith, and then reopen their own theatre with Britten's *Peter Grimes*. He had much faith in Eric Crozier, whose praises he sang constantly to Clive, not least because he had ideas and ideals of his own, and certainly did not follow him blindly or uncritically. Dent appreciated Crozier's natural insistence that 'quite young people' like Britten should come first in his future plans.

When Covent Garden eventually opened – and the talk

188

was now of October 1945 – it was hoped to get the Moscow Ballet, the Paris Opéra-Comique and the Stockholm Opera for its first season. However, the Russians were reported to be very reluctant to allow their Ballet to come to London; one of the ballerinas had recently married an Englishman in the Embassy, and they feared that other ladies finding (what was carefully concealed in Russia) that life in England is altogether pleasanter, might follow her example. Perhaps the Moscow Opera might be more amenable, as the opera singers were less likely to rush into matrimony!

All this information was relayed at length, and at times repetitiously, to Clive in Melbourne. His replies were brief and not very informative. While Dent was 'missing him quite dreadfully', he was up to his neck in work, doing *Dido and Aeneas* with the two Conservatoriums combined, and *Riders to the Sea* – evening rehearsals on top of full days of teaching. This success confirmed his belief in the extreme value of the opera class, starting from the formulations of

Riders to the Sea: Powell Lloyd's design for Clive's production at Sadler's Wells, 1953.

stage technique. He was looking forward to getting back, but not expecting, or even hoping for, the senior posts for which Dent was so constantly recommending him. That Dyson wanted him back at the Royal College of Music was enough, and he would be glad to resume teaching there. Meanwhile his wife was reminding Dent that Clive had been unwilling to take over Sadler's Wells opera when Lilian Baylis had wished him to, and that he was now 62, and had no ambition and no wish for administrative responsibility, even if he did sometimes feel that his work for singers and for opera had received little recognition – 'in many ways he is as simple and as unsophisticated and gentle as he must have been at 20, and I would not try to change him for anything'. To Dent's list of classics Clive would have added *Iphigenia in Tauris* which he found thrilling.

Besides making efforts towards securing Clive's return to the College, Dyson had also thrown in his lot with Sadler's Wells, thus accepting the professional championship of English opera. He was a strong character, and as Steuart Wilson had just joined the Covent Garden committee, Dent felt himself to have more allies where he most needed them. When Clive eventually got back, a little late for term at the R.C.M., early in October, the future of Covent Garden and the Ballet were still uncertain, but *Peter Grimes* was playing to packed houses at Sadler's Wells.

Although the affairs of Covent Garden and Sadler's Wells were the foremost concerns of the London years, there were, as always, other activities and experiences. As an exercise in criticism Dent's two-page description of Tyrone Guthrie's production of *Hamlet* in March 1944 is a small masterpiece that it is kinder not to reproduce – Dent reckoned that he had 'never witnessed such an accumulation of dreadfulnesses since the days of Reinhardt and the Deutsches Theater in Berlin 30 years ago', though he conceded that, considering all things, Robert Helpmann as Hamlet did remarkably well to carry it all off as he did and hold one's sympathies somehow.

His own version of *The Beggar's Opera* gallantly performed largely by amateurs in Birmingham – Katharine Thomson and the Clarion Singers, a working people's choral society – enlisted his enthusiasm, although at the first rehearsal 'the band sounded like a fat man in creaky boots trying to walk across a room on tiptoe'. At least it

The Beggar's Opera at
Birmingham: 'Fill every glass'.

gave him an idea what the score would sound like, and what
he would have to alter – too much of the flute and oboe in
the higher regions, and the horns rather high, sounding
like trumpets. Eventually the Lord Mayor and Corpora-
tion took over the performance, which took place, not in a
theatre, but in a 'Big Top' erected on a devastated area near
the station; it provided an auditorium as big as Covent
Garden, but no adequate protection against rain, wind,
cold or outside noises. There were two performances – and
luckily no rain on either night: on the first night they had
only motor buses to cope with, but on the second there
were two hours of church-bell practice to contend with
('just like Cambridge'). 'The singers were quite good; they
knew their stuff perfectly and sang the rather difficult duets
with complete assurance and certainty. The two girls were
very pretty and quite bright as actresses; Polly had just the
sort of innocent charm that is wanted. Macheath – a
railway lorry driver by occupation – looked very well in
costume, sang well and acted well too, on the whole. Of

191

The Beggar's Opera at Birmingham: Macheath and Polly.

course they came on in leaps and bounds as soon as they got into their dresses, and by Tuesday night the very demure "ladies of the town" were letting themselves go thoroughly! As you know from the Vic, the very nicest and properest girls simply love acting the part of a harlot.' The orchestra, under a young schoolmaster who 'never lost his head, even in the most hair-raising emergencies, and never lost his temper, which meant a good deal', consisted of the wind section from the Police Band – 'everything that policemen should be – absolutely safe and reliable, but rather stolid' – and strings, mostly women 'no doubt competent teachers and schoolmistresses, safe enough for a

Haydn trio or Popper's Gavotte, but just hopeless when confronted by my score of the *B.O.* ...: These good females, who were always looking at the stage instead of the conductor, invariably missed the bus, and ran for dear life to catch it up, producing a most uncomfortable sense of anxious hustle in every song.' Anyway, it sounded very well when it *was* played right, and Dent learned that his experimental scoring as well as his orthodox scoring sounded rather attractive and always quite safe. He was very thrilled and grateful. It was to have had a London performance in October 1944 but 'bomb trouble' led to its postponement till after the war. The arrangement was published by the Oxford University Press in 1954.

Besides that there were committees, irksome because of all the 'Government hush-hush', which usually was not concerned with military secrets at all but just with trivial personalities – 'for total lack of humour commend me to the British Council!' The oddest of jobs was a request from the B.B.C. (and the British Council too) to write three scripts of lectures on musical form for the Chinese; Dent chose to give three lectures on 'Sumer is icumen in'. He also had to write introductory 'blurbs' (about 100 words in each) to accompany scores and records of British composers to be sent to Argentina – 'I was particularly ingenious about Elgar; it required some ingenuity to do that trick!' He helped a young naval officer to edit a book of songs for sailors. He was also asked to write a preface for a little book about church music for young organists, very devout too; 'I sent the author some notes and said I thought a preface from me would damage his reputation rather than improve it.'

10. *Reluctant Decline*

The two friends' reunion had to be postponed, for Dent was ill with another gastric attack, 'overdoing things and seeing too many people, I suppose'. Then he went to Liverpool to give five lectures. Malcolm Sargent was very friendly, inviting him to rehearsals and concerts: 'the only really interesting item was the new orchestral concerto of Bartók which is a very good entertainment. It is a sort of divertimento in five movements written obviously to show off virtuoso orchestras in America – and needs wonderful oboes, horns, brass and everything. But it is not at all difficult to follow, and is brilliantly amusing (v. often beautiful) without being flashy or cheap. We also had two concertos for pianoforte of Rachmaninoff which both start with beautiful ideas and gradually become cheaper and showier and end up as a hash-up of Liszt at his worst.'

Clive Carey had taken up a short-term appointment as Director of Opera at Sadler's Wells, the post he had never sought for himself. Dent was full of advice and encouragement: 'I hope you will go round everywhere keeping an eye and ear on everything, telling everybody – stage-managers and conductors too – what they ought to do. *Words to be clearer* everywhere; more attention (especially in such things as *Rigoletto*) to *piano* and *pianissimo*. I always say to people "the softer you sing the more trouble you must take in articulating your words, so as never to let down the *intensity*" . . . Don't hesitate or be undecided; then the dangerous outside forces will get in. *You* are now sole director with supreme authority.'

But it was an unhappy time, and there were bound to be hurt feelings when some of those who had borne the heat and burden of the day during the war (and before it) could not be reappointed with the seniority they felt themselves to merit; moreover, Clive was easily hurt by criticism, whether in letters – sometimes initially addressed to Dent and passed on with careful encouragement to disregard them – or in the press. '*Time and Tide*, I see, has a sniffy paragraph about Sadler's Wells, as if all sorts of disasters had happened: but don't let that silly women's paper worry you. Their acknowledged symbol is Miss Dartle out of Dickens – the lady who was always "asking for information"!' 'People often write things that they wouldn't say, and make matters worse by thoughtless management of the pen.' He wrote after a few months to tell Clive how very much struck he was by the way all the 'underlings', box office, doorkeeper, cloakroom etc. all seemed so pleased and happy and proud of the house. But it was no good; Clive was unhappy, and immensely relieved to hand over at the end of the year.

Rusteghi now re-emerged as *The School for Fathers* in Dent's translation made some years before and Dennis Arundell's production. Dent had suggested a number of other possibilities for the title besides the obvious 'Four Curmudgeons' – 'A Marriage of Convenience'; 'Parental Tyranny'; 'Home Discipline'; 'You Leave All that To Me' (a favourite expression of Sir George Dyson); he was not at the time well pleased with the plan (in which Clive acquiesced) to transfer the scene of the action from Venice to London, though two years later he was writing that he could see no harm in it at all, except that it could not be used appropriately in America, where 'you must always expect the background of *German* mentality. The London setting would certainly be quite wrong: more foreign than Venice, and not romantic.'

In 1946 he attended another I.S.C.M. Festival, the first since the war, but found it horribly exhausting; he also went to Glyndebourne for *Lucretia* and was rather bored by it; predictably, he was irritated by the whole atmosphere of the place. However, although he was now over seventy, he could still summon up great reserves of energy; when asked for a long chapter on Handel's operas for a symposium edited by Gerald Abraham he read 'some forty or fifty'[1] of them, reading every word and note carefully (in the R.C.M. library): 'the result has interested me a great deal and I got some new lights although I had not time to pursue all the investigations I ought to have made. I believe I have found two or three that we really could do at Sadler's Wells.' He was delighted when the Hungarian Government asked him (with Michael Tippett) to Budapest as vice-president of the Bela Bartók competition.

In 1949 he was back in Cambridge copying a Scarlatti

---

[1] As Dent must have known better than anybody, there are only forty of them, but the exaggeration is pardonable.

At the Bela Bartok festival: Dent
talking in Budapest, 1946.

opera at the Fitzwilliam – the wheel had come full circle –
and regretting that pressure of other work prevented Clive
from producing *King Arthur* there. The Purcell Society
had sprung into life again – its minutes revealed that it had
held only about a dozen meetings since 1888 – and he was
relieved to find not only that he was not the only surviving
member of the committee (for Clive and Jack Westrup had
been elected in 1937, since when there had been no
meetings) but also that three more volumes were practically ready for the engraver, and had been for about ten
years! Better still, there was an Arts Council grant to cover
the cost of publication. In the summer of 1951 he had four
weeks in Italy, nearly three weeks in Venice spent in idling,
which he realised had done him a great deal of good. He
carefully avoided all music, and had one lovely but tiring
day at Arqua Petrarca to revisit the house where Petrarch is
supposed to have entertained Chaucer – and the place
looked as if nothing had ever happened there since then.

He had an afternoon, too, in Mantua where he went to inspect Rigoletto's apartments in the Ducal Palace again. It was pleasant to be taken back in spirit forty years to his days of Italian tramping.

The old partnership was renewed over *Ballo in Maschera*, with at least half a dozen letters sending drafts of the translation for criticism. Dent had begun his research and translation in 1941, then put it aside. Even if the love affair was Scribe's invention, and not only unhistorical but also quite out of character as he had already noted, he was fascinated by the 'psychological situation most unusual in opera – the case of a man and a woman passionately in love while both married to other spouses, but rigidly restrained from committing adultery by scruples of duty and honour. Gustavus and Amélie (in Scribe's libretto) are perpetually obsessed by these honourable scruples, and "intimacy" never occurs even when they meet at midnight in snow under the gallows! . . . I have restored the historical names of Counts Ribbing and Horn, the chief conspirators. Anckarström was certainly the actual assassin; he shot the king at the masquerade with a pistol; he loaded it with rusty nails etc. so as to induce gangrene poisoning (of which Gustavus actually died, a fortnight later), and fired at very close quarters into the king's bottom. He had also provided himself with a sharp and purposely jagged knife in case the pistol did not take effect.' Dent continues the account with great vigour, stressing that a new version must do everything possible to bring out the recklessness, light-heartedness, generosity and humour of Gustavus's character, and also to make the most of Oscar's frivolity. On the other hand the conspirators ought to be a strong contrast – deadly serious, fanatical, sinister and cruel. Here Clive pencilled the comment 'but at the same time they are *young* and *noblemen*'. They discussed single lines which provide special difficulties; the ensembles were a jig-saw puzzle as usual, but the important thing was to give the characters something dramatic to sing when they had a phrase that stood out. Dent kept the Swedish names (to an Italian unpronounceable) but hardly ever used them on the stage. He knew that some of Gustavus's remarks, which simply wouldn't translate into orthodox operatic English, would raise a laugh at Sadler's Wells, he wished to goodness that Covent Garden would roar with laughter at them too, but Beecham's recent revival there of *Bo. Girl* was like a memorial service! He was interested too in

Francis Toye's observation that the tune of a trio in *Ballo* is also used by Sullivan, who probably knew it from a performance in London in 1861.

When the work was half completed, in October 1951, Dent was surprised to hear that Covent Garden had already asked Sophie Fedorovitch to do the décor and costumes for *Ballo* there, and had advised her to go to Sweden for local colour – 'Webster of course never says anything, but always with honeyed politeness!' Dent hoped he was learning something from Clive about the peculiar difficulties of turns and shakes; he was amazed to see how often he could get the same vowels as the Italian on important notes. The last scene was the hardest of all to translate; historically, after the murder Anckarström occupied his time before his execution mostly in religious exercises, still fanatically convinced that he had done his duty. Should he in the final ensemble and 'Orror' chorus though singing in unison express completely opposite sentiments to the other characters? There are precedents in *Rigoletto* and *Traviata*.

Eventually *Ballo* was produced in Dent's version at Covent Garden in 1952, with John Pritchard conducting, after an amicable discussion over a cup of tea. It was a major achievement to have switched the action away from seventeenth-century Boston to eighteenth-century Sweden, where it belonged.

Meanwhile Dent and Clive were involved in their last collaboration, *Seraglio*, produced for the first time at the Wells in 1952. Typically Dent justified himself even in matters of apparent insignificance: Blonda's song had been changed from

> But should her man abuse her
> Ill-treat her and misuse her

which Clive deemed unsingable, to

> But should her man be-rate her
> Annoy her, aggravate her,
> And quite infuriate her

'I have only just thought of the middle line' he wrote, 'which I suggest instead of repeating the 3rd as in the score. I find it a little weak, and line 2 would strengthen it. "Aggravate" in the sense of "annoy" is incorrect English, but very common usage among females of Blonda's social class! (see Dickens)'

There were still some tasks to be undertaken which could not be refused – 1,000 words for *The Musical Times* to commemorate Vaughan Williams' eightieth birthday, and in 1955, 2,500 words for the *Opera Annual* on the modern cult of Mozart, an opportunity to look back to 1911 and 1920 and to be thankful that, as well as being sipped, château-bottled, at Glyndebourne Mozart could also be riotously enjoyed as *vin ordinaire* at Sadler's Wells.

There was a delightful winter in Lisbon, with a German opera company doing *Parsifal*, *Dutchman*, *Flute*, *Freischütz*, *Seraglio* and *Salome*. He saw most of them: 'The Flute looked more like *Rosenkavalier* – quite dreadful – it is the new German stunt of returning to Wiener Barock. The three boys looked like "principal boys" out of a Strauss operetta. The German singers all seem to bring their own costumes, which don't agree amongst themselves in style or period. The Portuguese chorus wear any cheap draperies . . . but for that reason the Prisoners in *Fidelio* were very good – the raggedest and wretchedest I ever saw. One man appeared wearing a tattered shirt and nothing else . . . Inge Borkh is a fine-looking Leonora . . . she rather knocked the rest silly. But why do all these grown women in breeches parts stand with their legs wide apart? It is quite suitable for Hansel when he says "I am a boy and know not fear", but the ordinary grown up men don't stand like that.'

He looked forward to hearing the Italian company which was to follow the Germans, and hoped the Director would invite him to rehearsals too. At the same time he was most anxious that Clive should give him news of *Orpheus* at Covent Garden; he had been to the dress rehearsal and thought it rather a mess and a muddle – 'good singers, good dancers, good orchestra, but no intelligence and no sense of an organic unity. Barbirolli seemed to treat some of it like Beethoven and the other parts like Gerontius; and the chorus singing "Cet asile" in Elysium were as bumpy and stiff as the Glyndebourne chorus in "Placido e il mar" under Busch! What a pity! The audience will find it all so tedious and boring when it might be profoundly moving and beautiful.' Clive's reply is not extant; Dent himself had a bad relapse through trying to do too much in Portugal – 'more mental and nervous, I think, than physical – an indigestion of beautiful and wonderful experiences of all kinds'.

Back in England Dent saw a few more operas, but his sight and hearing were most uncertain, though he still saw and heard some things that others missed. He collapsed

A last visit to Percy Lubbock: Clive at Lerici, 1957.

after seeing *The Consul* in 1954 – inconveniently just as he was going to pay the bill at Kettners! – but during that winter he went to *Hansel and Gretel* enjoying the very Florentine angels with golden pea-shooters, covering the Babes in the Wood with golden leaves – and then clearing them all away before going upstairs. He went (a second time) to *Troilus* but was stone-deaf – 'it was all complete silence except for some odd Chinese noises in the orchestra which were certainly not composed by Willie'. It was good to find a full house for the seventh performance. He found he could enjoy a life of pretty complete silence, and was reading Metastasio for his chapters on Italian Opera for the *New Oxford History*, and found one drama very like another. He had not been fit enough for the performance of *Deidamia* in St Pancras Town Hall, but wanted to know what Clive thought of it. Kubelik came to talk to him about the forthcoming *Flute* at Covent Garden; he was president of the Theatre Research Conference in London and hoped at least to meet the foreign delegates.

In 1956, thanking Clive for eightieth birthday greetings, 'If I have ever done anything useful for opera', he wrote with his usual generosity, 'I could never have done it without your help, ever since the *Flute* of 1911 and probably before that.' He described the lunch he had been given on the occasion in King's. He had to reply to Boris Ord's proposal of his health but could hear neither Boris' voice nor his own. It was a most thoughtful gesture, with a car provided by the college to take him both ways.

His strength was running out now, but not his enthusiasm nor his intelligence. He was sad that he couldn't hear Clive sing folk-songs at the Oxford and Cambridge Music Club, but there was no point as he could not hear a note; however, he went once or twice to the Ballet – *Pagodas* and *Petrouchka*. He wanted to see *Benvenuto Cellini*[1] which he had last heard in 1936 when he translated it for Chisholm in Glasgow; his chief memory of it was that they were rather frightened that there would be a disturbance by the Irish population when Cellini says 'Au diable ma statue, et le Pape à L'Enfer' which he had translated literally, 'The Devil take my statue and the Pope may go to Hell!'

In August 1957 he was staying at a hotel in Tunbridge Wells to give his invaluable companion, Michael, a chance

---

[1] He did see it, performed at Sadler's Wells by the Carl Rosa company; by now he was almost blind as well as deaf.

200

Edward J. Dent: drawing (1941)
by Edmond Kapp.

of a holiday. John Denison of the Arts Council had asked him to translate *Idomeneo*. 'The fact is that Varesco's original Italian of 1780 is pretty bad – you know the whole story of Mozart's letters to his father about it. And it is much too long (as Mozart knew himself too!) But if I could make a really good version it might be (artistically) worthwhile. Of course, it will never *pay*: but it might be done eventually. The trouble . . . to begin with is that the only available edition (which I possess) is the Breitkopf of about 1880 or so, *very small print*, and my eyes are still in rather a bad state. It is all rather a gamble, my health and everything else.

'I should love to see you sometime. I want to hear all the backstage talk and scandal of the opera at C.G., S.W., Glyndebourne and everywhere! But people who *know*, like John Denison and George Harewood, are all much too busy to talk to a deaf man!'

It was the 415th letter that Clive had received and kept, and the last, for Dent died a fortnight later on 22 August. At his cremation – for which naturally so staunch an agnostic had left no instructions – the organist played the Angels' Chorus from *The Dream of Gerontius*; it was an irony that Dent would have enjoyed.

Clive lived on till 1968, teaching singing pupils until he was eighty; among the last of his enterprises was to begin to assemble the letters which have formed the staple of this biography.

Some notes on the illustrations

Unless otherwise stated all illustrations are from the author's collection.

p. 1   Reproduced by kind permission of the Provost and Fellows of King's College, Cambridge.

p. 3   A recent painting by Julian Barrow. Picture kindly lent by Major Geoffrey Dent.

p. 4   The photograph was taken in Edward Dent's boyhood. The piano, a Broadwood of burr walnut with rosewood inlay, which had been acquired by Dent's grandmother, is in the far corner. At the age of five, Dent is reputed to have struck his mother over the knuckles with the light ruler with which he was conducting her performance of one of his compositions, because she attempted to 'improve' it instead of playing the notes in front of her. In the family it was assumed that his musical talent came from her side of the family, the Woodalls. Photograph lent by Geoffrey Dent.

p. 5   Photograph lent by Geoffrey Dent.

p. 6   There was 3½ years between the brothers. Gordon Carey was later a Fellow of Clare College, Cambridge, and Headmaster of Eastbourne.

     The house in the background is The White House, Sible Hedingham, at which Clive Carey was born. The spectators are presumably a nanny and a governess for the five children.

p. 7   The group of Dent's contemporaries includes E. M. Forster, not surprisingly in the background (on the left) and, much more prominent, Lawrence Haward (centre, with monocle) who later became Curator of Manchester City Art Gallery and a music critic – certainly Dent's closest friend outside the circle of performing musicians – and compiler of the bibliography of his writings. The Dean, M. R. James, is seated at the centre of the group; he became Provost in 1905. Photograph kindly lent by Nicholas Furbank.

p. 10 The postcard, typical of its period, refers to a C.U.M.S. rehearsal of Vecchi's *Amfiparnaso*, one of Dent's favourite works for whose revival he was often pressing.

p. 11 Pen sketches of Clive's gyrations during his performance of the Parabasis, for which Parry had composed new music for this occasion. The Greek script is Clive's; the sketches are by his sister Margery.

p. 14 *Edwin and Angelina*, words by Winifred Carey, music by Clive Carey, performed at Burgess Hill and at Bedford by a company consisting chiefly of Careys and Stareys.

p. 15 At the New Theatre, 23 and 24 February 1904. A 'town and gown' occasion, under distinguished local patronage, in aid of the District Nursing Association and of the Girl's Friendly Society Lodge. The other items in the programme were *The Bugle Call*, a one-act play set in London during the South African War, and *Hal the Highwayman*.

p. 16 Photograph taken by Clive in Venice, in the days when one's gondolier (Angelo, in this instance) became one's personal chauffeur for the duration of the stay.

p. 20 A snapshot taken by Clive 'from my bedroom window, Hotel Riva San Lorenzo', the room from which he was evicted, possibly later making a plot for E. M. Forster.

p. 26 Snapshot, presumably by Clive, taken in 1906. In the foreground E. Alexander and M. C. Hawtrey (identification probable); in the background M. R. James with Walter Fletcher and Maisie Fletcher (Pamina in 1911).

p. 27 Barges seem to have been not solely the perquisite of Oxford; Mrs Wright's features in snapshots over a number of years. Among the ladies are one of Clive's sisters and two of his Clare contemporary C. V. Durell's.

p. 29 The postcard of 1906 consists of brief exhortations from four correspondents, the 'Busoni school', Tagliapietra ('the barefoot dancer'); Dent, who mentions that Busoni is 'utterly disgusted and loathsome with you' for not writing to him; O'Neil Phillips, who bids Clive come to Berlin for a week instead of giving 'very indifferent lessons in singing to young ladies in stuffy old London'; and Busoni himself. Presumably the restaurant (with guitarist) was a regular meeting-place.

p. 31 Clive Carey as Athena; his lifelong friend A. F. Scholfield (who was also George Worthing to Clive's Lady Bracknell in a contemporary A.D.C. production) played Orestes. Rupert Brooke's appearance in *The Eumenides* led to his first encounter with Edward Marsh, later his literary executor and the writer of the well-known Memoir of him. Years later Marsh remembered how 'the radiant youthful figure in gold and vivid red and blue, like a page in the Riccardi chapel, stood strangely out against the stuffy decorations and dresses'. Percy Lubbock, less impressed, noted his curious hop to the right or left each time he raised his property trumpet.

p. 32 *The Graphic* tells its readers that there was 'a scholarly, vigorous assemblage of Chorus, of elders, maidens, attendants and citizens, all personated with appropriate feeling by the Cambridge undergraduate; and it is, perhaps, noteworthy that the supernumeraries were greater in number than at the 1885 performance, and that on this occasion Athena was personated by a member of the University, whereas in 1885 Miss J. E. Case took the part'.

p. 38 A programme kindly provided by Sir Geoffrey Keynes. This is the 1907 performance, produced by (male) members of the university; Dent devised the music.

p. 39 Reproduced by permission of the Marlowe Dramatic Society and the University Library, Cambridge.

p. 43 Inserted for its period flavour, a commercial photograph by Mason and Basébé of Cambridge. The diners, except Winter, are all Clare contemporaries most of whom entered the college in 1900. Left to right, J. F. Hall, C. E. Winter, Carey, W. W. Morrice, F. W. Chambers, F. P. Croshaw, J. Strachan, C. V. Durell, H. S. Berry, L. Starey, G. F. Thomas-Peter, H. Pettit (with whom Clive used to sit at Clare dinners some fifty years later). The occasion was F. P. Croshaw's 21st birthday in May 1904. The set of rooms, lodgings presumably, are a fine example of contemporary undergraduate and landlady taste: centre lamp (and shade); épergne; pictures (suspended at length from the picture rail) of mountains, pyramid and sphinx, a Frans Hals-y cavalier; pot plant in Benares brass bowl; and photo-cards of contemporaries. Undergraduates are all clean shaven, the gyps finely moustached.

p. 51 Mrs Jenkinson, wife of the University Librarian, was in her day regarded as a little old-fashioned in her tastes and dress. Photograph kindly lent by Mrs Frida Knight.

The Mozart programme, with the wreath hand-stencilled in colour, exemplifies another feature of the period, the custom of printing programmes and menus for small private occasions.

p. 53 Part of a notice in the *Westminster Gazette*, to which Rupert Brooke was a regular and privileged contributor. Hence, perhaps, a surprisingly long and laudatory review of the 1910 'bi-sexual' performance of *Dr Faustus* (not of 'Faust'). Kindly lent by George Rylands, King's College, Cambridge.

p. 55 The Esperance group were 'working girls' and the folk-dancing and singing were thought of by their promoters partly as 'social work'. The centre illustration is in colour.

p. 56 A snapshot by Clive. Robert Beadle was the singer from whom Clive and Mary Neal collected Lemady ('One midsummer morning') on this occasion in October 1911. It was published with his accompaniment in 1915 and became especially popular.

A group taken at Ralph Vaughan Williams's home on 10 June 1910; Clive in the foreground, with Margaret and Bobby Longman.

p. 57 Clive playing (or over-playing) Comus at a private party while staying at Bob Maltby's home shortly after the success of the Marlowe's *Comus* in Christ's College garden.

p. 58 Photograph kindly lent by Mrs Anne Hopkinson.

p. 59 Off-stage. There appear to be no photographs taken at the actual performance. Presumably camera shutters functioned too slowly.

p. 60 The programme was designed at the Cambridge University Press; the introduction and synopsis, often used afterwards, were by Dent; the circular design on the back was by Mrs Cockerell.

p. 62 Review with pictures provided by the Cambridgeshire Collection, Cambridgeshire Libraries.

p. 63 Snapshot taken by Clive Carey in Switzerland, January 1913.

Boulestin's caricatures (for so he described them) were intended for the *Bystander* but it had no room and they were eventually used to illustrate his article in the journal of the Société Internationale Musicale. His review describes Dent as having produced from the libretto 'une traduction exacte, charmante, naïve et absurde et qui sut conserver les plaisanteries comme l'accent tonique de l'original'. The misprint in Clive's name gave special pleasure to Jean de Reszke, who sometimes used to address him as Olive.

p. 65 Photograph by Sydney J. Loeb, reproduced by kind permission of the Provost and Fellows of King's College, Cambridge.

p. 66 An agreeable occasion at Port Ballintrae, Ireland, of which this may well have been the first and last example. Among the folk-dancers, besides Clive himself, are Percy Scholes, Ernest Bullock, and Edward Bairstow.

pp. 69–70 Costume designs reproduced by permission of the Syndics of the Fitzwilliam Museum, Cambridge.

p. 72 Crayon sketches of his designs, given by Lionel Penrose (later a distinguished psychologist) to Dennis Arundell, through whose generosity they are reproduced here.

p. 74 A snapshot taken at St Jacut-sur-Mer, where Clive and a group of friends used to assemble annually. Iolo Williams was at this period a colleague on expeditions in search of folk-songs and dances, the Toyes were concerned in various musical enterprises in London, and Marcel Boulestin was still plying his trade as a music critic; he was later to make a reputation as a connoisseur and provider of good food.

p. 75 Clive's companions in Italy, of whom he took this indifferent snapshot, were all prominent in the movement for women's suffrage, into which he had first been drawn by his sister Winifred. Emmeline Pethick Lawrence, a close friend of Mary Neal, with her husband (later a member of the Attlee ministry) were also vigorous campaigners in the 'stop the war' agitation. Olive Schreiner, author of *The Story of an African Farm*, also wrote powerful condemnations of British imperialism. Clive was never much concerned with active politics, but in old age his interest in the peace movement revived.

p. 93 Cartoon kindly lent by Jasper Rootham.

p. 102 From the album of Frida Stewart (now Mrs Knight).

p. 103 Reproduced by kind permission of the Theatre Museum.

p. 104   The poster was designed by Lovat Fraser. Clive sang Death and produced the opera on a number of occasions, eliciting Holst's comment in a letter of 11 October 1926; 'it is good to hear that *Savitri* is still in your hands and I should feel easier in my mind if both it and other things of mine were always being produced by you.'

pp. 106–7   Photographs, sketches and advertisement kindly provided by The Cambridgeshire Collection, Cambridgeshire Libraries.

p. 107   The sketch is by Frida Stewart's sister Jean, then aged sixteen.

p. 110   Picture kindly lent by Miss Irene Seccombe, Secretary of C.U.M.S.

pp. 114, 117   Reproduced by permission of the Provost and Fellows of King's College, Cambridge.

p. 121   A cutting from *The Sketch*, 18 February 1925, kindly lent by Dennis Arundell, who comments that Dent was 'rightly amusing' about the Arcadian scene.

p. 125   The snapshot of the poster hoarding advertising the production was taken at Charlottesville. Sylvia Nelis had sung (as Victoria Hopper) in the Cambridge *Magic Flute* in 1911. Audrey Mildmay (Mrs John Christie) was greatly instrumental in the foundation of the Glyndebourne opera.

     The photograph at Cambridge in 1933 was kindly lent by Miss Irene Seccombe, Secretary of C.U.M.S.

p. 128   Picture kindly lent by Jasper Rootham.

p. 130   Reproduced by permission of the Provost and Fellows of King's College, Cambridge.

p. 139   Picture kindly supplied by the Mander and Mitchenson Theatre Collection.

p. 141   Reproduced by kind permission of the Theatre Museum.

p. 142   The scene includes Sumner Austin (Count), Joan Cross (Countess), Ronald Stear (Antonio), Audrey Mildmay (Susanna), Arnold Matters (Figaro), Powell Lloyd (Basilio), Harry Brindle (Bartolo), Edith Coates (Marcellina), D. Morgan Jones (Curzio). This was Rex Whistler's only commission for opera at Sadler's Wells.

p. 145   Clive Carey's production at Sadler's Wells; designer Powell Lloyd.

p. 149   Clive Carey's production; stage designs by M. Doboujinsky; negotiations were under way in 1938 for him to return (from America) for *The Queen of Spades*, but these had to be abandoned because of the political situation. It was his only – splendid – Sadler's Wells venture. Reproduced by permission of the Theatre Museum.

p. 150   A review of *Boris Godounov* from *The Bystander*, 3 March 1937, kindly supplied by the Mander and Mitchenson Theatre Collection.

p. 157 From a review of *Der Rosenkavalier*, March 1939, kindly supplied by the Mander and Mitchenson Theatre Collection.

p. 162 Photograph of the rehearsal kindly lent by Miss Irene Seccombe, Secretary of C.U.M.S.

pp. 162–3 Charles Cudworth's snapshots kindly provided by the Cambridgeshire Collection, Cambridgeshire Libraries.

p. 165 From an article about the Royal College of Music in *Weekly Illustrated*, 11 March 1939.

p. 170 From the *Cambridge Daily News*, 20 September 1939. Picture kindly provided by the Cambridgeshire Collection, Cambridgeshire Libraries.

p. 174 From the *Cambridge Independent Press*; the air raid took place in June 1940. Picture kindly provided by the Cambridgeshire Collection, Cambridgeshire Libraries.

p. 180 Photograph supplied by the Hulton Picture Library.

p. 185 Reproduced by permission of the Press Association.

p. 189 Drawing generously lent by Harry Lloyd.

pp. 191, 192, 196 Reproduced by permission of the Provost and Fellows of King's College, Cambridge.

p. 201 Picture reproduced by permission of the Syndics of the Fitzwilliam Museum, Cambridge.

Index